MY DIARY

HARRY, EVIE AND CHARLIE'S GREAT ADVENTURE

By

Gary Johnston Smith

This is a work of creative nonfiction. While all the stories in this book are true, some names and identifying details have been changed to protect the privacy of the people involved.

This book is dedicated to both my Grannies
and especially my Auntie Rose.

I'd also like to make a special dedication to all the wonderful people I've met
in my life. The ones I've loved and had special moments with, even the ones I
might have annoyed or driven away, all I ever wanted was for you to be happy....
Best regards love and kisses, Gary

CONTENTS

Charlie, Harry and Evie ♡

1

It was early, still dark outside, and I could hear the fan whirring away at the side of me. I always had the fan on when I went to bed, whether it was warm or not. I had just become so used to the noise of the fan, it reminded me of being in an aeroplane, trying to get some sleep, my head up against that small window with my eyes closed, the sound of the powerful engines as we comfortably sped along at five hundred miles an hour...

Harry was lying across my legs and Charlie had managed to snuggle under my arm; when I looked round, there was Evie, lying on the pillow next to me. "Geez, these dogs have got a good life," I thought to myself. Usually I'd get up, stumble through to the kitchen for a drink of water and go straight back to bed, doing my best not to disturb my furry friends. But not today – I had a little bit more packing to do, and the dogs, well, they were in for the biggest shock of their lives. Little did they know that they were about to begin the biggest journey of their lives – 2500 miles by boat and road, most of the time spent cooped up in their cages. There would be stops on the way for them to stretch their legs and take in the lovely fresh air, but this was something none of them had ever experienced before – and here they were, stretched out with not a care in the world. I could tell they had no idea what was about to befall them. Many a day I had tried to explain what the great plan was, foolishly lecturing them while I was sure they were listening intently, understanding every word, but this morning, I realised the reality of the situation – they did not have a clue.

I started my morning like every other – filling the kettle and trying to squeeze a lemon at the same time. I had a set routine, more a rigmarole of flounder and blunders. I always squeezed a lemon into a large solid pint tumbler, adding a little bicarbonate of soda, quickly trying to beat down the ensuing bubbles as they would sometimes overflow the glass, then adding turmeric and ginger with just a little honey to sweeten, all topped up with hot water and a good amount of cold water so I could drink it down quickly. I would then squeeze two oranges this time only adding turmeric and ginger, no water or honey needed – oh, I forgot to mention a little ground pepper which helps activate the turmeric. It will come as no surprise that my next move would be to rush to the loo as these drinks go through you very quickly. Yes, that was the way I started most of my days. But today was going to be quite different.

Harry, who was thirteen years of age, Evie aged five and Charlie, who was just heading into his second year, are all Yorkshire terriers, born and bred in the sunny climate of Fuerteventura. When I say Yorkshire terriers, they were all very different variations of their breed and the three of them had quite distinctive characteristics. Harry was the biggest weighing just over eight kilos, Charlie a little less at six kilos, and 'Princess' Evie was a little under four kilos; regardless of her size, she always gave as good as she got – in fact, she had a terrible habit of occasionally biting Harry's ears so hard he'd screech out in pain. Don't get me wrong, she loved Harry and could not bear to be apart from him, but like all cheeky little girls, she just needed to let him know it was her that pulls the strings. Charlie, on the other hand, loved them both, they were his best friends in the world and he just dearly wanted them to reciprocate. His boundless energy would push them both to the limit. Harry was getting old now and didn't always enjoy Charlie's enthusiastic charge on life – in fact, dare I say it, there might even be a little jealousy involved as Charlie was beginning to grab a lot of the limelight with his doggie good looks and charm.

I knew they had a long day ahead of them, so I had to make sure their walk was suitable enough to burn as much energy as possible.

With Charlie I would usually try and avoid the seafront, a lovely path with views across to the island of Lobos and our busier neighbour, Lanzarote. Being on the northern tip of Fuerteventura there was usually quite a strong swell which would bring lots of massive waves crashing onto the shoreline. The island's surfers would be up early trying to take advantage of this popular reef break, which was certainly no place for beginners – if the big waves didn't get the better of you then the hardened regular surfers would certainly tell you that your amateurish skill set was not appreciated around these parts. Thankfully, most of the time, common sense prevailed, and these young newbies knew their place and would stay on the shoreline and admire from afar.

The front coastal path was also extremely popular with people running, walking, skateboarding and the constant stream of enthusiastic cyclists. This gave Charlie a perfect excuse to get overexcited and not just bark but literally scream at these fitness fanatics. As an impressionable young puppy, we were sure he learned this awfully bad habit from Harry who would joyously bark at any passing skateboarder and other dogs. Charlie decided to take it to another level. The truth is though, Charlie just really loved people and other dogs and, as far as he was concerned, they were all his best friends. We decided it was best to avoid this place during its busy times.

However, today was different. Knowing I had to burn as much of his energy as possible, this was exactly the place to do it. I would have to put up with trying to calm him down while failing miserably. In the past when we were passing people on particularly busy days, we would draw long stares from them. I knew what they were thinking: "Can't you control that noisy dog of yours!?" Nope. Impossible. I would always look back with a defeated shrug of my shoulders while offering an apologetic "Perdon". But today I was not too fussed as I was on a mission. I even took a walk down one of Charlie's favourite streets where he could enjoy looking under the cars and going mad at the local street cats – making sure to keep him on a short lead so he didn't lose an eye! The cats didn't seem too bothered, they seemed relaxed and even bewildered at his over excitement. One cat in particular, a rather nice-looking young ginger tom, followed him down the street, keeping his distance and sneaking from car to car until we got to the end of the street which frustrated Charlie even more. Eventually, we returned to the house with Charlie panting like mad; as soon as I unclipped him, he made a beeline for his water dish with Harry and Evie following in hot pursuit, desperate to find out what smells he had picked up on the way.

Then it was the turn of Harry and Evie. Normally, my partner and I walk them all together, but Nicky wasn't here and, being on my own, it was not possible to take them all together as Charlie's enthusiasm would spread throughout the pack like wildfire. Harry may decide to bark at another dog which would cause Evie to have a go at Harry, which in turn would make Charlie have a go at Evie. This could be quite amusing for the passers-by; on one fateful occasion I had taken all three of them out together and had become uncontrollably tangled up in leads and barking dogs, helplessly trying to unravel myself as they all decided to head off in different directions. I had returned to the house feeling a mixture of uselessness and defeat. So, there was no other way of doing it. Taking them out in two different stages was my easiest option.

Walking Harry and Evie was a much more relaxed task and now that Harry was older, he was less inclined to bark at other dogs and passers-by. It would only happen on the odd occasion if Evie inspired him to do it, the little troublemaker. But most of the time we could amble along for quite a distance. Evie's one major fault is she would never walk in a straight line, always getting tangled up with any passing benches or lampposts – hence her nickname: Evie 'Weavie'.

This walk was different today. One that I'd been dreading for weeks. Little did he realise, but it was Harry's final walk in Corralejo.

I was not so fussed about Evie and Charlie. They were both still young and I knew they should settle into their new environment fairly quickly. But this was Harry's home, his patch as they say, the place he had been all his life. When the tide was low, we would take him down to the warm rock pools where he'd spend hours chasing little fish. Some of the pools were quite expansive and he'd have to literally swim after his little fishy friends. And of course, he was always at his happiest on the coastal path where he would recognise all the regular passers-by.

Harry was always a very lively dog. We were sure his eyesight was not great from a youthful age which had made him a little defensive from the off, and unfortunately he began to suffer from epileptic seizures from the age of two. These could sometimes last for quite a while and we would have to quickly rush him up to the local vets for help. As you can imagine it was very distressing and we felt so helpless watching our little best friend suffer. Thankfully, things began to improve through the years as Nicky made sure his diet changed so he didn't eat certain food which could trigger these horrible seizures. If he did have a fit, we would quietly and gently take him through to our bedroom, squirt a little prescribed liquid valium up his rear end and lie with him till it passed. Over the years his fits began to lessen, and we could lie with him without having to use the valium. Ensuring his diet was better seemed to help with his general health and fitness. He was extraordinarily strong, especially for his age. And despite his barking and unsure reactions towards strangers, he was the most loyal and loving dog you could ever have. Although he was often very unsociable with other dogs, for some reason they'd all warm to Harry and would by-pass Charlie and Evie just to get to him... Yup, for some reason they all loved Harry.

Once they had settled down after our final seafront Fuerteventura walks, I could see the three of them all staring in my direction, expecting me to fill their dishes with their usual breakfast. As I filled their bowls, I did my best to explain to them that things were going to be a little different today. They would be getting an exceedingly wholesome breakfast consisting of carrot, boiled fish and their usual dry dog biscuits, a meal which had all of the nutrients they required but that left my hands smelling of bad cod liver oil so I'd be forever washing my hands. (I'm probably showing my age here but my gran used to give me a tablespoon of cod liver oil most mornings: one for me and one for the dog, insisting it was good for me. How something so putrid could be good for you I just couldn't understand!)

Once the dogs were fed, it was time to make sure I had got absolutely everything we needed for our long journey, which was primarily paperwork. If we didn't have that sorted down to the finest detail, we were going nowhere.

This long arduous trek wasn't going to be easy and just to make it even more complicated, we were doing it during an unprecedented pandemic.

Okay. Dog passports? Check. All dogs fully vaccinated? Check. All dog worming tablets taken? Check. And last but not least, Pet Fit to travel documents completed? Check!!! Dog muzzles were also required by law for certain parts of the journey, though fingers crossed we wouldn't need to use them.

It wasn't just the dogs' details which needed close inspection, it was also my own. I had my passport, ferry tickets, Covid vaccination certificate, Day Two Covid test confirmation for when I arrived in England and another certificate which I needed to get me across the French border. Good. All of that was in order. Nicky's suitcase that she had left with me to take on the journey was very heavy and there was no way I was going to even attempt to open that up to squeeze anything else in it – a Pandora's box if ever there was one. It would just have been a clothes explosion, I would never have got it closed again, so I just wheeled that straight to the front door. There was just one more bag to pack. A small amount of my things and more importantly (as Nicky reminded me!) the dogs' belongings: little jackets and jumpers for the chilly weather and some of their favourite toys, not forgetting a big bag of their food and their bowls to eat and drink from. Still in the back of my mind was the dreaded thought that the driver taking us on this hugely important journey might refuse me access with these two heavy bags.

I found three old blankets that I could throw in the pet cages to help my little fellow travellers be as comfortable as possible for the trip and finally, I couldn't forget Humpy. Humpy was Harry's favourite toy, a rather scruffy looking stuffed toy dog. It was actually bigger than Harry when he was a pup, but that didn't stop him from dragging it around with him everywhere he went. As the years passed by, we always knew when Harry thought it was time for us all to go to bed as he would be staring up at Nicky and me with Humpy faithfully hanging from his mouth. Harry eventually managed to pull most of the stuffing out of this pitiful thing and, in the end, it resembled a badly designed pillowcase with its missing ears, nose and tail – but no matter, it was still Harry's Humpy. I will leave it to the reader's imagination as to how it got the name Humpy.

It was now nearly half past eleven and we weren't due to be picked up till 3.30 pm; it was time to phone Nicky to go through the checklist one more time just to make sure I hadn't forgotten anything.

The reason Harry, Evie, Charlie and I were travelling this way was simply down to Harry's epilepsy – there was just no way we would have got a fit to fly certificate for him. This journey was something Nicky had been looking forward to, researching and looking into, for years. Not me, I had been dreading it – I was hoping a million pounds would just fall into my lap and we could book a private plane and off we would go into the sunset like conquering heroes. But no, down in the world of reality, that just wasn't going to be. And now, due to health reasons, Nicky was not going to be able to make the journey with us — it was horrible and this was not the way we had planned things originally. Nicky was massively disappointed that she wouldn't be travelling with us, but unfortunately it was what it was, and we were just having to get on with it. Fortunately, Nick's health was improving and that was important, but for now, I had to forgo my dread of this journey — it was a case of knuckling down and getting on with the job at hand.

It was now getting close to 3.30 and my stomach was full of nervous energy as I paced backwards and forwards, constantly speaking to the dogs and asking them to please behave and hoping that they understood me when I told them that this was going to be the journey that reunited us all with Nicky. I went frequently to the front door and looked out over our communal swimming pool, hoping it was going to be quiet; I really did not want to make a fuss. We had not told our neighbours about our intentions, and as nice as they all were, it would not be long before they were all chattering about seeing Gary and the dogs leaving en-masse. Like any small town or village, it did not take long for people to notice your actions and then wagging tongues would start trying to piece together your reasons, your motives. For me, this was something personal and I did not really want half the town knowing our business and that the apartment was lying empty even if we were living in a quiet part of town.

I looked again at my watch — twenty minutes past three, our driver Jim could call at any time. A last visit to the toilet as I tried to gather my thoughts and a last look around to make sure nothing was left to chance. I could still see lots of things lying around that belonged to the dogs and Nicky but there was no way I could pack it all in. I felt a wave of sadness coming over me as I saw a nice big woolley jersey that Nicky would wear as we watched late-night television; in every corner were well-chewed toys that Harry, or more likely Charlie, had pulled to bits as I constantly threw them from one part of the room to the other just to keep them amused. Suddenly, I was pulled out of my thoughts as my phone rang. I almost jumped with the realisation that it was probably Jim. Yup, I could see his name on the front of my phone.

I was filled with a sudden rush of excitement. "Hi there, is that you outside!?" I asked. "Yup, I'll just be parked on the corner," Jim told me. "Okay, I'll bring the dogs first Jim," I exclaimed. "No problem, take your time." I think Jim could tell by my voice that I was in panic mode. Quickly I picked up Evie's bag as I hurriedly grabbed her. I had left their harnesses on ready for this moment. I pleaded with Evie as she wasn't making things easy for me, but I got her sorted, and into her little bag and onto my back with her little head poking out. Charlie had started barking – he didn't know exactly where he was going but he certainly knew he was going out. Thankfully, Harry was a bit more relaxed. I made sure I had my keys and we quickly made our way out of the door. There was only one of my neighbours sunbathing by the swimming pool as I rushed past with the dogs, hastily making our way along the terrace to the main entrance.

As I left the gate, I could see Jim opening the back doors of the van, making preparations for the dogs to be put in their cages. I couldn't help noticing that it was a brand-new Ford Transit Custom, all shiny and new; it looked great which helped lift my spirits to a more positive level. "I've just got to go back to get Nicky's case and a bag with some stuff belonging to me and the dogs, Jim." He could see I was on a mission. "Look, don't panic, slow down, we've got plenty of time," he said, trying to settle my nerves. "Cheers Jim," I replied, relieved that there didn't seem to be any problem with the extra baggage.

I opened the gate and ran back along the terrace; my mood had certainly improved as I sensed everything was going to plan. I opened the door and grabbed the three blankets which I had left on the back of the couch, wedged them under one arm and swung the hold-all over my other shoulder. It was quite big and heavy but most of the weight seemed to be balanced on my back. Finally, I went for Nick's case. "God knows what's in there," I thought to myself; it certainly wouldn't have passed the check-in desk at any of the airports.

Luckily, the wheels on it were in decent shape and I hurriedly wheeled it along the terrace. As I turned to look back at the swimming pool, I could see our neighbour now sitting up and looking at me in a perplexed fashion. "I'm just off to visit Nicky," I shouted to her. Not waiting for a response, I carried on down to the gate, overloaded with bags and blankets. With no free hands, I raised my leg and used my foot to press the buzzer which unlocked the gate; I let go of the case and swung one of the gates open.

Jim had now opened the side door of the van for me and I cleverly passed the blankets to him and used all my brute strength to get the case into the van. I was hoping I'd made that look easy, whereas I was lucky I didn't put my back out. I picked up the hold-all and threw it next to the case – just one plastic bag containing the dogs' food and their dishes and that was it.

I quickly ran round to the back of the van to see the dogs – they were all just sitting looking at me from their separate cages. The two bottom cages held Harry and Charlie, with Evie on top of Harry's cage – she'd got the best seat in the house, from her position she could even see out of the front of the van.

Jim looked at me. "Now calm down, is that everything!?" With a big grin on my face, I replied: "Yup, that's it, we're good to go."

So that was it, we were on our way! I had been dreading this day for months; my reluctance to talk or even think about it had dogged me for ages but luckily the operations manager (Nicky) had made sure every T was stroked and every I dotted. Yes, just to repeat, Nicky had been meticulously thinking and planning this journey for years – the only worry for her now was leaving the rest of the operation in the hands of her scatter-brained partner.

In my defence, once put into these situations I seemed to have the strength and common sense to step up to the plate. Yes, I could be relied on to get the job done. I knew it was a big responsibility, and failure was not an option.

From the passenger seat, I turned to the dogs who were again all staring up at me from their cages. "Right you lot, we're all off to see Nicky," I said – and with that, Jim started the van.

2

Even as the journey started, I could tell Jim's new van was not going to let us down, you could feel it moving swiftly with insignificant effect on the REV counter. As you can imagine, being a person who worries about the slightest thing, every possible scenario had already played out in my head – for instance, what if we broke down in the middle of Spain, even worse in the middle of France!? What would happen if the ferry started to sink on the way to Cadiz!? What would happen if we were abducted by aliens from outer space while we were out at sea – would the aliens allow me to call Nicky to let her know things were not going to plan? Yes, some of my concerns were downright silly – my fertile imagination could be very annoying to me at times.

I kept glancing back at the dogs, feeling happy that they and the bags were all safely in the van and that this great adventure I was reluctantly on had finally started. Of course, I'd often focus more on Harry – he was thirteen now, and all he had ever known was the same apartment he had been brought up in, and the fantastic walks and swims he'd had around Corralejo. Another favourite of Harry's was being taken round to the beautiful little town of Cotillo on the west coast, where he could run freely and jump into the gorgeous pools of sea water. There was a real sadness in my heart knowing we would never do that again. I had to snap out of it though, there was no turning back, we were on our way to see Nicky.

Feeling fresh and alert, my mind was settling in for the long journey, which I had been led to believe would be about five days in total. Even though this seemed quite daunting, I was going to handle it one stage at a time – first we had to get to Puerto Del Rosario and safely onto the ferry; that would be the first big test.

As we were making our way to Rosario, it was noticeable that the van itself was very capable; with a 2.300 litre engine, it effortlessly sped along the dual carriage and, although it was very warm outside, the air conditioning system was fabulous. I could tell Jim was immensely proud of his new high-calibre machine as he decided to give me a run-down of all the fantastic accessories he had at his disposal.

It felt like I was being shown around a pilot's cockpit as he pointed out all the elaborate controls, even the adjustable arm rest which came in very handy as he flicked the wonderful machine into cruise control. There was even inflight entertainment which all came through the infotainment system, which to me looked like an iPad; it allowed him to access the apps on his iPhone and, using a hands-free system, he could have it call anyone anywhere in the world.

Now I must point out Jim was not just a driver; Jim was joint owner of Woodside Cargo S.L. and was very much involved in the day-to-day running of this well-oiled, well-established business. They had come very highly recommended, and I was quickly beginning to realise why. Unlike me, Jim was very efficient and acutely focused on the job at hand. I had only met him once, very briefly, but I could tell he was not the sort of guy who suffered fools gladly and, knowing it was going to be a long journey, I had to remind myself that it was important I did not do my usual and waffle on relentlessly.

It was not just me I was worried about as Harry seemed to be barking a lot. Thankfully, Jim picked up my concerns. "Don't worry," he said, "they'll settle down." Of course, I thought to myself, Jim's done this journey more times than I've had hot dinners with lots of animals. But in the back of my mind, I was still concerned as I knew Harry could be quite a demanding wee dog. But sure enough, even before we had got to Rosario, they had all settled down; if it hadn't been for me looking back at them every five minutes, you would never have known they were there.

Eventually we started to move into Rosario, the capital of Fuerteventura. Thankfully, the roads were not too busy as it was still quite early and people were just starting to awake from their siestas, so getting down to the harbour was quite easy. Had it been a little later, I am sure the roads would have been far more congested.

My nerves picked up a little as we approached the harbour. In my mind, I was wondering how closely they would need to check the paperwork and dogs, whether Harry would start barking, would that then set Charlie and Evie off as they had a habit of copying Harry? But just as these thoughts were running through my mind, we pulled up to the main entrance and Jim started talking away with the security people. They all seemed really friendly with Jim, it was just like old friends meeting, and with a laugh and a joke, Jim carried on to our parking place. "Brilliant," I thought.

We seemed to be right at the front of the queue, apart from one other car that was parked next to us. It was a small sports car, and the owner was sitting on his bonnet enjoying the late afternoon sun. He looked young and well-tanned and seemed very relaxed with his long drink in a plastic carton next to him. It was only half past four, so we still had plenty of time before we all boarded the ferry which hadn't even docked into the Rosario harbour yet. "Ahhh it's not too far away now," Jim shouted. "It's fairly close to the harbour." He was staring into his phone at an app called Vessel Finder.

I decided to climb out of the van and stretch my legs. As I looked around at the vastness of the harbour, I was quite surprised to see how big it was; I'd certainly never seen Rosario from this view before. The first thing that really grabbed my attention was a humongous cruise ship parked just across from us – it was massive, a P&O ferry called *MS Iona,* the sixth largest cruise liner in the world. I wasn't sure I'd ever seen a boat as big as this one. Jim, who had done this trip so many times before, was quick to give me a run-down on the size and capacity of this luxury liner – he said it was only just over 18 months old and had taken about a year to build; it was 350 metres long and could carry just over 5200 guests; P&O had to employ 2000 staff to cater for so many people. It stood proudly high in the harbour and no wonder as it had sixteen decks. I just stared at it with my mouth gaping open in amazement. I was used to watching the little boats coming in and out of Corralejo harbour; even our two regular ferries that ran back and forth between Lanzarote and Corralejo could not compete with this.

I decided I would try to get some pictures of this wonderful boat and quickly ran to the water's edge which was a good fifty metres from where we were parked. Looking across another two hundred metres of water to where this wonderful ship was moored up, I got an even better understanding of its magnitude. It was magnificent. I still could not get over the size, or the amount of people that could be on that boat at any one time – it was like a large floating town in permanent party mode. Sadly, it was proving difficult to get the right pictures as the sun was now behind the boat which was casting a large shadow across the water but, undeterred, I snapped away with my camera as best I could.

Suddenly, my attention was distracted by a fast-paced noise behind me. I turned and saw large metal containers being driven at speed across the harbour, between me and where the van was parked. The driver of this strange machine had obviously been shifting these containers for many years. He seemed at ease as he flew past me with the large container trailing behind him. Just at that moment, I saw someone waving and shouting at me to move away from where I was standing. I could see by the way they were dressed that it was one of the Port authorities. I waved back and carefully but quickly made my way back to the van before I was crushed by this quick-moving container-shifting machine.

Just before I climbed back into the van, something else caught my eye – as I looked beyond the van I could see a compound area, obviously a place of storage with its large aluminium roof and big solid gates at the entrance, but as I looked further in, I could see about thirty young lads all being kept under the watchful eye of the Guardia Seville. There didn't seem to be any commotion, in fact it all seemed fairly relaxed, most of the lads were sitting quietly, their faces motionless as they stared into nothingness; they were probably all tired and hungry, completely drained of energy. I suspected they'd not long arrived from West Africa, travelling over in fishing boats. It is a terrible journey for them as a high percentage do not make it simply because a lot of the boats break down mid-journey and are then carried off by the currents further into the south Atlantic. Very noticeably, it is usually young lads who make this journey, and most of them are barely into their twenties. Lots of people wonder why it's always groups of young lads – well, there's actually a good reason for this.

Only sixty miles across the water from Fuerteventura is the largest continent in the world, Africa; not only is it the largest continent but it has the largest concentration of valuable resources and minerals, including oil, gold and diamonds. Africa's resources are used by all the world's most powerful nations; some are used for nuclear power, bauxite is used to smelt aluminium, and electronic devices contain tantalum, which is originally derived from coltan. These resources are hotly contested in the commodities markets of the most powerful nations in the world and sadly these small African nations are powerless to stop their countries from being pillaged by their larger neighbours. This inevitably leads to proxy wars being fought out in their own backyards and swathes of land being turned to waste as the people living on the ground are pinned down by these disease-like wars.

When these poor people's towns and villages are being destroyed, there is just nowhere for them to run to, especially if they have young families; and it is even worse for the elderly. Sadly, it is something we in the West either never get to hear about or even worse just turn a blind eye to. Their only hope is to send their young off to find pastures new, somewhere safe that their families will be able to follow on to in the future, and it is a terrible gamble that many pay with their lives. This is nothing new – it has been going on for years – but at the time of writing this, sadly the number of people trying to make that crossing has increased immensely.

It certainly made me think about my journey – although I was uncertain about everything that was going on around me, it put things in perspective, watching these poor souls all huddled together, a long way from their families. They had no idea what their futures held, the only thing they knew was that at least they were still alive, for the time being anyway.

As I turned to look back over in the direction of the cruise liner again, it didn't escape me the vastly different lifestyles of the people in my immediate vicinity. There was the young lad proudly sitting on his fancy sports car, and the people looking down from up on high on board the beautiful ship the *MS Iona*. Then there was me, worrying about getting through all the border stops, hoping my paperwork was all in order and praying the dogs would behave and not bite any jobsworth customs officer. And finally, the Guardia Seville and their 30 friends hopelessly staring into space, probably with their fingers crossed that if anything they might at least receive a decent meal while in their provisional captivity.

Jim again grabbed my attention. "That's our boat, just about to pull into the harbour now," he said, watching its progress on his phone. And sure enough, there it was. I could just see the top of the boat over the high harbour wall, making its way into dock. Jim had told me that this was a new ferry, built just 12 months before. I could see the whole ship now as it sailed into our dock. The ship was called *Cuidad de Valencia* and it had Naviera Armas Trasmediterranea in big letters across its side; it was just over 200 metres long and, at its busiest, it could carry 600 passengers and 240 vehicles depending on their size.

This information was all being relayed to me as the ship was being speedily emptied. Jim assured me it didn't take long to get everyone disembarked, and just as he said that, six guys ran up the ramp where the vehicles were unloading. "What's that all about?" I asked Jim. "These are the guys running on to get the hired cars off," he answered, and no sooner had he said that than suddenly all these brand-new VW cars came speedily out. The guys drove quickly past us, carefully parked them up and went running back up the ramp for more. I could tell everything around me was happening very efficiently, everyone seemed to know exactly what they were doing. This made me feel better about this particular part of the journey. Jim was also very aware of what was going on around him, watching everything with a beady eye; he had been in this situation before and literally knew their every move. There were quite a few people around making sure everything went smoothly and again Jim knew nearly all of them and it was not just a nod and a hello, they seemed genuinely pleased to see him.

Seeing Jim being so focused and understanding everything that was going on around him made me feel like I was in good hands. "Here's the guy coming over to tell us we're just about to board, and it looks like we'll be on the top deck," Jim said in a calm and knowing voice. And right enough, we were off and moving onto the boat. "We'll need to keep to the left as we will be going up the ramp which will take us onto the top deck," said Jim, and sure enough he was right on the button as a man in a hard hat guided us up a very narrow ramp to the higher deck.

This was something else I could not get my head around; I knew I was going to be spending two nights on the ship with my own cabin. But I was more concerned about the dogs and them having to be shifted from the van to allocated kennels on the ship. This seemed cruel to me, the poor dogs having to stay somewhere in the lower decks – would it be dark, or even noisy, would they be close to the ship's engines, cramped into small, enclosed spaces? My mind wandered back to all the old films I'd ever seen, one in particular was the film *Das Boot* about life on a German U/boat; it was all dark, damp, dingy conditions, almost squalor, unfit for human habitation, and on top of all that, they were trying to fight a war in heavy seas. Yes, my mind was wandering again, my imagination was running riot and thinking of all the worst scenarios.

It was a small relief to know I could visit the dogs whenever I wanted, but I was still dreading the idea. I thought about taking only one dog at a time up onto the upper deck for a walk so they could do their business – these dogs were used to a life of luxury; I just couldn't imagine them enjoying this situation. How was I going to manage this? And it wasn't just for a few hours, this was for two full days and nights – the dogs would never trust me again I thought. What if I was tired and it was late at night and one of their leads accidentally snapped and one of the dogs went overboard? I was now imagining myself being lowered from the ship in a lifeboat, into the dark, massive waves crashing around, helplessly shouting "Harry, Harry," thinking, "Geez, Nicky's going to kill me, oh my god, big waves." All of this while suffering from seasickness…

Thankfully, Jim had got to the top deck, having expertly pulled a tight right-hand turn, and had parked behind another vehicle. He jumped from the van, made his way to the back and quickly opened both doors, just as another car drew up behind us. Ahhh brilliant, I could see why he had moved so quickly – the crew like to get the cars parked as tightly as possible, something they must learn as the summers can get so busy and congested. But thankfully for me, Jim was one step ahead of them, making sure there was plenty of space so we could get in and out of the back doors.

The kennels were also on the upper level so once everyone was on board and the cars and vans were all in place, I went to inspect them. They were bright but smaller than the cages the dogs were already in. I quickly realised that the good thing about Jim's cages was that the dogs could see each other and the back of the van was very warm and spacious. With their blankets and the familiar smells coming from our bags, they'd become familiar with that environment and there seemed no need to start moving them again; furthermore, I could climb through the side door and comfortably sit and spend time with them which was not really an option in the ship's kennels. "Are you sure that is what you want to do?" Jim asked. I'd made my mind up. "Yup, they will be fine in here Jim," I replied.

Thankfully, the parking bay was large and spacious and, being late October, the ferry was a lot quieter than it would normally be; this would come in handy when I had to walk them. I filled their dishes with water and then prepared some of their biscuits. Charlie and Evie seemed a bit lost and didn't seem to be fussed about eating but Harry was not hanging about and got stuck in straight away, he didn't seem to be fazed by it at all. I pleaded with Charlie and Evie to eat something, but to no avail. I told them to behave and that I was just going to sort my cabin out but would be back soon, and just to make them feel better I said, "Remember this – all of us are off to see Nicky." They were all staring straight back at me, looking rather vague. I could only hope they understood what I was saying. As I left the van, I checked my watch – 6.45; it was still hot and sunny outside and there was only fifteen minutes before we set sail.

The cabin was better than I thought – there were two single beds and a toilet with a shower and it was spotlessly clean; each of the beds had little reading lights which made the cabin look comfortable.

My mind went back to the dogs – wouldn't it be great if I could just bring them all up here, but I knew there was no chance of me getting away with that, I could just imagine the three of them barking with excitement. Suddenly I realised the boat was beginning to move, so I quickly made my way out of the cabin, past the bar, which was not yet open, and out onto an upper deck from where I could see down to the van. But my eyes were now looking across the whole harbour as we gently pulled away from the quayside. In the distance I could see Puerto Del Rosario; the town had grown and there were new buildings dotted all over – in fact, it was looking nicer than I had ever seen it. I remembered when I first arrived 26 years ago, it was quite industrial, not somewhere you would want to stay on your holidays.

We were only ten minutes out of the harbour and I began to see how mysteriously beautiful the island could be. The sun was just beginning to sink in the west and it looked like it had got caught in between the volcanoes where some clouds had begun to gather. The colours were fantastic, all reds, yellows and browns, and the volcanoes were eerily perched across the skyline. It was still warm with no breeze and thankfully the sea was like a millpond, it was wonderful. I scrambled into my pocket to get my phone – I just had to get a picture of this, I had to capture this moment.

I looked down towards the van – my god, the dogs were in there. Suddenly, I was hit with this massive wave of euphoria as the magnitude of what was happening really hit me. How did I get here, to this point? Destiny was dragging me along and I was powerless to stop it, I was going through an explosion of different emotions. Looking down at the van again, I thought of all the years Harry, Nicky and I had spent in that apartment, Saturday nights making fajitas and always remembering to make a special Harry chicken; again realising that it was all over, it was horrible knowing that it would never happen again. I was staring back out into the distance now, feeling a sad emptiness. Charlie and Evie were still really young, it would be easier for them I thought, they still had their best years ahead of them. I began to realise it wasn't just Harry I was worrying about, it was actually myself. I felt I was out of my comfort zone, but there was no turning back even though this incredible journey was only in its infancy.

Suddenly my mood changed as I stared back at the island. I felt an air of excitement, a feeling of hyperfocus euphoria was exploding inside of me, a crazy mixture of sadness, acute loneliness and a strange feeling of well-being. With my mind so elevated, it felt like all the answers to everything were in front of me – I couldn't see them, but I knew they were there, something just felt right. With the combination of my feelings and these incredible views, and even though I was smiling I could feel the tears welling up in my eyes, I knew deep down that this was a pivotal moment in my life. Although I felt rooted to the spot, I knew I couldn't live in this moment forever, I was going to have to walk away. Thankfully, my stomach decided to remind my head that there was going to be food available at eight o'clock, so I took one last pic, turned and walked away from that moment, but there was one thing I knew for sure – it was something I'd never forget.

With everything that was going on with the dogs and my concerns for the journey, I hadn't realised that not only did I have a cabin for the whole duration, but I had three meals a day, breakfast, lunch and an evening meal, included in my ticket. This would make things much easier for me because, with my head overthinking what could and could not happen on the journey, I had not really considered the idea of food.

Back in my cabin, I made sure I had the essentials, toothbrush, change of clothes, cable for charging my phone and, most importantly, the folder with all our travel documents. It was now five to eight, so it was time to go down to grab some grub. Once I had shut the cabin door behind me it was just a short walk along a narrow corridor, down a set of stairs and straight ahead into where the food was being served. The room was quite spacious and there were lots of tables and chairs, plus three or four TVs positioned around the room, with small groups of people huddled around peering up, all of them watching the news. Everyone seemed to be eagerly watching the latest ongoings from the island of La Palma where the volcano Cumbre Vieja had erupted; lots of people and livestock had sadly been evacuated from their homes.

I was also extremely interested in this story as it had been something I had discussed weekly while doing a volcano walk. Being an entertainer for a hotel in Corralejo for over twenty years, once a week I'd organised a walk up a dormant volcano called Bayuyo; it certainly wasn't the largest of the volcanoes on the island, but it was high enough to give everyone fantastic panoramic views around the north of the island, and with Lanzarote only being twenty kilometres away, people were able to get fantastic pictures on a clear day. It wasn't easy getting up there, in fact the walk would take just over three hours; climbing almost to 1000 feet, it wasn't for the faint hearted. It was one of the youngest of Fuerteventura's many volcanoes at only eight thousand years old – it was a baby compared to some of the other volcanoes that were further south on the island, the oldest ones being thirty-six million years old. My talks would expand to the rest of the seven Canary Islands, and would climatically finish by talking about Cumbre Vieja on La Palma, explaining that at some point in the distant future, this old volcano would collapse into the sea creating a tsunami that would have a devastating effect on the east coast of America and would even reach the south coast of Ireland and England; it would also be catastrophic for the six other main Canary Islands as the resulting waves would engulf us before we could really do anything about it.

As you can imagine, when the news broke about the first eruptions on La Palma a lot of people were excitedly messaging me saying, "Oh my god, you were right, it's actually happening". Now I'm neither a geologist nor more to the point a volcanologist. I was only giving information I'd learned about the islands over the years and had a lot of them listened to me properly, they would've heard me say that scientists believed that it would take several major eruptions before this disastrous event would take place. Now that's not to say it wasn't happening, but realistically it was highly unlikely. A lot of people were very relieved as they thought their holidays were going to be cancelled and of course you had some people who were disappointed that this disaster wasn't happening. Sadly, a lot of people were missing the point that a lot of the local people of La Palma were losing everything – their houses, their livelihoods, it was devastating for them. There were heroic efforts being made to rescue livestock but unfortunately nothing could be done to save their highly successful banana plantations as the molten lava and ash were destroying everything in their path.

As my attention turned away from the TVs and their terrible news, I could see there was a queue beginning to build; it was then I realised it was self-service, so I thought I'd better join in sharpish. Looking around at most of the people gathered, it did not seem like there were too many people travelling as part of their holiday, it looked like people were travelling on business or delivery drivers. The atmosphere was very sombre and business-like; few people were smiling and there certainly wasn't much in the way of eye contact. Yes, there were some seasoned travellers, but they were outside the restaurant sitting around eating food that they had prepared themselves, backpacks close at hand as they gazed into their phones or laptops; they had that motionless composure, almost invisible. But everything around them had been carefully placed, all very close at hand and cleverly set out so it was not in anyone's way.

Being a hungry Horace I was looking forward to my grub but on first appearances it wasn't filling me with excitement. It certainly wasn't a case of "Oh my goodness, what a great selection, so what will I choose!?" It was more a case of "There must be something here that I might like"; realistically, it was a case of just eat something, because I knew I had to keep my energy levels up for the long journey ahead. Thankfully, my initial worries about the food were unfounded – as I got to the cashier's desk to show my ticket, I realised I'd managed to squeeze a three-course meal onto my small tray, plus a drink and an orange. Turning to find a seat in the restaurant, I could see Jim had managed to find a quiet table and was tucking into his food. As I was looking over in his direction, he spotted me and shouted, "Hey Gary, come and sit here" as he pointed to the seat next to him. We were both in good spirits as Jim filled me in on all the procedures we may go through while aboard the ship.

I felt comfortable in Jim's company as he was truly knowledgeable, and I felt reassured that if anyone was going to help us complete this long journey safely, Jim was the man. It made it easier for me to use my ears rather than wittering on in my loquacious fashion. I knew we had a long journey with so many border crossings and so many different pieces of paper, dog passports and muzzles –yes muzzles, it didn't matter how loving your little pooch was, these were still a legal requirement. In Harry's and Charlie's cases, lots of different border guards all dressed in uniforms were ideal targets for their sharp teeth. Oh, the fun and games just trying to put them on – I'd had one trial run at the vets and let's just say it was less than successful. They would regularly go mad when strangers came to the door so I knew this was going to be a worrying test for me; my overactive mind had already been through all the different shootout scenarios that could possibly happen at any of the border crossings – the ending of the film "Butch Cassidy and the Sun Dance Kid" comes to mind. I think Jim noticed that I was starting to drift off into my little world of panic, and he was quick to snap me out of it with his reassuring "Don't worry about it Gary, everything will be fine." I looked back at him and smiled, thinking to myself, "Well, we got through the first test easy enough. I suppose there's only another four to go."

After finishing my meal, I said goodnight to Jim and went the short distance back up to my cabin to make sure everything I needed was there. Again, I was fairly impressed, it was a lot nicer than I had anticipated. I wasn't expecting a well-worn hammock covered in stains from the previous old sea dogs that had slept in it before, but I remembered when Nicky and I were first booking the ferry it had got me thinking back to the one time I'd taken the sleeper train from Edinburgh to London – it was like trying to sleep on a plank as we rattled along the tracks, always being woken as we shunted our way through the stations we stopped at. I had imagined having a cabin on a boat could be much worse – picturing the boat rocking back and forth as we crashed our way through every massive wave the cruel Atlantic could throw at us, trying to grab onto something secure in my cabin as the other hand held onto the plastic bag I was violently throwing up into. The thunderous noise and flashes of lightning coming in from the port hole as the sea water sloshed back and forth between the cabins. But this was nothing like that – in fact, if it wasn't for a very gentle motion, you'd never have thought you were on a boat. Everything was pristine and, if anything, it reminded me of the Yohotel Nicky and I would use at Gatwick Airport. We would always land late so it was lovely to have somewhere we could put our heads before we caught the Gatwick Express into London for our yearly week-long holiday. The rooms in the Yohotel were very futuristic, more like smart pods in a spacecraft, but still very comfortable, equipped with a shower very similar to the one in my cabin. After I'd finished admiring what was going to be home for the next two days, I just had to check that everything I needed was in my bag. That done, it was time to head down and visit Harry, Evie and Charlie.

The cabin doors opened using a key card system, so I made sure I had my card in my back pocket before making my way along the narrow corridor and down the stairs. The boat decks seemed quiet, just the odd person sitting around looking at their phone or trying to get some sleep, but the main thing on my mind was what state the dogs were going to be in. Quickly checking my watch, I realised I hadn't seen them in nearly two hours. I felt terrible – this was not what they were used to, being nearly ten o'clock on a Saturday night, they would usually be stretched out on the couches or lying curled up in a place of their choosing, but not tonight.

Tonight, the poor dogs were holed up in cages in the back of a van on a boat in the dark, with only the slightest shimmers of light coming in through the van's windows. Outside the van, it was quite noisy as we were parked close to the ship's funnel and you could hear the large diesel engines powering away as they expelled their light fumes into the night sky. We were heading into a blustery warm northerly wind, so it was difficult to hear the noise coming from the propellers, but I'm sure it was playing its part in the ship's cacophony of sound.

To get to the van, I had to first pass through the boat's reception and then through an extremely heavy door which took me out onto the deck. There were already a few people walking around with their dogs. They all seemed very pleasant and were making the effort to chat with each other. The dogs were all very friendly as they sniffed each other with their excited wagging tails; it was very noticeable that these dogs were all well looked after and all very well behaved. "Geez, wait till they get a load of my lot," I thought to myself. The one saving grace that I knew might help was that I planned to only have one dog out on the deck at a time; there was no room for any slip ups, I was determined to complete this mission without any disasters, although the words (simple mistakes) were never too far away from my usual repertoire.

The van was facing south, meaning it was facing to the back of the boat. As I turned to my right, I passed the back doors of the van; the side door was facing the sea. As I heaved the side door open, the middle light came on, and I quickly climbed into the back of the van, pulling the door shut behind me. Straight away I was relieved to hear the furore of all the different noises outside had dissipated and I could see all three dogs were sitting present and correct. Harry was the only one to bark which actually made me feel better – he was the whole reason we were all in this van in the first place, so it was great to hear he was his usual chirpy self. One of the main worries was that all this excitement could bring on one of his epileptic fits. I did have plenty of Valium if needed, but it wasn't the ideal place to be if he did have a fit, it wasn't like I could just pick him up and carry him through to the usual quiet tranquillity of the bedroom till it passed.

Charlie seemed fine but not as lively as he can be, but noticeably Evie looked a bit out of sorts: her long fluffy ears were drooped, and she seemed rather lost. It would have been great if I could have opened all the cage doors to let them out but unfortunately the cage doors were all facing the back doors of the van. I was able to get myself comfortable on one of the seats in the back of the van. I inspected my surroundings – around my feet was Nicky's suitcase, the large hold-all containing a mixture of the dogs' things and mine, a large plastic bag which contained all their food and a smaller plastic bag with their muzzles. These silly things just filled me with dread – on the first and only experimental time I tried to put them on, well, let's just say Harry and especially Charlie were less than helpful.

Looking into their cages, I could see Harry had scoffed all his food but had managed to overturn his drinks dish, Charlie had eaten most of his, but Evie's dish seemed rather untouched. It dawned on me rather quickly that it might be Evie who I was going to have to pay particular attention to. I tried talking to them, hoping I'd lift their spirits with "Now don't worry, this is us on our way to see Nicky." I began to consider the possibility that I could probably get comfortable enough to sleep with them in the van, but I was reminded of what Jim had said to me – the more you visit them, the more they become over-excited. He had rightly said to not over-do the visits so they became more accepting of their predicament, but I still couldn't help feeling sorry for these little friends of mine being stuck in the van.

One thing I had to do was get them out of their cages so they could have a walk along the deck and out in that lovely fresh sea air; obviously they were going to have to do their doggie business, so I was armed with water and plastic bags. I knew there was no way in this mad blustery wind I was going to manage all three of them at once, and to leave just one dog in the van while I walked the other two would have been unfair, leaving the solitary dog to panic, so the only option was to walk them one at a time.

With Harry surprisingly being the liveliest and the one that seemed like he had it all together, I thought I'd take him first as the other two would then smell his track, giving them the slightest feeling of familiarity with their surroundings. So, with that plan in mind, I climbed out of the side door, carefully pulling it shut behind me. Nothing had prepared me for the difficulty that lay ahead once I'd got round to the back doors. Straight away as I opened the right-hand door, I realised how difficult this was going to be – with the back of the van heading with the forward motion of the boat into the blustery wind, the doors would be ripped off their hinges if you didn't hold on to them. So, with Harry being in the cage just underneath Evie's, I had to somehow take control of the right-hand door with my shoulder while trying to keep control of the left-hand door with my left hand, while at the same time opening Harry's cage and getting his lead on with my right hand. Oh, did I mention the wind? Then, when Harry jumped to the ground, I had to carefully close the left-hand door and then the right. Wow, this was a challenge.

Once we had passed some of the other parked cars and got onto the more open part of the deck closer to the reception, everything seemed fine. Harry was in great fettle and not too fazed by his experience, he was even being well behaved when introduced to the other dogs who were walking around with their owners. Thankfully, even though it was extremely windy, it was still very warm, and the ship was moving along at a steady pace. Usually by this time of year, the heavy Atlantic winter swell would be in full swing, and our shorelines would be alive with the throngs of eager surfers fighting over the crashing waves. I did have two little travel sickness tablets with me, but these would have been little consolation while trying to deal with those doors had there been a large swell. If that had been the case, I would have had to put the dogs straight into the ship's allocated kennels.

Again, returning Harry to the van there was just no easy way of getting him back into the cage, and of course with me struggling with the van doors, I was only making things worse by panicking Harry. Then it was the same rigmarole again with Charlie. Getting Charlie out onto the deck was more of a lively affair as he chose to bark at the other larger dogs, but the owners didn't seem to mind as his tail was wagging and his ears were back in a submissive fashion. More importantly my plan had worked, Charlie had picked up on Harry's scent and he chose to pee in exactly the same spot as Harry had. Before taking Charlie back, it dawned on me that this was just the first time on the first night of moving the dogs in and out of the van – I had another two days of this more than arduous task. I realised I was just going to have to knuckle down and get on with it. Getting Charlie back into the van was not as difficult as I was only having to use the one door on the left-hand side, but there was no way I could entertain complacency as I had to go through it all again with Evie. Eventually getting Evie out on to the deck, I could tell she was still out of sorts; she was just not settling into this journey very well at all. I could only hope as the hours progressed, she'd become a little more comfortable in her surroundings.

Once I'd got the dogs all safely back in the van, I made sure their water and food dishes were replenished. I climbed back into the van, entering once again through the side door, and looked around just to check there wasn't anything I'd forgotten to do. The three dogs were staring at me from their cages; once again, Harry seemed the one most at ease. In a stern voice, trying to kid them that I was in total control, I told them I was off to the cabin and I'd be back in a few hours. In fact, I actually said to them, "I'm just popping to the shop, I'll be back soon" as this was something that they would hear on a regular basis as Nicky and I would say it repeatedly before we made our way to our local supermarket, Hyperdinos.

After checking the doors were all secure, I started to head back to the cabin, but as I was making my way along the open deck, and just before opening the heavy door to the boat's main reception, I happened to look down at my jeans, actually they were fawn-coloured chinos, only to see they were covered in dirty black marks. On further inspection, I could see my once lovely bright white t-shirt was in the same mess – to any passer-by, it must have looked like I'd been rolling around on the deck. I quickly about turned and made my way back to the van where I knew I had a change of clothes in the bag.

The dogs welcomed me back like I'd been away for a week, although it had only been two minutes. I apologised to them and told them, "Sorry but I've got to go back out again." I changed into a pair of shorts as it was obviously warm enough and there was no point in ruining another pair of jeans so early in the journey. I couldn't really see into the bag that easily as the light was poor but luckily my searching hand came across a dark blue t-shirt which was a more ideal colour for getting the dogs in and out of the back of the van. Don't get me wrong, the van was spotless and very new, it was only the inside door fixings that had got me into this mess – had the van been pointing in the other direction, this whole operation of visiting and taking them for a walk across the deck would have been a lot easier, but it was what it was so I just had to get on with it.

Finally getting back out onto the deck and making my way back to the cabin, I noticed the boat was a lot quieter as most people had hunkered down for the evening. Again pulling open the heavy door, I passed through the reception. I could see a few bodies in the seated area, either curled up trying to get some sleep or still staring at their devices, again with all their worldly possessions close at hand. Getting into my cabin, I sat on the bed, thinking isn't it just nice to relax but looking at my watch. I had promised the dogs I'd visit them in a few hours. I could see it was twenty to one, so I set the alarm on my phone for three o'clock. I was sure the dogs would be fine until then.

Lying in my cabin bed I could still feel the slight movement of the boat with a slight noise and vibration from the two powerful engines. Even though the lights were out I wasn't getting much in the way of sleep, just lots of weird dreams closely related to this strange journey I had begun. Rolling about restlessly I began to feel really thirsty so my hand began to scramble around the cabin floor searching for my bottle of water, but I just couldn't find it. I had no other option – I had to put the light on. I could now see my water bottle lying on the other bed where I had left it. Checking my watch I saw it was nearly quarter to three so after having a big drink of water I realised there was no point in trying to get back to sleep, I may as well get up and get ready to visit the dogs. The struggles I'd had with the van doors were fresh in my mind, so I thought I'd have a shower and see if I could freshen up for the challenge ahead. Surprisingly the shower was quite powerful and instantly began to make me feel better. I must have spent a good five minutes just enjoying the warm water and it was a real pleasure getting out the shower to find a lovely fresh clean towel, which certainly helped to lift my spirits.

Leaving the cabin in spritely fashion I felt refreshed and more prepared for the mission ahead. I knew what I had to do and this blustery wind wasn't going to get the better of me, I said to myself, although after passing through reception I realised I'd forgotten how heavy the door was leading out onto the deck.

Even though it was early in the morning, it was still really warm, but I noticed there was no let up with that blustery wind. I could see the lights on the deck were very bright, but outside of the boat there was nothing but darkness. Making my way to the van there was that worry in the back of my mind – would Harry be okay? Instead of opening the back door straight away I knew it was better to enter through the side door just to see how they all were. On entering the van my eyes first focused on Harry, but there was no problem at all, he was glad to see me, same with Charlie, he was also looking lively, but Evie looked much the same as when I'd left her earlier. She was the smallest of our three dogs but for a small Yorkshire terrier she had the biggest of ears, and with them both being lowered and pointing away from her head she looked like a sad little gremlin. It was also noticeable that she hadn't eaten much of her food. "Come on Evie," I said to her out loud, "you've got to eat something, we've still got a long way to go" and with a last plea, I said, "You know Nicky's going to blame me if you're not eating."

It was hard to tell if they had been drinking enough water as they had all managed to spill their water and get their bedding wet. But this I couldn't sort till I got to the front of their cages. First things first, I had to get Harry out for his walk and then I'd try and sort their cages out one at a time after each of them had been walked. Getting Harry out was the same hassle as the first time, the only difference being I was prepared for all the hassle that came with it; this actually helped, being a little more positive and just getting on with it. Harry was fine in himself and was off as soon as we got walking – his head was up and he was raring to go. I wanted to take a picture, but I felt it was safer not to as there were still little places around where Harry could disappear off the side of the ship and into the sea. The thought of that filled me with dread. I'd like to think I would have jumped in after him and that both of us would have been rescued, leaving me with another heroic story to tell at some illustrious dinner table.

Given that it was well after three o'clock I was surprised to see so many other dog owners up and about walking their dogs. I thought most of these people would've been tucked up in their cabins fast asleep. But then suddenly there was a face I recognised, it was Maria, our vet, standing there with her small Jack Russell, Tia – yup, that's exactly what I thought when I heard her dog's name: Tia Maria!

Now it shouldn't have come as a surprise that Maria was on the boat, she had told me numerous times that she was going to be making the same journey, I just didn't realise it was going to be the exact same one. Nicky and I had spoken about how handy it would be if Maria was on the same boat, especially with Harry being the way he was. Although obviously this wouldn't be fair on Maria as she wasn't working and had told us she would be off visiting her family in Valencia.

Nicky and I had got to know Maria really well as she was the one who had first diagnosed Charlie with a damaged cruciate ligament. After his operation we had to go through a long process of cage resting him, and with him being a young puppy this was extremely difficult, we felt so cruel putting him in a cage for long hours and of course it didn't make any sense to him either but it's what we had to do. When we let him out of the cage, we had to make sure the whole house was knee friendly and I can assure you that was no easy task, it meant moving a large coffee table into our main bedroom which was replaced by a mattress so when he did jump on and off the couch his knee was cushioned.

The bedroom was another concern as we always allowed our dogs to sleep on the bed, and yes, I know what you're thinking: "Dogs shouldn't be allowed on the bed". And yes, you would be right to say that. One, it's probably unhygienic, and two, once you start letting them sleep on the bed, they see themselves as equals, they literally think they own the place – and now times that by three! Yup, as far as Harry, Evie and Charlie were concerned, they owned a three-bedroom house in Fuerteventura with two able servants; I say two able servants, but I think they saw one of them as pretty useless but always good for a laugh. Of course, there was the issue of the bed as well; there was no way Charlie could be allowed to jump on and off the bed so there was only one thing for it – the bed base had to go so the mattress would be on the floor. I was okay with that, I remember back in my younger days it was actually quite cool to have your mattress on the floor, but now, nearly 40 years later, it was a completely different proposition. The reality was a lot of moaning and groaning as I tried to pull my old frame up from the floor – that electric-paced single jump to my feet like a ninja warrior was certainly a thing of the past. Don't get me wrong, I was still keeping pretty fit but this was making it more than obvious I was getting older.

Nearing the end of his treatment, once a week mid-afternoon we would walk him up to our vets where Maria would give him laser treatment on the damaged knee to help reduce the chances of him suffering from early signs of arthritis when he got older. It was a little quieter late afternoon as most of the locals would still be mid-slumber with it being their siesta time, so it was an easier time in the vets for the women who worked there, and they seemed a bit more relaxed. So, Nicky and I would often chat happily away with Maria on all different subjects. But with everything that had been going on, it had slipped my mind that Maria was going to be on the same ferry journey. I must admit I was surprised to see Maria out with Tia on the deck at that time of night, as Maria had booked a cabin for herself and the dog. I would have loved to have done that but having three dogs with me there was no chance. I could imagine every time someone passed the cabin door our three all barking in unison, which would obviously end up with us being put out to sea in a solitary lifeboat or even worse being made to walk the plank.

Maria seemed genuinely pleased to see Harry and me. "Hey, hiya Maria" I said in my usual jovial fashion. "Hiya, I wondered where you'd been, I haven't seen you, and where's Charlie!?" she asked. Maria obviously hadn't forgotten we were all going to be on the same journey. I explained that I was only able to walk one of the dogs at a time; straightaway, Maria offered to help. I said not to worry, I could handle it. I knew there was a long way to go and I felt there was no way I could burden her with my problems – it was okay having a laugh and a joke back at the vets in Corralejo, but this wasn't fair, Maria was supposed to be on holiday. But Maria was insistent. "I'm not doing anything else," she exclaimed. So, very apologetically, I accepted her offer of help.

Once we had made our way back to the van, Maria could see my predicament and thankfully helped me with the doors. Even with two of us, it was still quite a difficult task to get all three dogs out at once. It was great getting all of them out onto the deck together, especially Charlie and Evie, they seemed in much better form. Charlie recognised Maria straightaway which must have been a pleasant surprise for him although a mite confusing. I couldn't thank Maria enough. I told her that I recognised she was on holiday and that I felt really guilty, but she would hear none of it and again she insisted it wasn't a problem and it would help pass the time.

I was surprised to see how many other dogs were travelling the same journey, but it was very noticeable that my three were the noisiest. I didn't mind too much as it was a sign they were happy; sadly, Harry and Evie had had their tails docked at birth, but their stumpy little tails were wagging away profusely. After a short while, Maria helped me back to the van with the dogs; it was so much easier filling their dishes with water and food with Maria's help. Once I'd got them settled and got the van all locked up, I walked back to the reception area with Maria and little Tia. It was nearly 4.30 in the morning and still dark outside the ship; when I looked up, I could see all the stars brightly shining in the sky. I turned to Maria to say goodnight and just at that moment she asked, "When will you need to take them out again !?" I said, "Oh don't worry, I've got it covered; you've done enough for me tonight." Quite nonchalantly, Maria said, "Look I'll need to get Tia out for half-six just before they start serving breakfast" and with no resistance I replied, "Aww great, I'll see you then, thanks Maria."

I felt much better with Maria's help, life had just got a whole lot easier, and now that I was able to relax a little, I realised how tired I was. But there was still one thing I wanted to do. While we'd had the dogs out of the van, I had noticed there were lots of stars in the night sky; the visibility wasn't great because of all the light pollution coming from the ship's car deck. Not hanging about, I ran up the stairs to the terraced area on deck seven. It was really dark up there and there wasn't a soul around, so I quietly grabbed a sunbed and just lay back and looked up to the sky. The view was amazing, just millions of little bright speckles filling the night's skyline. Now before I get carried away, can I just say I'm not a cosmologist, or an astrophysicist, I know nothing about quantum mechanics, but I get really excited about the universe and all its unanswered questions. I don't mind listening to all the different theories even though I don't understand them. I just stared up at the sky in wonderment, the little knowledge I did have just filling me with even more questions; it's in these moments I really wish my retention of information was a bit more organised. There seemed to be a similarity between the space inside my head and the vast space I was looking at – there's a lot of it and not a great deal of intelligence to be found.

Now for any of you other folks who ever take time to stare up at the sky you might be amazed to know that there's only a total of five other planets you can see with the naked eye, everything else is stars, similar to the sun in our solar system and some massively bigger. All the stars you see (and there could be anything up to four hundred billion of them and ten times as many planets) are all within our own galaxy (The Milky Way). We can't see any stars out with our own galaxy, this could only be done if you had a powerful telescope. Having said that, if you're in the southern hemisphere on a moonless night you can sometimes see Andromeda which, although it looks like a weak hazy star, is actually another galaxy, bigger than our own. Our two galaxies are both hurtling towards each other at an incredible 402,000 kilometres an hour, but don't panic just yet, as both galaxies are about 2.5 million light years apart, so we shouldn't crash together until about 3.75 billion years from now. They even think the earth might survive, well that's if our life-giving sun doesn't blow up first, which will ultimately mean the end for our beautiful little planet. Both galaxies are called spiral galaxies and will spin into each other like two slow-moving Catherine wheels. Andromeda may be bigger than us, but we are still a whopping 52,000 light years in radius. Now if you're wondering what a light year is, especially regarding distance, well in human terms, each one is about six trillion miles in length. It just makes everything here on earth so insignificant. So if you have a little problem, trust me – in the vastness of this ginormous universe, yup, it's small.

Now surely after reading all this you can understand my amazement at this cosmological conundrum, even you must be asking yourself, where did it all come from? Is there a beginning, is there an end? Well, let me give you the littles bits I do know. The universe started around 13.7 billion years ago from something that scientists call the big bang. Now this is where stuff begins to get even more mind blowing. The universe before the big bang was a million times smaller than an atom (for any of you who don't know, an atom is around a million times smaller than the thickness of a hair). Yup, the word small doesn't really cover it – maybe the word infinitesimal might do the trick. Then in a millionth of a second there was something called an inflation (which again is a scientific theory) and boom – the universe was off and running. Ironically, we use the word bang which in actual fact is wrong as there's no known noise out in space, reason being, the vacuum of outer space has zero air, so crashing asteroids, exploding planets and bright supernovas make no sound at all because there's no vibrating air. So how big is the universe now, I hear you ask. Well the known visible universe (as much as we have been able to discover) now stands at around 93 billion light years, so when you think our own galaxy has possibly four hundred billion stars in it, they believe the known universe could have as many as two trillion galaxies, and it does not finish there.

The universe is still expanding at a phenomenal rate, in fact many years ago the sky at night would have looked far more congested with stars than it does now, but because of expansion everything's moving further apart. You would be forgiven for thinking that after nearly fourteen billion years this expansion was beginning to slow down to a cumbersome rate but no, you'd be wrong, it's still fizzing along at an incredible 70 kilometres a second, I mean we are literally living inside an explosion. So, when we hear stories of some bloke walking on water, or even turning water into wine (after all we know about the physics of the universe) it doesn't seem that farfetched.

I didn't lie too long on the sunbed, but I certainly felt a bit more relaxed or at least a bit happier about the whole situation; the boat journey was going to be okay, with the help of Maria, the dogs were going to be well looked after. There was still the concern that Evie hadn't settled into the journey very well, but I had noticed she was a bit better when we were all out on the deck together, so again things in general were looking up.

Returning to my cabin I began to realise how tired I was. Looking around my spick and span surroundings, it seemed luxurious compared to the back of the van, although I still felt guilty that I'd left the three dogs caged up in some stranger's van. I thought for all my efforts I deserved a little respite, so climbing into my clean and comfortable bed was quite a relief but in the back of my mind I knew I wouldn't be there for very long; I certainly didn't want to sleep in and miss the opportunity of having the help of Maria with the dogs, and my stomach certainly wouldn't forgive me if I missed breakfast. Resting my head on the pillow I realised I had better set my alarm as I could only sleep for two hours.

It wasn't long before I was checking my watch – only 15 minutes till the alarm went off so there was no point in trying to fall back to sleep again. With a slight feeling of annoyance that I hadn't had much sleep, I realised the best bet was to get up and jump into the shower, it had certainly worked the day before. Making my way back down to the car deck I once again felt quite refreshed which was amazing considering I'd be lucky if I'd slept for an hour. That big stiff door at the reception which led out into the open air hadn't got any lighter. Right in front of me I could see Maria was already there, chatting away quite happily with one of the other dog owners.

It was still dark outside with just a glimmer of light now coming from the east. Looking around me I could see I had been late for the party as all the other dog owners seemed to be out and about with their dogs; it was nice to see, because they were all very friendly and chatting away. The wind around the deck although warm, which I thought was surprising for that time in the morning, hadn't changed and was still very blustery so I knew what to expect when we got to the van.

My main concern of course was what condition the dogs were

going to be in, especially Harry, with all this change of environment on top of all the excitement, there was always the chance it could trigger a fit, but I had good cover – I had boxes of Valium if needed and I now had the very capable Maria at my side. But once again I was pleasantly surprised to see that Harry was up and ready, almost like he had been expecting me. Charlie looked well but Evie still had these drooped ears. I could tell she wasn't really enjoying this at all, although once she was out on the deck and mixing with all the other dogs, she picked up again. Mind you I also put that down to her keeping an eye on Harry as she gets so jealous, there was no chance of Harry getting a girlfriend on this journey.

Once we returned to the van, I could see Evie still hadn't been eating much, Maria said not to worry too much as this can happen with certain dogs as the travelling can make them feel very unsettled which can put them off their food. That certainly didn't seem to be a problem for Harry –I'd noticed that he had managed to scrape the top of his nose trying to retrieve his biscuits that had fallen through his cage. It was great to see he had a raging appetite, we always found that was a good sign he was in a good place. Charlie's dish still had some biscuits in it, but I put that down to him not running around as much and not getting to burn his usual amount of energy, but Evie's dish had hardly been touched. "C'mon Evie, you've got to eat darlin', we've got a long way to go," I pleaded, but she was still in that droopy eared way.

Once I had the van all locked up and secured, I headed towards the restaurant where I was looking forward to my breakfast. I wasn't under any illusion, I knew it wasn't going to be exactly five-star quality with table service, and this became more apparent when I entered the restaurant and found myself at the end of a very long queue. The place still had that industrial feel about it; people were looking very sombre and were probably still tired as it was early in the morning. Some were looking nonplussed, staring at the news on the TVs, still reporting on the volcanic eruption in La Palma. The staff were all standing behind the buffet waiting to serve up the food on show. The food all looked very bland, the scrambled egg, tortilla, bacon, beans and sausages failed to impress, even the fried tomatoes did little to give it any colour. There was a little more life at the end of the buffet with yogurts and a modest selection of fruit and that wafting smell of warm coffee. It was unfair of me to get too judgemental; as anyone who knows me would tell you, I'm not the fussiest of eaters, in fact if you had thrown all my food into the one bowl, I would be happy to get down on my knees and chow down with the dogs. It didn't take me long to finish my breakfast and after all was said and done, I quite enjoyed it. I made sure I took away an orange for myself and a small carton of natural yogurt, just to see if I could tempt Evie to eat a little more.

3

My next plan was a simple one, all I wanted to do was go back to the cabin and see if I could catch up on a couple of hours of sleep. Thinking back, I was amazed at the lack of sleep I'd had over the last twenty-four hours, and surely there was no way I could keep this up for the rest of the journey. But before I did that, I had to see if Evie would try some of this yogurt, I was hoping it would get her back into her usual habit of enjoying her food, and there was plenty there to give Harry and Charlie a little treat. Making my way past the now open reception, I could see there were a few more passengers milling around, so I had to make sure I didn't make a fool of myself struggling with that heavy door which led directly out onto the open-air car deck. Luckily for me, just as I approached the door it began to open. I could see there was a lady using all her might to try and heave it open, so I quickened my pace so I could help her. "No problema," I uttered, trying to make it look easy. "Gracias," she replied. So I'd made myself out to look like I was the helpful good guy, but I realised in my haste, I'd nearly destroyed the yogurt carton and some of it was now halfway up my arm. "Shit," I said despairingly; the lady was now laughing loudly as she could see I was covered in yogurt. I had also managed to amuse some of the other people standing around with their dogs out on the deck; all I could do was raise my eyebrows and smile as I tried to lick the yogurt off my arm.

Thankfully there was still enough left for me to offer Evie so I quickly made my way back to the van, feeling a little embarrassed. Climbing through the side door of the van I tried to explain to the dogs what had happened before realising they probably didn't have a clue what I was on about. I put what was left of the yogurt carton down on the van floor, grabbed a large kitchen roll, ripped off a few pieces of clean paper towel and wiped the yogurt off my arm and hands.

Still feeling silly, and slightly sticky, I proceeded to stick my finger into what was left of the yogurt carton and offer it to Evie. At first, she sniffed at it but then decided to lick it off my finger – brilliant, I thought to myself as she eagerly waited for more. Sadly for Harry and Charlie, they missed out and didn't get any at all, as Evie had the lot. My only worry was that it would give her squishy guts that could leave a smelly mess to clean up, so I wasn't too fussed that Harry and Charlie didn't get any. The great news was that it had the desired effect; not long after licking all the yogurt from my finger, I found Evie tucking into some of her biscuits. That was such a relief for me, it meant my mission to get all three dogs back to the UK alive and all in one piece was fully back on track. I couldn't get too excited as I realised I hadn't even completed the first twenty-four hours yet, there was still a very long way to go.

I hung around in the back of the van a little longer, wittering away all sorts of nonsense just knowing they would feel a little more secure hearing the familiarity of my voice; their ears would always prick up every time I mentioned Nicky's name. I suppose deep down I was really hoping they had some understanding of what this mission was all about, knowing how happy the three of them would be when they saw Nicky again and, of course, I couldn't wait to see Nicky's face as they all come bounding out of the van when we eventually got to our final destination

As I left the van, it was still quite early, but the sun was beginning to rise and the blustery breeze seemed a little warmer. From the open port holes it was just a beautiful ocean for as far as the eye could see, only the odd ship some way far off in the distance. Another real bonus for me was that fortunately the sea was still relatively calm, something else that had played on my mind before the journey had started – the idea of me spending two days at sea on my hands and knees puking into a plastic bag feeling extremely sorry for myself, but thankfully for the time being everything was going along quite smoothly.

Getting back to the cabin I wasted no time in throwing my clothes off. I didn't even bother to fold them up or place them tidily on the spare bed next to me, I was just happy to quickly bunk down and feel comfortably stretched out. Normally it takes me a while to get used to a strange new bed I've never slept in before, especially as I'm not a great sleeper at the best of times, but not this morning. I didn't set the alarm on my phone. I was going to take a chance and see how long I'd sleep for, knowing in the back of my mind the dogs seemed quite settled in their strange new surroundings which added to my more relaxed frame of mind.

I climbed into my bed, rolled onto my belly and thankfully I quickly drifted away into the land of nod. It seemed like no time at all before I was awoken by some people passing my cabin door. Not knowing the time or what day of the week it was, I checked my watch and saw that I'd managed to catch a couple of solid hours sleep. Feeling satisfied that this would do me, I didn't lie too long and quickly jumped into the shower. I spent a good five minutes refreshing myself with that lovely warm water. The two hours' sleep had really helped recharge my batteries and I quickly dried myself and put on some clean shorts and a t-shirt. I tidied up the clothes I'd flung off earlier, and made my way out of the cabin.

It wasn't far to the elevated deck seven, and I couldn't wait to get out there and take in the views. Getting out onto the deck I could see the sun was high in the sky and looking out beyond the back of the boat we were protected from the northernly breeze. The first thing I noticed was there were quite a few people out there. I recognised a lot of faces I'd seen previously down in the buffet, only now they seemed a bit more relaxed, even happy as they sat around chatting. I noticed a good few were now making use of the sunbeds that were casually dotted around this warm and very sunny deck.

I spotted Maria. She was sitting on a seat with her feet up and her back to me, chatting away on her phone, so I knew not to disturb her, not that I wanted to anyway. I just wanted to take in the fresh air and enjoy the vastness around me. Every direction I looked it was just lots of sea and sky, nothing else apart from us and the boat churning along at about twenty-two knots. It was wonderful. There weren't even any other ships in sight. I'd downloaded an app on my phone called Vessel Finder and usually when I looked at it, the sea just seemed to be crowded with ships, especially around Cadiz, which was where we were headed, but from where I was standing, I could see nothing. Again I was being hit with that euphoric feeling of well-being. I could see down to the van and knew I couldn't stay on the top deck for long, I had to go down and visit the dogs. But with the way I was feeling, I was confident they would be fine. I stretched my head over the side of the boat and looked in the direction we were headed. I still couldn't see any other ships. I got my phone out, I had to grab some pics, I maybe couldn't record the feeling of euphoria, but I could certainly grab some memories.

While I was taking the pics, I began to think of the last time I was actually on a ferry. I thought back to the very first time, way back in 1976 when, as a young boy only aged thirteen, I'd travelled to Guernsey from Portsmouth with my mum and dad and two brothers Michael and Kenneth. Eventually docking in St Peter's Port, we then had to get a smaller boat over to the beautiful little island of Herme.

Herme was an incredible little island. It only had one hotel and a small handful of holiday cottages dotted around the island, and there was only one shop which was close to the little harbour. We were lucky enough to stay in one of the holiday cottages which was high up in the middle of the island. With its fantastic views we could almost see all around the island. The cottage was big even for the five of us; it was pretty isolated up there, but there were lots of lovely tracks to all the little special beaches and coves in and around the island. Something that vividly sticks in my mind from that trip was the popularity of Rod Stewart's "I am sailing" – he didn't write it, but it became a massive hit; the BBC used it for a documentary they made about HMS Ark Royal, and the Scotland fans made it very anthemic as it was sung during all our international games. Yup, there was just nowhere you could go at the time without that song playing in the background.

Once I'd finished taking pics around the ship, I found myself positioned somewhere near the middle of deck seven, which gave me a very good panoramic view of my surroundings. Again, I was just blown away with the endless views of sea and sky.

Spending so much time on social media and keeping a close eye on current affairs, I was becoming very aware of some of the terrible things that were happening around the world. My inquisitive interest in geo-politics was certainly broadening my mind. Wherever countries were geographically, whether it be eastern Europe, the far east, the middle east, the Southern hemisphere, south America, central America or even North America, the world begins to look a lot smaller and very interrelated. I wasn't interested in taking sides, I was just concerned these selfish power-greedy lunatics could destroy this beautiful world. Like many others, I liked the place, so what right did they have to destroy it? And if that wasn't enough to worry about, along came a devastating pandemic that no one seemed to fully understand. Some people believed it was all part of a big plan to take control of the world and protests began to spring up from city to city, while the money men all claimed that weak governments were dealing with it badly which was costing business a great deal of money. All over the world, rightly or wrongly, everyone had an opinion that needed to be heard. Newspapers and news channels around the world were all sharing the same headlines, it had all become a bit globally claustrophobic, which in turn was turning a lot of people globally paranoid. So just for a few days it was nice not to be looking at my phone, and to be enjoying these breath-taking views, and breathing in all that lovely fresh air. It was great at this moment just to feel the world was a much bigger almost happy place.

As my mind was floating around in the white fluffy clouds, I was just standing staring out into nothingness with some weird gooey look on my face when suddenly I heard, "Shall we let the dogs out!?" It was Maria. I obviously hadn't seen her coming. "Yeah, brilliant Maria, cheers." Looking at me again she asked, "You, okay?" She had obviously noticed when she approached that my mind was somewhere else. "No, honestly, I'm fine, I was just really enjoying the views." I started to tell her about the last couple of times I was on a long-distance ferry journey, but realising I was probably beginning to sound really boring, I quickly changed the subject and started asking her how she was finding the journey and how far she had to travel once she got off the ferry. I was amazed when she told me she had over seven hundred kilometres to drive once she got to Cadiz, it was a long way to drive. Mind you it was only a fifth of the distance of our journey.

I was looking forward to eventually getting to Cadiz, although I was still a little apprehensive as there was still the challenge of getting all three dogs safely through customs. I was sure we would all pass with flying colours. My only other possible problems were that the rules and regulations were changing on a daily basis, or maybe a technical issue with the van. The idea of me and the three dogs being stuck somewhere in the middle of France with incomplete paperwork didn't bear thinking about. I realised it was best not to think about it and stay positive, things were working out at the moment, so let's just hope it stayed that way.

Maria like Jim had also done this journey a few times so she was always reassuring me, and kept telling me things would be fine. It may sound like I was always going on about it, but to be honest it was all part of my sense of humour, I was just whinging on about it in jovial fashion. One other thing that put my mind at rest was when Maria explained that she was quite happy to help me with the dogs – having done this journey quite a few times, she made it very clear that it can get quite boring and that it was a refreshing change that she was on the boat with something to do. It was certainly a massive help for me, the journey would've been so much more difficult without her, so once again (literally) lady luck was smiling on me. Okay, she wasn't the Roman goddess Fortuna, but she was Maria from Valencia.

If I've got this right, Maria had studied to become a vet at the University of Zaragoza and once she completed her studies she then travelled around parts of England and other cities in Europe, but wherever she went, she always used to get herself into some sort of veterinary work. So not only was she honing her veterinary skills but also learning new languages at the same time. She was obviously a very intelligent young lady, who loved the work she did. That reminded me of the old saying, "Choose a job you love, and you'll never have to work a day in your life."

4

People always say you should never have regrets, but I'm sorry, I do. I'd love to have been in the position where I could have learned some skill and honed it like Maria did through the years. I've literally skidded through life by the seat of my pants, bouncing from pillar to post, eventually ending up on the beautiful island of Fuerteventura to ironically become a professional idiot. Now in my own defence, through some previous writing I had learned that I had a form of ADHD. It all happened purely by accident. After I'd written my first couple of chapters I decided to send it off to a friend not only for his approval but just to test the waters as they say.

My friend Dougie was working as a university lecturer at the time but was writing articles for a few different publications so I thought to myself, who better to go to than Dougie? My first move was to contact him and tell him that I had been doing a little writing, and to ask if he could look at it and, in his esteemed opinion, let me know what he thought. Dougie was one of life's good guys, he just didn't have a bad bone in his body, always greeted you with a smile and of course said it would be a pleasure. Dougie was a well-travelled man, but whatever corner of the world he found himself in, he always shared his experiences through teaching, so I felt I couldn't have picked a better guy to turn to. Being my first attempt at writing, I wasn't sure how I was doing.

My biggest concerns were that I'd not really taken advantage of a decent education system, and also the fact that getting me to sit down for more than five minutes and focus was a challenge. I didn't lack confidence and I certainly wasn't one of those people who would go on to claim how they hated school, or how they really disliked their teachers. Neither was I a big guy, so I didn't exactly pose a threat to anyone. In fact that hasn't really changed, I'm still only about five feet eight inches with shoes on. But getting close to my preliminary exams in my third year I found out that because my birthday was in February, I could qualify as an early Christmas leaver. I foolishly thought I'd hit the jackpot – not only could I leave school early, but I could avoid all forms of examination. As far as I was concerned, everything would just eventually fall into my lap anyway – I mean, I was the sort of guy if I fell out of a window, I'd probably go up.

Yes, I was a confident happy-go-lucky guy with a very positive outlook on life, just unfortunately there had been a little oversight regarding reality. When anyone tried to explain that I'd maybe need to start thinking through a bit more carefully before I made decisions, I would just shrug my shoulders and say, "Ach, don't worry, no problem."

So, after sending off my first attempt at writing to Dougie, I was quite excited. I knew if anyone could find the remotest positive thing to say about it, Dougie was my man. Well, it didn't take him long to reply, it must have been about three days later that he got back to me. I could see that he must have read it, so as I was excitedly opening the email, I was anticipating which parts he might have enjoyed the most. But on opening the email, I realised it wasn't the answer I was hoping for. In fact, it was worse than that, it read, "Hi Gary, I've read through it all, here try doing this!" and underneath his less-than-informative comments was a link to an online ADHD test! I was devastated, I felt betrayed – not Dougie, if there was anyone who could find something, anything positive about my writing, I was sure it would be him! On further inspection of the email, I noticed that just under the ADHD link Dougie had said, "Once you've done it, give me a video call on Friday."

I stared at the comment for a little longer: "try doing this"!? My mood of devastation had started to change, I was now in a more inquisitive mood; one thing was for sure – it didn't look like it was a joke. Dougie had been teaching for years, and okay, maybe listening was never one of my strong points, but I always listened to Dougie, he always had a wealth of knowledge on a range of different subjects. So, with that all in mind, there was nothing left to do apart from take the test. It was all straightforward, a multiple-choice test, and even as I was working my way through the questions, I was beginning to get a sense of realisation – and it wasn't a bad feeling. I felt I was learning something about my reactions to things, the way I thought about stuff. It came as no surprise to me once I'd finished the test and their final analysis came through that it was highly probable that I had some form of ADHD.

After doing the test it wasn't long till I was doing further research on the subject. The more I read about it, the more my life's jigsaw puzzle was coming together. I was always one for big ideas, I never got round to completing things. I struggled to hold my focus, my whole way of being could frustrate me at times, the more agitated I became, the less I can sit still, sometimes my mind is racing and I feel like I'll never be able to switch it off. If you hand me a packet of chocolate biscuits, I'll eat the lot, there's sometimes no filter there to say hold on, you don't need to eat them all. The bigger my worries are, I can be susceptible to drug dependency, and I certainly enjoy drinking – sadly these things are great for dulling an overactive mind, but the downsides are another dangerous hazard to your health, but on the upside, there are positive ways you can deal with it. Thankfully I enjoy my cycling and swimming and getting out and about, and all these activities help balance it out. Of course, my job – no wonder I had managed the longevity, it was ideal for me, speaking to twenty different people on twenty different subjects. Okay, I'm slightly exaggerating there but I'm sure you get the idea. I am always at my happiest enjoying myself in the company of other people, I got a contentment when I feel people around me being happy. Of course, it was a great relief – I knew there was an air of intelligence about me, but in the back of my mind I knew there was something wrong.

Eventually getting through to Dougie on the Friday was great, he even knew what my reaction was going to be. The first thing he said to me through his big beaming smile was, "Hey, how are you man!?" Without realising it, I was babbling away excitedly. Dougie had just been recovering from a terrible illness, but I was glad to see he was looking and sounding much better. One of the first things Dougie explained to me was that he sometimes comes across students and friends who have different forms of ADHD, and he says my reaction was typical of someone who's just found out. Dougie was also quick to point out that it was a massive help when adults find out they have ADHD because the questions they've always had about themselves are quickly answered; people begin to look back, picking out moments in their past where, had they known about their ADHD, they might have done things differently.

Once the dust had settled on the subject of ADHD it was time to get down to the main item of business, my writing. I was still a bit apprehensive about what he was going to say. I wasn't sure if all this positive talk about my new disposition was just a way of letting me down gently. But I was actually pleasantly surprised when he repeatedly told me to keep at it; there was obviously issues with my grammar and punctuation, and structure was another issue he brought up, but he was pleased to point out that he loved the content and said I had a flair for getting my energy and passion across in my writing. All in all, I was pretty pleased with the way our conversation about my writing had gone.

We then discussed some of the stuff he had been working on, and as quick as a flash he sent me over a few of his latest articles. Dougie and I had enjoyed many evenings in Corralejo so there was a lot to talk about; he still had lots of friends on the island of Fuerteventura who he was very close to and many that he stayed in contact with. As usual with me and Dougie, we had been talking away for ages. For me it was early evening but for Dougie it was smack in the middle of the day, so on that, I promised I'd send all my writing when it was finished. His last words were, "Hey, stay in touch man!!" to which I replied "Of course." Sadly that was the last conversation I was to have with him. It was only a few months later the news filtered through that Dougie had passed away, that horrible disease had come back. Like many of Dougie's friends we were left devastated at the news. I just wish I'd had the chance to thank him for his inspiration. I'm sure we have all lost close friends, we all understand that cruel feeling of loss, but I truly believe Dougie was one in a million and I'm sure there must be many other people who can tell you Dougie was a great help to them.

After gazing out to sea, and taking the last of my pics, it hadn't escaped my attention that the deck had become a little quieter as people had begun to head off for their lunch. I wasn't in a particular rush, although my stomach was demanding that I go and join the queue straightaway, but my head was telling me to relax. There was no point in rushing down there just to join in with all the other people, elbows out, jostling their way into a better place in the queue. We were all stuck on that boat for nearly another twenty-four hours so there was certainly no rush. I had noticed the smarter ones coming in a little later for breakfast, when there was no queue and it was much more relaxed, and of course the buffet was always being replenished.

Going down for my lunch just that little later was much better. I was able to take my time, my selection of food was better balanced, and I also made sure I chose the chicken. I only ate a little as this wasn't for me. I spent ages sucking on the chicken meat to get rid of any of the flavourings and seasonings before wrapping it up in a servette for the purpose of using this to coax Evie to eat something. The restaurant was much quieter, everyone around me had plenty of space to themselves, and the televisions were not on either which I think helped make it a bit more relaxed and of course the sunlight from outside seemed to stream in through the windows and brighten the whole place up.

After finishing my lunch, it was time for me to once again visit the dogs. Even this seemed a little less stressful now as it was quite apparent that they seemed to be settling into their situation, especially Harry, who was obviously my biggest worry. Heading past the small reception I was determined not to let this solid heavy door make a fool of me again, so with both hands I assuredly opened it, knowing there would be a small crowd of people standing on the other side. This time I'd walk by without making a scene, but just as I got through the door there was Maria to greet me. "Hi, I was just about to come looking for you," she said. "Aww sorry Maria, I was trying to give you some peace," I said laughingly. I'd made a point in the morning not to arrange anything with her regarding the afternoon as I'd thought she'd helped me enough. "No don't be silly, it's not a problem me helping you," she again reiterated, although I was fully geared up for dealing with the dogs myself.

I must admit I was glad to see her, even though I felt a bit more alert and things were obviously a lot brighter with it being the middle of the day. But that now-warm blustery wind would still have been a challenge when it came to dealing with those van doors. Even Maria's dog little Tia seemed happy to see me, so we all trotted off to the van. On getting there, I climbed in the side door first just to see how they all were. Harry started barking away first in his very lively fashion, which was great news, Charlie also seemed in good spirits, but I could see little Evie was still feeling sorry for herself.

My first reaction was to quickly mention to Evie that I'd brought her some chicken before realising I should have tried to give it to her quietly – I'd only alerted Harry that I'd brought in one of his favourite things which only made him even more excited. Thankfully I had enough to give each of them some. Charlie was new to the word chicken, he just knew by Harry's reaction there was something good on the go, so both Harry and Charlie got a little while Evie got the most. It was still noticeable that Evie hadn't touched her biscuits, so I was relieved when she ate all the chicken; the chicken from the buffet wasn't ideal, but at least she was eating something. I could only hope that if she persisted in not eating her biscuits I'd find something nice for her when we landed in Cadiz.

Once we got the dogs out on to the deck, they all seemed fine, and even with Tia there they all seemed to get along fine. Although it was now early afternoon and the sun was beating down on us, thankfully that blustery sea breeze was keeping the deck area nice and cool. When I wasn't walking them around, there was plenty of sheltered areas out of the sun where I was able to let them lie out in the fresh air, and of course it was important to make sure they were drinking plenty of water.

The deck was quite busy with other passengers out walking their dogs; they had all become very friendly, and everyone was sharing stories about their journey, where they had come from, and where they were going. From what I'd gathered, most of the people we talked to were heading home to mainland Spain, or like Maria they were travelling to visit family or friends. Most of them were quite impressed when I told them our gang was travelling to England, all the way through Spain then France, then getting the ferry from Calais to Dover and then on to the East Riding.

I mentioned to some of the other passengers that I was quite concerned about Evie who was a little down and not eating her biscuits. I think they were quite surprised to hear this as Evie had joined in with Harry and Charlie who were barking at a rather large bird who had decided to join us for part of the journey. She was obviously showing no signs of any ill effects and was just doing this to embarrass me; thankfully some of the people I spoke to said this can be quite normal with dogs who are a little more sensitive. I was fortunate to have Maria there if I needed any real advice, and by the way Evie was behaving once she was out of the van, there didn't seem to be much wrong with her. She was always first to the big water dish every time I filled it, so I knew she was being well hydrated.

It was late afternoon by the time Maria and I had got the dogs back securely into the van. It was the longest they had been out in the fresh air since we had left Corralejo, and I hoped that all the fresh sea air and the excitement of meeting all these different dogs – and let's not forget the barking at that large sea bird – might be enough to help them settle down for the rest of the afternoon. After arranging to meet up with Maria later I decided to head back to the cabin.

Looking around me, it was certainly the strangest Saturday afternoon I'd had in a long while. Here I was on a boat out in the middle of the ocean. Usually about now I'd be feet up after getting back from a cycle, or not long out of the sea after a swim; I'd probably have had a quick shower, then hit the fridge to see if there was anything there I could stuff my face with, before checking the football results to see how all my preferred football teams had been getting on, with the three dogs cuddled up around me.

I was quite happy to get back to the cabin. I was feeling tired, and I really fancied the idea of just stretching out and relaxing. Having a cabin that was very central in the boat meant I didn't have a port hole to gaze out of. I didn't mind this, it helped me forget I was on a boat. I had this daft notion that if I could see the skyline going up and down through the port hole it would've made me feel seasick. Like I said before, there was hardly any motion from the sea, so you'd be forgiven for thinking you were just in a very small comfortable hotel room. So this was psychologically working for me, and if things did take a turn for the worse, I still had the two seasickness tablets I could take. The good thing was we were now nearly halfway through the journey so it wouldn't be too long before we were docking at Cadiz. On a funnier note, I think it was Spike Milligan who once said the best cure for seasickness is to sit under a tree.

Now lying comfortably on my back, I was doing what millions like me were doing – staring at my phone. Yes, I was another slave to social media, yes, I probably spend too much time on my phone, but let's be honest, they are great. You can almost keep up to date with everything that's going on in the world, whatever you are into – sport, war, cooking, hillwalking, sex, boats, booking holidays, weather reports, checking your finances, buying or selling, just about anything you can imagine you can research online. Yes, there is a downside, in that you can't always believe everything you read on the internet, everyone rightly or wrongly has an opinion, and the legions of keyboard warriors are endless with their Facebook pages, websites and the immensely popular blogs so the waters of truth, opinion, conspiracy and propaganda can all become very muddied. But in their defence, some of them are brilliant – in fact, you'll find a substantial number of football fans rarely use or listen to mainstream reporting. Yes, the large satellite TV channels still have the monopoly when it comes to showing live football, but swathes of fans are turning to their preferred bloggers for news and information. Clubs and players alike are seeing the importance of these bloggers and many are now invited to the clubs' press conferences and allocated questions. And it's not just in sport that this revolution is taking place – politics, the arts, and especially music have all demonstrably changed since the online digital pathway opened up. The record industry has been turned upside down since the evolution of the internet – CD sales alone have disappeared like snow off a dyke.

Back in the day, I can remember excitedly waiting on the latest release from my favourite bands, going into a record shop and finally getting my hands on the prize and rushing home to stick it on the turntable or latterly putting it in the CD player. As the first sounds came out of the speakers, my eyes would be gazing down at the album cover, fixated on the written lyrics as the music washed over me. Always making sure that it was nice and loud so the bass was heavy enough to punch my heart out.

Yup, when I was younger, I liked my music big, loud and fast. I haven't changed really – yeah, I have grown up a little, and I've become a bit more open minded and respectful of the many different types of music, but as I just pointed out, it's all changed. The record shops have gone, there's no more going through the aisles, flicking through an artist's back catalogue; the whole format of making music has changed from top to bottom, so in turn the artists themselves can't sit back and rely on their recorded music sales. The great, the good and the bad for reasons of survival have all had to dust down their touring gear and get back out on the road, which to be honest has been great for the fans and venues. Live music is back on the menu, that's if you can afford the ticket prices – no more picking up your tickets at the venue a few months before the gig. In fact, the face value on the ticket doesn't really mean anything, it's what price the middleman agencies demand, and these new exorbitant prices are all determined on particular seating arrangements, not one square inch of your chosen venue goes un-costed.

But for your average music listener, every piece of music you've ever loved is now available at the touch of a finger, whereas the melomaniacs of old would have had shelves stacked with huge record collections which could reach into thousands and take up massive amounts of space in their houses. These formidable, cherished collections, gathered lovingly over a lifetime, have now been surpassed by a form of technology which was beyond their wildest dreams only a decade or so before. Hundreds of thousands of quickly accessible songs can now be stored inside a computer chip not much larger than a postage stamp. These small chips can be hidden away inside your computers, laptops, mp3 players and even inside your new smart phones.

Personally, I was always hanging on the coat tails of this new technology. I still use an iPod classic and an iPod nano, which at the time of writing were still regarded as old school. I always tried to make sure I had the best earphones, but I wasn't geared up for their latest wireless technology and still used the old-fashion cables that were thankfully still provided. I try to keep up to date with the latest phones, although it all just seems to happen so fast – as soon as you've finally decided to invest in their new technologies, they're already working on the latest model. Had I been a bit savvier regarding all the fantastic new editing apps I would have been one of the high-flying kings of social media, with their classy videos and snappy podcasts. But as a member of the older generation, it's hard to remember how we survived without it, especially if you meet someone who just lost or broke their phone. You can see that look of helplessness in their eyes, there's nothing you can do to console them, they can even become hysterical, a feeling of total panic just seems to set in. Of course these are the worst-case scenarios.

There's also that idea that the phone gives you a feeling of protection, you can call someone to let them know that you are safe. I suppose a lovely side of it is you can video-call loved ones, you can take endless amounts of memorable pictures and videos of your holidays, you can even edit the pictures or videos straightaway then post them on to social media – within minutes, anyone, anywhere in the world can share your fabulous experiences. On the other side of the coin, they can be intrusive, not everyone wants their picture taken, not everyone wants to be videoed; people in the world of sport and entertainment are constantly harassed, having phones rammed in their faces. It's fine if you ask, and the recipient of your intrusion is willing to have their picture taken, but it's not always the case. Some people will argue, that's what you should expect if you are always in the media spotlight.

I can remember back in my day when things were oh so different. When we were kids, we would disappear into the countryside for almost the whole day; nobody knew where we were, but we would always knowingly return around teatime. Oh, some of us would return a bit battered and bruised with the odd scrape and scratch, but we were happy with not a care in the world. We would all be rosy cheeked from our energetic adventures, ready to gulp down our tea (evening meal) as fast as we could so we could get right back out again to do even more running about. A lot of us would play football until too many of the players were told in no uncertain terms that it was late and it was time for bed. There were no computer games to sit and play with, you couldn't sit online with your friends around town or even around the world for that matter, while simultaneously talking to some other friend on another social media platform. If you were out and about, you had no mobile phones to send your mum a text letting her know where you were, and what time she could start getting your tea ready.

For me, Sundays were the worst day of the week. My freedom was always curtailed because it was a family day, and my dad would have it all planned out. As we would drive out in the car I'd see the other kids gathering together getting ready to organise a game of football. Now had I been left to my own devices, and they had left me with my friends, I would have probably turned out to be one of the best players in the world, or so I thought anyway.

Even if we got back early enough, I still couldn't join in as it was the day my dad would cook our big Sunday dinner. But the worst part of all was the television – just three channels of abject misery. It would start off with old people crammed into church, all dressed up trying to outdo each other. And with the TV cameras there it was obvious they were just trying to see who could sing these boring hymns the loudest, even I could recognise these people had gone to great efforts to look as good as they could. But to me, all it really did was exemplify their oldness, as they righteously belted out their songs in such a way you could almost lip read from their exaggerated facial expressions, and I'm sure some of them were standing on their toes for that added attention. Even the other two channels were no help whatsoever, with one showing bleak pictures of cold wintery farms where the conversations got no more exciting than the year's milk production figures. Although in their defence, I loved milk, especially a brand-new bottle, you would take off the silver top and your first couple of glugs would be that gorgeous thick cream. Yeah, I'd literally drink pints of the stuff when I was a child, but even this wasn't enough to get me excited about farming programmes. Your final offering would be politicians arguing about stuff you didn't care or have a clue about. The afternoons wouldn't get any better, in fact sometimes it could be worse with the monotone drone of the cricket commentators, as the game moved along at a snail's pace. It was either that or staring at the little girl with the teddy bear on the test card. Yup, there was no twenty-four-hour television in those days.

The pain would carry on into the evening, in fact it might be even bigger churches this time, sometimes with people you used to enjoy laughing at on TV. But now they were turning their backs on fun and laughter, with no semblance of their usual entertaining selves, they were traitorously joining in with the really old loud singers. It didn't look like it had been accidental either as these once proud entertainers were even trying to dress like them, this would make it very hard for me to forgive them when I'd next see them in some other TV programme, sadly I wouldn't forget their act of treachery, as far as I was concerned their card was marked.

Our next course of doom and gloom would come in the form of what they called costume drama. It was always the same sorts of actors who played the same stereotypical parts, the settings were always dark cold candlelit rooms, and the actors would vigorously throw their arms around as their sneering faces inevitably spewed out Shakespearean promises of death. It was all just too much to handle, these gloomy downtrodden feelings of despair, magnified by the realisation that this was the night before the dreaded Monday morning, the beginning of another full week back at school.

Okay, there were little glimmers of light and hope that would shine through in the form of a very colourful programme called "The world about us". This was a BBC 2 television documentary series on natural history, with the calming steady voice of the great David Attenborough. You were taken on these magical trips to these fantastic places that seemed to be millions of miles away from home, jungles filled with gorillas, elephants, zebras, giraffes, tigers, monkeys, lions, snakes, fabulously coloured birds, rivers filled with hippopotamuses, piranhas and crocodiles. But the ones I really felt sorry for were the wildebeests and the gazelles, especially during times of the great Serengeti migration, for me and my delicate mind it was horrible. Not so much meals on wheels, more meals on legs as they ran the gauntlet of Africa's greatest predators, all these beautiful animals with their Bambi-like features being slaughtered in this horrific blood fest. It could be argued that out of a number nearing a million fleeing animals the death toll might only be reaching hundreds, but it still wasn't nice to watch and little comfort to the poor ones that were caught, and I remember this horror show was still being calmly narrated by the silky overtones of David Attenborough.

Another spectacular side to this programme was when they showed "The Undersea World of Jacques Cousteau". He was a French marine scientist who just seemed to have the best job in the world. He was grey haired with a deep brown tan and was always surrounded by a team of likeminded men, all experts in their profession. These were hardworking guys who were also very well-tanned and happy to drop into a shark-infested sea at the drop of a hat. Living a life like this was just beyond my comprehension, they certainly weren't teaching anything like this at my school. Mind you, they might have been – knowing me, I was probably daydreaming, the one thing I was very good at in school.

My favourite thing in the show was when they would bravely lower themselves into the sea in protective cages just to observe these sharks. Anyone reading this who was also young during the seventies will obviously be an expert on sharks, yes, we were the generation who were around when the blockbuster "Jaws" came out, probably one of Steven Spielberg's finest films. (Spookily enough, this is Nicky's favourite film.) The world just seemed to go shark mad after this film was released, everywhere you looked, if it wasn't magazines, it was documentaries on TV. We all inadvertently became experts regarding these fascinating creatures of the sea, and of course we were only interested in the dangerous ones, whether it be makos, tiger sharks, bull sharks, hammerheads or the king of them all, the great white. Of course, there were so many other species, but these were not ridiculously dangerous; in fact, some of them were as docile as their plankton-eating cousins, the whales. This of course did not excite us, these creatures were more what we would call the tree huggers of the sea, we only wanted the dorsal-finned man-hungry serial killers of the sea up there on our walls. Sadly, these poor creatures were unfairly given a bad reputation with everyone chasing sensationalised stories about shark attacks when in truth the number of attacks was ridiculously low. There has been a massive increase in people taking up water sports hobbies, especially surfing, and all that extra splashing in the water can grab the attention of these very sharp-toothed predators, but in general you've got more chance of being attacked by a hippopotamus than a shark, according to the statisticians anyway.

Now rubbing my eyes and peering at my watch I could see it was just after five o'clock; as far as I could tell I'd fallen asleep for nearly an hour and a half, this was good as grabbing any bits of sleep was a bonus. My phone was just at the side of my pillow, and I realised I must have nodded off while looking at it. No harm done, again I was quite happy that I'd managed to grab some sleep, it already felt like it had been a long journey and a feeling of permanent tiredness was hanging around me like a heavy coat. I knew my next move was to jump into that shower. I'm usually not one for spending much time in a shower, it was always a case of needs be, and anyhow the thirty-litre tank in our apartment in Corralejo was always the deciding factor on when it was time to get out. But the shower on the boat seemed to run hot water forever.

Once I'd finished and dried off, I instantly felt refreshed, that heavy coat feeling had gone, obviously that little amount of sleep I'd managed to grab had really helped. Grabbing my card for the door lock I left the cabin in spritely fashion. Before visiting the dogs, I thought I'd have another visit to the higher positioned deck seven.

It was now early evening but out on the deck it was still sunny, so there were quite a few people just lounging around on the sunbeds either chatting or speaking on their phones. The atmosphere felt quite relaxed as everyone appeared to be well settled into their journey. Although our position at the back of the boat was quite protected, the ship was still battling its way through a head wind so I knew once I eventually did get down to the van, I still had these awkward blustery conditions to deal with. Fortunately looking out to sea I could tell there still hadn't been any change to the swell, it had been the same for most of the journey, I could only cross my fingers and hope it stayed that way. The views were still fantastic, the sun was very much to the west and with no clouds, it was all blue sky and seas, with still not another ship in sight.

Making my way back down inside the ship I came across Maria and her small dog Tia; they were heading in the same direction as I was. "That was handy, I was just coming down to meet you," Maria said through a smile. "Ah, good timing Maria," I replied. Tia was non-plussed as she walked obediently at Maria's side. "Geez, I wish our three could be like that," I thought to myself. Walking through reception I prepared myself for that heavy door. Yup, there was no change there. I laughed through my struggle. "I'll get it right one of these days," I said, as Tia passed through as though I'd been holding the door open just for her. I was glad to hear Maria say, "It's been the same every time I've done this trip, it's always been hard work." As Maria said that, I thought to myself, "Wow, Maria's done this quite a few times." In fact, I knew Maria was doing the same trip again in a week's time, as she was going to have to make the return ferry journey all the way back to Fuerteventura.

Now we were in mid-October at the time and were really lucky that the winter swell hadn't been its usual massive self. Unfortunately, I had done some research about the boat I was travelling on and the company I was using, and some of the reviews were not brilliant, and the bit that worried me the most was really nobody's fault but mother nature itself, the idea of sitting in a large metal tub while trying to negotiate our way through thirty-foot waves for two days just filled me with dread. Oh I'm sure there are some strange people out there who enjoy the feeling of sickness but I'm certainly not one of them. When reading about some people's experiences on the ferry it really got my fertile imagination ticking over again, stories of people sharing cabins with people they had never met before, and all being sick at the same time. This was the stuff of nightmares to me.

After spending more than twenty-five years on the island of Fuerteventura I'd witnessed some huge waves, in fact I'd spent plenty of time enjoying being hurled around by these brightly bubbled breakers. Yes, I'd dabbled with surfing but never really focused enough time on mastering the sport. In my defence, my job would have me committed during the days and nights, so my time wasn't my own. I do regret not applying myself more to the art of surfing as I really loved spending hours in the sea and loved it when the swell was massive. Sometimes I'd drag poor Nicky out there with me as we would swim out into the deep water and let the big waves wash us back in. And yes, sometimes you didn't get it right and these waves came tumbling down on your head. It could be a very exhilarating experience, you could feel the energy as this force of power dragged you helplessly along, it almost felt like you were in this gigantic washing machine not knowing whether you were up nor down. Finally, as we both thankfully rose to the top, we would find ourselves metres apart gasping for air but still managing to excitedly laugh at our dalliance with nature. But sitting on a boat for any length of time as it rocked back and forward usually led to me feeling very weak and horribly sick.

So my journey had been more than satisfactory as far as I was concerned, and regarding the service on the boat, I could hardly complain. Nicky had managed to book my ticket online, and because

I had Spanish residency it only cost me just over forty euros, that was a cabin for two nights including breakfast, lunch and my evening meal. Yeah, I could probably harp on about the food selection, but for forty euros, how could I?

As Maria and I walked across the warm but blustery car deck I decided just to go straight to the back of the van. I'd usually climb in the side door first just to see how they all were, but I was confident that they would all be fine. Sure enough as I opened the door, Charlie was staring right at me wagging his tail and behind the other door, I could hear Harry barking away like mad, which was a great sign. You could always tell when Harry was in good fettle by the volume of his barking. Just above Harry in the other cage was little Evie; she was obviously glad to see me, but she still had that look on her little face that everything wasn't right. She was panting a lot and her usually alert ears were slightly wilted looking, and I could tell she had hardly touched her food – in fact it looked like she hadn't eaten anything at all. Harry on the other hand had eaten everything, I even noticed he had a little pink mark on the top of his nose where he had obviously scraped it trying to get the biscuits that had spilled over and had fallen just outside his cage.

Once we got them out onto the car deck, they all seemed fine; even Evie had perked up and was barking at some of the other dogs. She had taken complete ownership of Harry and would get incredibly jealous of any other dog getting too close to him; it would catch other dog owners unawares sometimes when for no evident reason little Evie would fly at their dogs to chase them away from her Harry. Charlie on the other hand was great with other dogs, in fact the more the merrier, and the good thing was he had taken a shine to little Tia and was of course obviously very familiar with his other friend Maria, so everything in the little world of Charlie was just fine. Evie was a lovely little dog and always seemed so independent, certainly not as needy as the other two, so I wasn't really expecting her to be the one we would have any bother with while travelling, I just felt terrible for her, especially when leaving her in the van, she just looked so lost. Before closing the van door, I promised her I would bring her back something nice to eat. Mind you, that was a tough call as down in the restaurant I was struggling to find myself something nice to eat, but surely there would be something I could find for her.

After Maria and I left the van, we parted company at the reception area; she went off to her cabin while I made my way down to the restaurant. I was on a mission – I had to find something suitable for Evie, at least something to tide her over. I thought once we get docked at Cadiz, I should be able to find a shop where I could get her some decent food, but I felt it was imperative I find her something for the time being. Everyone I had spoken to on the boat had told me not to worry, but these little doggies were like our babies, I just couldn't rest till I knew she was feeling happier within herself.

By the time I got into the restaurant I could see it was quite busy which wasn't a bad thing as there was no long queue of people waiting to get served. I noticed Jim sitting with his little collection of plates, happily eating away, keeping one eye on the telly up in front of him. "Hi Jim!" I shouted. "Alright Gary," he replied. "Remember, it'll be an extra early rise tomorrow, I'd try and get down for breakfast early if I was you." That was music to my ears. "Yup, I'll be up early Jim." This put me in a good mood straightaway – it was getting close to us hitting the road, and I just knew Jim wasn't one for hanging about: no messing, no faffing around, just up and ready and let's get going. It was a great attitude to have.

During the boat journey, I intentionally made sure I gave Jim plenty of space. I knew he had thousands of miles to drive, and I didn't want him feeling distracted or tired, especially with me around. I knew I was a very loquacious character at the best of times, and I didn't want to annoy him with my endless talking. I knew straightaway when Jim first came to pick me up that I would like him, he was very knowledgeable, and it was obvious he wasn't one for hanging about.

I briefly told him about Evie and my plan to see if there was anything suitable I could give her till we reached land. Like everyone else, Jim told me not to worry. He had taken lots of dogs on this journey and he assured me that from what he had seen of Evie there was nothing to worry about. I knew I was panicking for no reason but in the back of my mind I wasn't going to give up on my mission. (This was probably another symptom of my ADHD, my mind still needlessly buzzing furiously and worrying about nothing.) It hadn't escaped my attention that Jim had chicken on his plate so that gave my overactive mind a bit of a break.

After being served my food, I managed to get the chicken and some pasta which was free from the tomato sauce that was served with it. Once again, I wrapped it all up in a serviette and carefully put it in my pocket. The restaurant seemed a little noisier than it had been previously, people seemed to be a bit more relaxed and were chatting more than they had when they first boarded. Up on the television, the news was much the same – more and more people's houses were being engulfed by the lava that was relentlessly flowing from the volcano on La Palma. The ash had also been covering the banana plantations; this popular fruit was delivered to all the other seven Canarian islands and was a big part of their economy. Lots of other local people were working hard to relocate belongings and livestock as their homes were being devoured by this slow-moving incredibly hot lava. In the back of my mind, I was still wondering if that old volcano called Cumbre Vieja was going to finally collapse into the sea.

Leaving the restaurant, my first port of call was to go and visit Evie with my little collection of goodies – if you can call cold pasta and chicken that I had already chewed on to get rid of any oily residue a treat. Regardless, I knew it would be something she would enjoy. I quickly made my way across the brightly lit car deck. It was dark around the outside of the ship with it being night-time.

I could see a few lights out at sea where there seemed to be other boats. I took this as a good sign as we must have been getting closer to Cadiz. Opening the side door of the van I climbed in. As usual, Harry was glad to see me – it was like the first time he had seen me in weeks. Harry was always like that though – if we left the house and realised we had forgotten something like a wallet, he would greet us like long-lost friends when we went back to the house. Charlie was also standing on all fours looking alert and barking at me, but poor Evie was just sitting looking at me, panting slightly with wilted ears, so she was the first one I went to.

"Hiya Evie, I've got some Harry chicken." Obviously I was trying to excite her with the idea of chicken but of course in my rush to please I realised it was the wrong choice of words as Harry and Charlie knew what the words "Harry chicken" meant. Whenever we made a chicken dish, we had always boiled a little extra to give to Harry; even once we had the three dogs, it was still known as Harry Chicken. A quick change of tack was needed. I decided to tempt her with the pasta first as the small amount of chicken I had was now going to have to be shared between the three of them. Thankfully, after sniffing the pasta hesitantly, she decided to eat it like she hadn't eaten in weeks. That was handy as I had quite a bit of pasta which allowed me to share the small amount of chicken between the three of them.

I didn't hang about in the van too long as I knew I didn't have long to wait before I'd be down with Maria taking them out for a walk across the deck. The one great thing I noticed just before I climbed out of the van was Evie taking a big drink of water; this really gave me peace of mind, as it looked as if my little chicken pasta treat had worked. Again, I was reminded that this journey had come together all because we were worried about Harry; all the planning, the passports, all the paperwork for all the different border crossings, and finally the money it all cost. Yup, it was a very expensive adventure once you totalled it all up, and after all that, the only one giving me any concern was little Evie. Just before closing the van door I shouted to the three of them, "I'll be back with Maria, and we'll go walkies."

Heading back across the car deck I was feeling much better, knowing Evie had eaten something and I was doubly pleased I'd caught her drinking some water. In my mind I knew I could go back to the cabin and relax a bit with a little less to worry about. I passed what had now become some familiar faces who were standing with their dogs chatting. The one thing I had to remember when opening that heavy door was to try and not make a fool of myself as I was sure they were all waiting and watching me. Thankfully someone was coming out just as I approached the door, so it was an easy manoeuvre for me to dart through while the door was open, avoiding any more embarrassing moments.

Getting back to my cabin I realised that time had flown past very quickly as it was now just about eleven o'clock and I had agreed to meet Maria for one o'clock. Feeling quite good about myself and not too tired, I reckoned there was no point in trying to get any sleep. My phone had a few messages on it so I decided to reply to them and check out what else was going on with the world. My dad's message was brief, he had been tracking my journey on the same app that I had and had noticed that the ship was making good progress. My dad loved this sort of thing. I'm sure he thought it was my fault he'd had to leave the Merchant Navy because of my mum falling pregnant – yup, it seems I was a thorn in my dad's side from the very beginning. Nope, I wasn't planned, true to form I was actually a mistake! I mean technically it wasn't exactly my fault, but I definitely played a part in why he had to leave.

My dad had loved the Merchant Navy, travelling to most of the important ports around the world, in fact my dad had circumnavigated the globe twice. One of the more controversial places my dad managed to visit during his time at sea was the infamous Pitcairn Island, hidden somewhere in the Pacific Ocean and made famous by the mutineers of HMS Bounty. It's so off the beaten track that hardly any ships ever passed it, therefore the crew members of the Bounty were able to stay hidden for so long. Mind you, there's lots of stories about most of them going mad because of their strange antics and self-imposed isolation.

My dad's ship which was named the Paparoa and was there delivering supplies in the late fifties. It's strange to think that there are ancestors from the Bounty still living there as the crew members had struck up relations with some of the Polynesian women who were first settled there. The island was relatively ignored right up until 1996, and sadly it has a rather dark and sordid history littered with stories of rape and inbreeding.

Another controversial place my dad visited was Christmas Island, not long after they had tested a nuclear bomb there. My dad was only dropping off supplies, but he spent a little time actually staying on the island. I only found this out when my dad suffered from cancer; it would really interest me to know how all the other crew members got on in life – in honesty, it would be no great surprise to hear many of them had eventually become ill with cancers. Fortunately, my dad's cancer was diagnosed very early and, after a successful operation, he managed to fully recover.

So, my dad has always had a passion for anything nautical, he would always tell stories of his days at sea with great affection. And of course, it wasn't just my dad who was following my line of travel – yes, I had to keep Nicky up to date with our progress. I didn't want to worry her, so I just mentioned to her that Evie was being a bit fussy with her biscuits, which was true, but I wasn't going to tell her that I was worried, just in case I had been overreacting. There was no point creating a fuss about nothing all because Evie wasn't enjoying the journey.

The cabin was still warm, but I thought as we moved further north the temperature would start to drop, especially being out at sea, but even the blustery wind that we seemed to be heading into hadn't changed either. Luckily things had been going rather well; the two travel sickness tablets that I'd brought with me were still in my bag and with only eight hours left on the ship it looked like they were not going to see the light of day.

After writing a little more in my diary, then checking through my Facebook and other social media apps, it wasn't long before I was needing to get ready to take the dogs for another walk along the deck. I was certainly beginning to feel within myself that this first part of the journey was nearly over. I knew the dogs would need another couple of walks, then we would have breakfast, then into the van and off the boat we would go.

But it was important not to get too ahead of myself, there would still be all the customs checks, and there was always the worry that I was going to have to put muzzles on the dogs. Evie wasn't too difficult, Harry was a nightmare, and I could still remember my finger dripping with blood trying to put Charlie's on. It was only three Yorkshire terriers I know, but when the three of them kicked off they were like Tasmanian devils. My fertile imagination was throwing up images of it all ending up in a shootout with the Guardia civil, like some old American mid-west picture, where the sheriff and his deputies have their pictures taken as they are proudly stand over the bodies, firmly holding on to their trusty shotguns. Yup, I'd be lying alongside with them; even though we'd all be dead they would still have us tied up, it makes us look like we were all the more dangerous. To think I was going to have these same over-dramatic thoughts every time we got close to a customs check. I had even gone as far as to think about Jim sitting in a bar in Corralejo slowly spitting out the story to concerned listeners as he swigged on his whisky, fighting back the emotions as he talked about our last stand on that fateful day.

It wasn't long before I'd left the cabin and was bounding down the steps to get to the car deck. Apart from the noise from the ship's engines echoing through the boat and the slightest movement of the boat pushing through the sea all was very quiet. I was soon pulling on that heavy door to get me out onto the brightly lit car deck. Maria was already there with Tia, speaking with some of the other dog owners who were travelling on the ship. Thankfully with the upper car deck being a lot quieter than usual there was quite a lot of space which was allowing some of the dogs quite a lot of room to run about in. This wasn't always the case as when it's busy all you can do is walk between the little spaces between the parked cars, and again if the sea is very rough it can't be a great deal of fun. Something else I had found out from Maria which I hadn't ever thought about before was that animals can also suffer from seasickness (or motion sickness). Imagine me and the three dogs all feeling sick! It's something I just hadn't accounted for, not once in all our very detailed planning had it crossed our minds that the dogs could get seasick. I thought between myself and Nicky, we had covered every eventuality. I might have been spending all this time cleaning out sick from poor Jim's van – and remember that the van and the boat would be rocking backwards and forwards as all this nightmare would be unfolding. Now had that situation arisen, I would have been kicking myself to find out that you can get travel sickness tablets for dogs. In fairness, we were having this conversation as we were taking Harry, Charlie and Evie for a walk on the deck, so I was laughing about it at the time, we had all been very lucky with the journey on a whole.

I felt pretty positive – with each minute that passed I knew we were getting so much closer to Cadiz; the temperature and the blustery wind had stayed consistent for the journey so far, and I was sure it wasn't going to change anytime soon. I told Maria how much happier I would have been if I had been allowed to have all three dogs in the cabin with me, but the problem was that every time someone passed the cabin, they would all kick off and bark loudly. I could imagine a member of staff coming to enquire about the situation and telling me there had been a complaint, and me pleading ignorance and making up some silly excuse as to why I had them all up there. Mind you, even if I'd been able to keep Evie on her own with me, it would have been better. I had felt that the dogs would be fine being all together, I'd never imagined Evie was going to be so unsettled.

As we were taking the dogs back to the van, I said to Maria, "I think I might sneak Evie up to the cabin." I had obviously said it in a way that suggested I was seeking Maria's opinion, although it wouldn't really have mattered what she said as I'd already made my mind up. "Yeah, I'm sure it would be fine, she's just a small dog." I felt a little better on hearing Maria's approval.

Once we got the dogs back into the van, I made sure Harry and Charlie had enough water and biscuits; as soon as I'd put fresh biscuits into their dishes there was no stopping them. With their heads buried in their dishes quite happily eating away they hadn't caught on to my plans for Evie. I shut both the back doors securely whilst still holding Evie under my arm. I then quickly moved round to the side door to grab a small doggie blanket and a little dish for Evie's biscuits. I was sure that once we both got back to the cabin Evie would start eating her food. My thinking was that the cabin might seem a bit more comforting to her, and with her spirits raised she would start eating her biscuits.

The other two dogs didn't seem to take much notice as I frantically searched through the large hold-all for a small doggie blanket; it hadn't escaped my attention that the area between the dogs' cages and the driving compartment was becoming quite messy with plastic bags, a large suitcase, jackets and dogs' things I'd prepared for the journey. I knew I had one more visit to take the dogs for their last walk before we docked at Cadiz, so I'd have a chance to tidy it all up then. My mind was more fixed on getting Evie back up to the cabin in such a way that I didn't attract anyone's attention. To be honest, I'd rarely passed any members of staff in the time I'd been travelling back and forth between my cabin and the car deck; my main concern would be getting Evie past the reception.

As we were leaving the van, I bid goodnight to Harry and Charlie and told them I wouldn't be long. I could see them both staring back at me, probably wondering what the hell I was talking about. I did leave them with a slight feeling of guilt, but at the end of day I knew the pair of them were as tough as old boots and with only one more deck walk to do it wouldn't be long till we were all back in the van together, leaving the ship and hitting the road.

Heading back towards the big heavy door I was feeling confident that there wouldn't be anyone at reception, and if I walked closely behind Maria that should be enough cover. Evie was comfortably wrapped up in one of her blankets as I carried her carefully under my arm; she looked quite comical as all you could see was her little head with her cute smile and big ears.

Luckily as we approached that big old door there was a nice couple who were kind enough to hold it open for us; a quick "buenos noches" and off I went – the couple hadn't seen Evie under my arm as I'd passed them. There were two reception staff in the office but they seemed to be busy, so the front desk was clear. Getting past the reception I knew would be my biggest hurdle and we managed that no problem. There were still a few of the seasoned travellers camped out in little corners, but they were all looking solemn faced as most of them seemed more concerned with trying to grab some sleep. After climbing one floor of stairs I finally made my way to the cabin door. I quickly pulled my key card out of my back pocket and placed it onto the door handle; the little light on the door turned green and it was just a simple case of turning the door handle and we were in.

After unravelling Evie from her cover, I placed her on the bed. "What do you think of this Evie?" I said to her, almost expecting her to be impressed. Just at that moment, I noticed her ears going up as she stared at the door, and I heard her little Evie growl starting. I couldn't believe it, this was the first time throughout the whole journey that someone was passing my cabin door. I quickly picked her up and quietly made the ssshhhh sound with one finger pointed at my mouth as I glaringly looked down on her; thankfully she replied by licking me on the nose. In desperation I quickly but quietly tried to explain to her that if she was going to be sleeping in here, she was going to have to be very quiet as dogs were not allowed in these cabins. I could only hope she got some sense of what I was trying to tell her.

While I got changed for bed, she explored her way around the cabin, all these news smells she hadn't experienced before were grabbing her attention. As I finally climbed into bed, I could see Evie had decided to curl up into a ball down by my feet at the bottom of my bed. It was then I noticed the little paw prints all over the sheets – the floor of the cabin hadn't dried properly from my earlier showers. Well, there was no getting away from it, they were certainly going to know there had been a dog in the cabin, albeit a small one. I wasn't too worried – we would be long gone by the time the cleaner stripped the beds. In fact I'm sure they wouldn't be bothered, it was a one-way trip, we certainly weren't going to meet them on the way back.

It was nearing two o'clock in the morning so I thought it would be safer to set the alarm on my phone. I set it for four o'clock, knowing I must get the dogs walked, then get my breakfast, check the cabin and then climb into the van and off we would go. I was excited but at the same time filled with trepidation – we still had the longest part of the journey ahead of us, and it wasn't just a case of sitting in a boat watching the world float by. We were travelling through three different countries – even under normal circumstances this would have been a challenge, hoping the dogs' passports and paperwork, and don't forget their attitudes, were all up to scratch. But then we had the pandemic to concern ourselves with – rules and regulations were changing on a daily basis, all it would take was one person or one dog's paperwork not meeting the correct criteria and suddenly, we were in a disaster situation. Maybe the situation could be remedied eventually but one thing is for sure, it would cost a hell of a lot of time and a considerable amount of money. It was a lot to think about, but luckily my lack of sleep and bouts of exhaustion were taking their toll on my thought processes, and for once my brain fog was helping me stop overthinking things; it was just a case of one thing at a time.

Just before I switched my small bed lamp off, I'd noticed Evie had snuggled up on the pillow next to me. Over the last few months, this had become Evie's regular sleeping place, most mornings I'd wake up with her either licking my nose or just staring back at me, so hopefully she felt a little more at home, and to be honest it was nice for me to have her there as company.

It felt like I'd only just put my phone down and switched the light off and suddenly, I could hear my alarm ringing. Just for a second, I had to gather my thoughts and remember exactly where I was. As I switched the phone alarm off, I stretched up to switch the cabin light on. I could see Evie had moved from my pillow and was lying at my back. I looked down at her and said "C'mon then Evie, we better move, we have a big day ahead of us." As usual, she was just staring back at me with that funny but lovable little face of hers.

Even though I was still in a sleepy daze, I could feel the excitement inside me. I knew in just a few hours we would be leaving the boat and starting the next part of our journey. The only concern I had was that there would be customs checks as soon as we left the boat.

I had slept solidly even if it was for only two hours, and I knew the best thing to do was to jump into the shower, a fresh start to a new day was just what I needed. Through the steamed-up glass door I could see Evie sitting on the end of the bed. This reminded me that if she persisted in not eating her biscuits, I would get Jim to stop somewhere so I could pick up some soft dog food. I don't know if it was just the excitement, but I felt confident that Evie would start to pick up a little once we hit the road. With Evie's cage being on top of Harry's I knew it allowed her to see out of the front of the van so with her having a decent view and me constantly chatting to her I felt it would help raise her spirits.

By the time I had got out of the shower and gathered all our things together, it was nearly half past four. With my bag over my shoulder and Evie again wrapped up in her little blanket tucked carefully under my arm, I made my way down to the car deck. I had checked the cabin thoroughly, making sure I had everything, but just to be sure, I'd have one more visit after I had my breakfast. It was then that I realised I hadn't made any arrangements to meet up with Maria – not only was it going to be more difficult getting the dogs out for their walk around the deck, but more importantly, I wouldn't have a chance to say cheerio and thank her for her invaluable assistance, my journey would have been so much more difficult without her help.

I realised I was going to have to do things slightly differently. I would take Evie for a walk around the deck first, then I would only have to struggle with Harry and Charlie. If I was lucky, that blustery wind would have died down which would make things a lot easier when opening the van doors. Getting to the reception area I could see there were quite a few people hanging around. I wasn't too worried if anyone noticed Evie as I had a raft of excuses as to why I was walking about with her under my arm.

With my one free arm I heaved the heavy door open and made my way out onto the deck, and to my surprise, there was Maria with Tia. Before I could open my mouth, Maria said, "Morning, how are you?" All I could do was smile back and say, "Morning Maria." I was so relieved to see her. I had prepared myself for one last effort to make sure I didn't have any disasters with the van doors, but straightaway I noticed that it still seemed very windy; had I been attempting this on my own, it would have been a nightmare. Maria noticed little Evie under my arm and kindly asked how she was. I told her she had been fine, and that I'd quite enjoyed her company. I looked down at Tia and said, "Morning Tia, how are you?" and at that I heard a little growl coming from Evie. Obviously, it was a jealous growl, but it was nice to hear her being so alert, it was a good sign that she was more her normal self. Without any questions asked, or discussions about not planning for this morning's rendezvous, we were both naturally walking towards the van.

Out on the car deck, nothing much had changed, it was still very noisy and bright, with that consistent blustery wind. Not that I was complaining, things could have been much worse; the boat had been steady for all the journey, with no change in the temperature, well not enough that I had noticed anyway. I was surprised at that, after all, it was mid-October and we were now over a thousand kilometres away from Fuerteventura.

Eventually getting to the van I could hear Harry barking as we approached; this was another great sign that all was well. Although Harry was often getting into trouble for barking too much, for the moment it was music to my ears. My mission was to get these three wonderful dogs back to Bridlington in one piece, and a large part of this journey was nearly over and thankfully there had been no need for me to search out Harry's Valium – or my travel sickness tablets for that matter.

As we opened the van doors there were Harry and Charlie, very alert and happy to see us. Harry in particular was looking quite funny with his little pink patch right in the middle of his nose; he had obviously been trying to get at the biscuits that had fallen on the outside of his cage again. Charlie's tail was wagging frantically – he was far more sociable than Harry and Evie and was probably looking forward to seeing the other dogs being walked out on the car deck. It was great to think it would be the last time we were doing this strange walk around a ship's car deck out in the ocean. The next time I'd have them out for a walk it would be on solid ground somewhere in the south of Spain, a completely new environment for them. For me, this seemed really exciting as I wasn't even sure what roads we would be taking never mind where we would be stopping.

Like a broken record I just couldn't stop repeating myself in thanking Maria. I just wished the dogs could've realised how lucky they were to have her on the boat, making sure they all got walked together. For one, I probably wouldn't have stopped to let them mix with all the other dogs as much if Maria hadn't been there, and of course there was little Tia, she was so laid back and had been very friendly with my three. Little Evie was the only problem at the moment – not that you could tell when we were all out on the car deck together, she was always jealously keeping an eye on her beloved Harry.

As I've pointed out before, Harry is the most unsociable dog I've ever known; don't get me wrong, he loves us to bits, but he just has no time for other dogs at all, but for some reason when we meet other dogs, Harry's the first one they go to, they all seem to love him. Small children are much the same, they are all drawn to him which was always a worry to us as he was a fiery little pup. Not that he ever bit anyone, but the idea of some small child pulling at Harry's ears just doesn't bear thinking about.

Once we were all out together on the car deck the atmosphere seemed different, maybe everyone was excited that Cadiz wasn't far away. We could certainly see the lights now shining in the distance and there were so many other boats all around us, lighting up the dark sky; we even had lots of birds flying along the side of the boat, possibly following us into the harbour. Evie seemed lively enough – one minute she'd be fussing over Harry, the next chasing off any of his admirers. Meanwhile, Charlie was just doing his usual thing – introducing himself to any other dog that would take notice – while Harry wasn't interested in any of them and was more concerned with barking at me. Right there it was so obvious that all three dogs had such different characteristics, all very aware of each other but all so different.

As Maria and I were taking the dogs back to the van it was very noticeable that the morning sky was beginning to lighten; it wouldn't be long until that big shiny faced sun began to rise in the east, not that I had time to watch. Yup, things were beginning to move along at pace. My final farewells with Maria were short and sweet as I thanked her for all her help for the five thousandth time. I mean, I could've hassled Jim, but with Maria being a fully qualified vet it just gave me so much peace of mind, especially having all those unfounded worries based around Harry's epilepsy. We both wished each other a safe journey as this wasn't the end of the adventure for either of us – it wasn't just Jim, the dogs and I that had a long way to go, Maria and her small dog Tia had over 750 kilometres to drive from Cadiz all the way to Valencia, no mean feat after a two-day ferry crossing.

After leaving Maria I hurried down for some breakfast. I was now quite hungry and didn't have a clue when and where my next meal would be after we departed the ship. Walking into the busy restaurant I could see a lot of what had now become familiar faces although the friendly smiles had all but gone; in their defence it was still very early in the morning and I would imagine most of them would be thinking about the long day ahead of them. Mind you, I would bet a lot of money that none of them had to travel as far as me this day.

The breakfast was much the same as it had been the previous morning; it still looked very bland and very uninviting, even the sausages managed to be the same colour as the scrambled eggs, but this wasn't a time to be turning up my nose as I knew I needed sustenance for the long day ahead.

Once I had my tray filled with what I'd managed to fashion together as a nutritious start to the day I made my way to a table. Luckily I'd spotted Jim sitting at a table on his own. "Hiya Jim, what time do you think we'll be docking?" I asked. "Hiya Gary, around eight o'clock, so try to get back to the van sharpish," he replied cheerily. I hadn't seen much of Jim during the time we spent on the ship, but he had also been down making sure the dogs were okay. One thing was for sure, there certainly wasn't a lot to do on the ship, maybe read, or sit on the upper deck and sunbathe or what Jim had cleverly decided to do – get as much sleep as possible for that extremely long drive that he had in front of him.

Jim briefed me on what we should expect when we disembarked from the boat. I listened intently; in my mind, this was massively important to me and the dogs – I had to get them through this customs check. Jim could see that there had been a quick mood change from me; even though I was eating like I hadn't been fed in weeks, my jovial smile and demeanour was now a sternly straight-faced stare. Without hesitation Jim said, "Now don't worry, it'll be easy, just leave the talking to me, and don't worry." Feeling a little more reassured, I said, "Cheers Jim," although trying to switch off that overactive mind of mine was not easy. It wasn't even the paperwork I was concerned about, it was me trying to get the muzzles on Harry and Charlie. Yes, they'd had all their injections, but I was still envisaging them both rabidly attacking port security men and police. I had to remind myself they were only Yorkshire terriers not Bengali tigers.

As I finished my breakfast, I told Jim I had to double check I hadn't left anything up in the cabin and that once I'd dropped off my cabin key card at the ship's reception I'd meet him back at the van. Jim also had to revisit his cabin for the same reasons. As I made my way back to the cabin, I was remembering what Jim had said about him doing a lot of sleeping. I envied him – how much I'd love to be able to say to someone, "I slept really well last night," especially the last couple of nights in particular. I had been kidding myself that I'd done okay for sleep, but truth be known, I was never in my bed for more than two hours at a time. I began to feel really tired thinking about it.

I didn't mind feeling tired, I was still excited about getting off the ship to start the rest of the long journey northwards. I knew we would be stopping somewhere along the way, but that was another niggling little worry I had – we still had another two nights ahead of us which meant three more days travelling. Jim and I hadn't spoken about where we were going to stop or which hotels we might be staying at. The major problem I had was the dogs – I couldn't envisage any hotel allowing me to have three dogs in their rooms, and I didn't like the idea of just leaving them in the back of a van all night, I would be in and out of the hotel every two hours checking on them. The reception staff would think I was mad, this strange Scotsman going in and out of reception every couple of hours throughout the night. What if someone broke into the van while I was sleeping in the hotel? I'd never forgive myself, or having to explain to Nicky that the dogs were stolen as I was sleeping in a comfortable bed – that certainly wouldn't go down too well. I made my mind up that wherever we stayed, I'd sleep in the back of the van with the dogs. If I was to be totally honest, I felt more comfortable with the idea of me being close to the dogs. Yup, we were in this together.

Just before going back down to reception, I decided I'd make my way to the higher deck seven. I could see that it was daylight now, and I was hoping I might get a good view of Cadiz. On opening the door I could feel the warm air rushing around me. I could see there was not a cloud in the sky, and the sun was already coming up in the east. But the first thing that grabbed my attention were all the other boats surrounding our ship, all heading in lots of different directions – cargo ships, cruise liners and yachts of all different sizes. Not too far in the distance ahead of us I could see what I could only imagine was the main ferry port, large cranes in a very industrial-looking area. I stood for a little longer than I had expected to, but Cadiz was beginning to reveal itself, the coastline seemed to go on forever, the reflection of the sun sparkling from the windows. I could see what looked like castles, fortresses even, this low-level city seemed to go on forever. It was like some magical place, and we had travelled back in time – well, apart from the very gorgeous and expensive yachts around us of course.

Cadiz was a fantastic place. One thing I had done during the journey was to check out a little of its incredible history – this was what drew me to the upper deck in the first place, I wanted to see Cadiz in all its glory, and with the early morning sun shining upon it, I certainly wasn't disappointed.

Although Cadiz was neither Spain's largest nor its busiest port, it was certainly its oldest and arguably its most historic. Cadiz was founded nearly 3500 years ago by Phoenicians from Tyre (which is now known as Lebanon). These people were traders who eventually based themselves around most of the Mediterranean. Even back then, they were using coinage mostly made from gold, silver and even brass. In fact, these traders would have descended from the original peoples of Mesopotamia whose first type of coins were called shekels, which is quite funny as I thought shekels was a Scottish slang word for money as you would hear it used by guys in pubs.

From what I read, I think the Phoenicians were quite peaceable people, very intelligent, and very productive. The old street markets in those days would be trading such things as fine linens, especially embroidered clothes (some dyed with the famous Tyrian purple, which actually came from snails' shells), salt, dried fish, wine and glazed pottery in the form of jugs, pots, tiles, or in some cases just things that were purely ornamental. The main port would also have been busy as the Phoenicians conducted an important transit trade with certain types of wood such as cedar and pine. They were also the first people to start mass producing ceramics and bricks, all of which was busily loaded on and off ships.

It'll come as no surprise that the Phoenicians built some fine cities in their time which would have drawn people from all over the world, and all that wealth certainly grabbed the attention of ambitious competitors. The city of Cadiz must have been very beautiful, but because of its very prominent location and being of great strategic importance it ended up having many visits from less than friendly Assyrians and Persians – I think even Alexander the Great had partied there at one time, and of course the Romans. Latterly the city would be visited by the Visigoths and the Moors, before it became a launching platform for the Crusades. Just imagine if they had all visited Cadiz at the same time!

Quite a few times, Christopher Columbus had used Cadiz as a final staging post before he made his way over to the New World. I don't think the peoples of the Americas really enjoyed their newfound popularity as the indigenous populations suffered irreparably. Mind you, I'm sure Cadiz could tell them a thing or two about unwelcome guests.

Talking of unwelcome guests, a certain Francis Drake also made a visit to Cadiz. He was only there for three days, but within that short period of time he managed to capture six Spanish ships while destroying another thirty. This delayed the sailing of the Spanish Armada for up to a year. When we were younger, we were always led to believe that the Spanish Armada was on its way to attack England only for Drake to receive this information during a game of bowls on Plymouth Hoe; he stopped what he was doing and quickly hit the high seas and put an end to the Spanish Armada. It certainly makes for good reading, but it couldn't have been further from the truth.

5

After enjoying these fantastic views of Cadiz, I left deck seven feeling quite upbeat and refreshed and really looking forward to the rest of the journey. There was just the small matter of getting the dogs and myself through customs. Thankfully there was no faffing around as I went to reception, it was just a case of leaving them my cabin key card. With a smile on my face I thanked them for a lovely stay which actually drew some strange looks from the reception staff. They obviously thought I was being sarcastic, but I was genuinely happy with my cabin and really enjoyed the use of the shower. I think I was just a little over excited to finally be getting off the boat and onto solid land. When we were out at sea obviously the ship was moving but when all you can see all around you is water you just don't feel like you're getting anywhere.

Going through that big heavy door I could see Jim was already at the van checking it over like a proud captain inspecting his ship. "Hiya Gary, if you want to give the dogs another small walk that would be no problem, we still have a little time before we dock." Jim seemed happy and very alert. "Yeah, good idea Jim," I shouted back.

Jim helped hold the van doors as I put the leads on the dogs; they too were quite excited and as usual it was Harry leading the choir as they were all barking in unison. Jim was smiling as he said, "This lot seem happy enough." I was slightly embarrassed at the fuss they were making and apologised to Jim for the noise they were making. "Sorry Jim, I hope they're not going to bark for the rest of the journey," I said, trying to shout over their loud barking. "Don't worry, they'll quieten down as soon as we get on the road," Jim said with an assured confidence.

By now we seemed to have a system in place – Harry would pee first and the other two would have to pee exactly on top of where Harry had peed. It was then just a case of waiting on them doing their number twos. Although I'm sure Jim was used to having dogs having little accidents in the van over the years, I was determined it wasn't going to happen on my watch, especially with this being a brand-new van.

All done and dusted, I got the three dogs safely back into their cages and filled their dishes with more water and biscuits. Evie's cage was still immaculate – her little blankets seemed to be lying in a tidy pile and there had been no water spillages; the only concern was that she had hardly touched her biscuits. Harry and Charlie on the other hand were a different story – their cages were a mess! It looked a little like when disgruntled prisoners smash their cells up in some form of protest. Some of their dishes were overturned, their blankets were wet in places with soggy biscuits stuck to them, and spilled biscuits littered the floor all around their cages. And of course, there was Harry with his pink nose where he had tried to get to the biscuits on the outside of his cage. I tided them up as best I could and apologised to Jim for the mess. "Don't worry about it," Jim said, "we'll tidy it all out when we get to our final destination." And with that I climbed into the passenger's seat and got my paperwork ready so we were all prepared to disembark.

It wasn't long before we were preparing to disembark. Jim had the engine running and was just waiting for his call to move, while I was hitting him with lots of questions: Will I need to get the dogs' passports out? Will they want to see my passport at the same time? Will I need to put their muzzles on? Have you ever had any of the dogs taken off you before? Have they ever pulled their guns out on any of the dogs you've transported before? Jim could hear I was starting to panic again. "Gary, don't worry, just let me do the talking." That seemed to stop me in my tracks. All I could do was nervously stare down at my paperwork and hope for the best.

Suddenly it was our time to move. You could see the ship's deckhands pulling out the stoppers that were behind the car wheels, though thankfully they had not been needed as it had been calm seas for all of the journey. And at that, Jim started the engine and pulled a sharp turn and then we were travelling down the steep narrow ramp to the lower deck. There was no shortage of people making sure everything ran smoothly as we vacated the ship. It was just like the harbour in Puerto del Rosario, all very well organised with no hanging about.

There was a big difference though – this harbour was massive compared to the one in Puerto del Rosario. There were actually quite a few large cruise ships docked around us, it was fascinating looking at all these different boats from all over the world. I couldn't get over how big and busy the place seemed. When I mentioned this to Jim, he informed me that the place was a lot quieter since the pandemic hit. It suddenly dawned on me, of course – the pandemic, I'd almost forgotten about that. Even though all around us people were wearing their masks, I was too busy worrying about our eventual date with destiny, the moment the Spanish customs officers would finally get to meet the gang, Harry, Evie and Charlie.

We were now stuck in a small queue waiting to hand over our paperwork that had to be checked over by the customs people. It wasn't just me, I could tell Jim was restless as well. He had done this so many times before, so he could tell when the customs officers were being a bit slow or inefficient when it came to getting things moving along. Jim just wanted to get out on the open road. Looking over the tops of the cars in front of us I could see the customs officers up ahead; they seemed to be checking everyone's paperwork but from what I could tell there didn't seem to be any rigorous searching of vehicles. Then I noticed some poor van driver being asked to park his van so they could have a better look through it.

At that moment, I happened to glance to my right-hand side

where I saw this most amazing yacht docked only a few hundred yards away. It was incredible – without exaggeration, it almost looked like a spaceship with these fantastically large shiny windows that were like some sort of glass visors protecting the front of this very sleek-looking ship. And no wonder it looked so amazing – a team of workers were cleaning the large glass windows, guys all wearing the same-coloured overalls, some hosing over the windows as the rest were hard at it cleaning off the water and some others were working hard to bring up the shine.

My mind was cleared of worrying about customs officers for the moment, I was just mesmerised by the size of this luxury yacht. My questioning to Jim was now completely different: what was it? who owned it? where had it come from? Jim could tell I'd become fascinated by this super yacht. He glanced briefly over to the ship; he had seen it many times before and was more concerned with the lack of movement coming from the customs guys. "Yup, that's the Yas, one of the most expensive yachts in the world. It's owned by Hamdan bin Zayed bin sultan Al Nahyan," he casually explained, again with only a brief glance over at the boat.

The Yas had formerly been a ship belonging to the Royal Netherlands navy and had been decommissioned and sold to the United Arab Emirates. I personally had never seen anything like it. My next question for Jim was, "How much do you reckon it's worth?" Again, with no hesitancy or excitement, he calmly said, "I think it's about a hundred and fifty million pounds." Jim said it like it was spare change that had fallen from his pocket. I turned my head quickly back round towards this fabulous yacht. In between all the lorry trailers and shipping containers that seemed to be scattered around the dock, this yacht looked so out of place. It was then the realisation of how the other half lived – here I was, in an albeit brand-new custom van, stuck in a queue with a host of other vehicles trudging along very slowly, almost being cattle herded from one post to the other, it left me feeling rather insignificant.

Looking back round to the back of the van, I cast my eyes over my bags which were now looking a little messy and dishevelled and then to the cages. I could see the three dogs all sitting to attention, staring quietly back at me. With that, my mind was quickly drawn back to the job at hand, these menacing little monsters looked like they were alert and ready to take on as many customs officers as Cadiz could throw at them. The enormity of the journey was again at the front of my mind, how nice it would have been if some kindly face had shouted from the expensive yacht, "Hey, Gary, just bring the dogs on here, there's plenty of room for them to run around; you just pop to our bar and we'll have you all home in a few hours."

I was brought to my senses as I realised Jim had put the van into gear, and we were moving towards the customs post. "Now let me do the talking," Jim said in an authoritative manner. I certainly wasn't going to argue with him. Jim rolled down his window and said hello to the young customs officer who peered over his shoulder into the back of the van. I waited patiently with my passport and the dogs' passports and vaccination papers. It all seemed to happen so fast – I handed the passports to Jim, the officer had a quick look at them then asked Jim where we were headed. The conversation was short and sweet and, before I knew it, the customs officer was handing back the passports to Jim who literally threw them back over to me, put his own passport up behind the sun visor and that was that – we were off.

I could hardly believe it. I didn't have to get out of my seat, the dogs didn't bark once, it couldn't have gone any smoother. I'd had the muzzles ready and was prepared for the eventuality of the customs officers checking their chips, the long wait as they scrutinised every last detail on their little doggie passports, but none of that happened. All this time I had been dreading these moments. First, I had panicked about how we would all survive the ferry journey, would we all make the crossing in one piece!? Would I lose any of the dogs due to them going overboard!? Or would we all just die of seasickness in a storm with massive waves!? The ferry journey couldn't have been any easier – well perhaps less wind would've helped, especially with opening and closing the van doors. Even if the ferry journey hadn't gone well, realistically I'm sure we would've all survived, although the inconvenient shortfalls could've been very unpleasant. But my biggest concerns were always going to be the customs posts – anything goes wrong there and the whole plan ends up on its head; being stuck in the middle of nowhere and not being able to get anywhere was a frightening scenario. Jim could tell I was massively relieved at our turn of good luck.

It was a beautiful day and we were now out on the road. I say road, but we were still in a very congested area and all to do with the busy port. It wasn't just me who was happy, I could tell Jim was quite lively and chirpy as he acted like my own personal tour guide as we tried to escape the throngs of traffic. One of the first things he pointed out was the Cadiz railway station which was the main station of Cadiz where, if need be, you can catch these super-fast high-speed trains to nearly anywhere in Spain. Obviously not all lines would suit these high-speed trains and it does change over to the more conventional rail line services at certain points, but none the less, this starting point could eventually lead you all the way to Calais in France if need be.

This little nugget of information struck a chord with me as I had wondered what might happen had Jim turned up in a rickety old van that broke down somewhere on the journey. What would I have done? It wasn't something I'd researched, I had obviously thought about the possibilities of Jim breaking down but had never considered my options. Obviously, me phoning Nicky with tears streaming down my face, pleading for help wasn't going to get me anywhere. In honesty, as we were driving past Cadiz train station, I was very confident that our mode of transportation was as good as any other we were passing on the road and you could almost feel the enthusiasm and love Captain Jim had for this super custom van he was driving, it moved smoothly and accelerated very quickly when needs must.

It was a beautiful sunny morning as we drove out of Cadiz. Jim had music playing from the radio which seemed to be in keeping with my very upbeat mood; the traffic seemed to be thinning out the farther we got from Cadiz which was leaving Jim a clear path out on this open road. The first thing I noticed were the hedgerows and trees lining our route out of town, this was certainly a far cry from the dusty desert roads of Fuerteventura which always looked like they had just been rolled out across the unkempt malpais.

It really felt like this journey was finally getting underway; back on the ferry, although we were moving, it didn't really feel like you were getting anywhere, just blue sea as far as the eye could see and everything seemed to be moving at a very relaxing pace. I suppose it was my ADHD that didn't allow me to fully appreciate the idea of relaxation – as soon as I sit down, my mind is ticking over at a rate of knots looking for something to do. The truth of the matter is, it's more likely I am trying to find an escape from my overactive mind until exhaustion finally knocks me out; even then there are no guarantees, unfortunately even though the body's burned out your mind keeps going, it reminds of the lyrics from Nirvana's Pennyroyal Tea   "I'm so tired I can't sleep". So now that Jim had his pedal to the metal and I felt like this journey was really underway, it was noticeable that it had left Jim and I both feeling very positive and upbeat.

I didn't know exactly where we were headed but Jim was quick to tell me we were headed in the direction of Seville, a distance of around 130 kilometres. We weren't going directly into Seville but would drive around it. Jim reckoned this part of the journey would take about an hour and a half. He suggested that once we had got past Seville, we would make our first stop for the dogs.

At that I turned to look at the dogs; both Charlie and Evie were sleeping but not Harry, he was sitting up, looking alert. I could see he was quite happy, so I wasn't surprised when he started barking at me.

"Alright Harry, quieten down, we'll be stopping soon," I said to him like it was some bribe to get him to be quiet. As usual, once Harry starts barking, it quickly spurs Charlie and Evie into action and they both joined in, all sitting to attention while they barked in unison. I turned to Jim and apologised for their cacophony of noise. "Sounds like they're all quite happy," Jim said with a smile on his face. I'm not sure if he was laughing at the dogs or my obvious lack of control. "They'll quieten down soon enough," Jim said reassuringly.

The road in front of us seemed quiet, although it was still early. "I thought there would have been a lot more traffic on the roads, especially with it being Monday morning," I said to Jim inquisitively. "It will get busier as we get closer to Seville I would imagine," he replied.

Now clear of Cadiz we were travelling along at a nice pace. Every now and then we would pass little bits of road works which didn't seem to affect us as the roads were free of any congestion. The excitement I had first felt when we arrived on the mainland had waned a little now. I was beginning to feel tired again and my mind was beginning to drift a little. I could see it was now nearly eleven o'clock and we were beginning to close in on Seville. All around me, I was astounded by the terrain, again so different from the island of Fuerteventura I'd left so far behind me. As we passed by some cotton fields, masses of them, Jim informed me that Spain was the second largest producer of cotton in Europe, only coming second to Greece. I knew nothing of this. I like to think I am a very worldly-wise, knowledgeable kind of guy on a range of different subjects, but this was something that had escaped me. There wasn't much cotton to be seen as most of it had been harvested in late September with just little amounts left on the plants.

It wasn't just cotton fields we were passing through, we were also seeing lots of olive trees or groves as they are known; they looked like mini forests with trees sort of scattered indiscriminately for as far as the eye could see. There was certainly no uniformity as to how they had been grown. It looked like a fantastic place to walk the dogs –

even with the sun beating down on your back, you would still have lots of places to take shelter as these small trees had thick foliage. It wasn't just the dogs I was thinking about, I thought back to my childhood, this would have been a great place for me and my friends to run around in. I imagined it would be great being there with all the local people helping out with harvesting, especially as it all had to be done by hand. Obviously every now and then you would be up and down ladders to get to the highest bunches of olives. Even if it was hard work, it would be such a beautiful environment to work in.

Coming from Scotland the only harvesting we ever got involved with was the very cruel and arduous task of potato picking. Out in the fields at the back of my coastal town of Kinghorn, it was horrible work – bent over, up to your knees in mud, fumbling through the cold earth to get to the potatoes that had just been churned up by the passing tractor. The weather was always awful, bleak skylines with cold winds blowing up from the sea, not that you would get time to enjoy the view as the farmer would be driving back round with that tractor again to churn up more potatoes, and woe betide you if you hadn't picked up the first lot.

It had seemed like a good way to make some quick money, but the reality was soul destroying. It had all come about because the farm was owned by the father of our friend Steven. Making some extra pocket money just for picking up a few potatoes had seemed like a great idea... I'll never forget the state of everyone at the end of the day, no one talking, just hunched over in the back of the van waiting to be driven home. We were all filthy from digging around with our hands to get to those potatoes, nowhere to wash your hands, clothes were dirty and damp from a ten-hour slog, and if that doesn't sound bad enough, we only got half the money because we were kids. So the idea of me and my small gang of friends getting to work in a sun-drenched olive grove sounds like luxury compared to the hardships we had all gone through in the harsh climate of a wintery October in Fife in Scotland.

6

The roads were now starting to get a little busier as we got closer to the beautiful city of Seville. Up ahead of us I could see the Centenario Bridge which stretched out across the left branch of the Guadalquivir River. Once we were up on the bridge we could look directly down on to the Port of Seville and just over to our right, rather higher than the river, we could see the castle of Alcala, or Castillo de Alcala as it's known in Seville. Unbelievably this has been the result of nearly 4500 years of human history on this very ancient hill.

Archaeological research has not found it easy to determine exactly what went on through history as the castle and its foundations have gone through many changes over the many hundreds of years of its existence. The Moors, the Romans and many of the past Spanish kings have all made claims to this well-fought-for location with its fantastic views that cover most of the surrounding areas of Seville. Amazingly, a lot of the battlements and walls you can still see to this day were built by the Almohad Caliphate and their Mujahidin army from North Africa in the twelfth century. Many years ago, much like the UK and my home country of Scotland, Spain was broken down into separate kingdoms which could cause a great deal of upheaval when lesser kings fell out; with Seville being a very sought after and prominent kingdom, there were many battles with armies fighting it out for a claim to this very famous hill.

I too had been part of a large army that invaded Seville, way back in 1982 – yes, the world-famous Tartan Army, led by our fearless leader, the late great Jock Stein. Sadly, it was to end in another glorious defeat as we fell to the swashbuckling and very cavalier Brazil. It was a warm clammy night at the Estadio Benito Villamarin, the home of Real Betis. The atmosphere was incredible, a mixture of Brazilian drumming and the skirl of the bagpipes and everyone singing at the tops of their voices. The stage was set for another footballing bonanza. We could only hope that we would put up a brave performance as we knew all too well how good this Brazilian team was. But in the eighteenth minute, there was an unexpected twist and our world was turned upside down. David Narey managed to put us ahead one–nil with a fantastic shot from outside the box that rifled into the Brazilian keeper's top right-hand corner. Yes, I was there, right behind the goal, a moment I'll treasure and never forget. Okay, it didn't last forever but for fifteen minutes, myself and the whole of the Scottish nation felt like we were kings of the world as we rejoiced and sang our hearts out. That was until Zico for Brazil equalised and made it one all and then reality came back with a vengeance as the second half turned into a footballing education for Scotland. Brazil scored another three through Oscar, Eder and Falco, all Brazilian legends, and if I was to be completely honest, we were lucky it was only three more that they scored. Just to rub salt into the wound, Jimmy Hill, commentating on the BBC during the game, actually said that David Narey's goal was a lucky toe poke. This obviously didn't go down well with the legions of Scottish fans as we added to our repertoire of songs "We hate Jimmy Hill, he's a poof, he's a poof". Yes, I know what you're all thinking, a rather homophobic jibe from us kilt-wearing Scots.

The great thing about we Scots is that we're as magnanimous in defeat as we are in victory and at the end of the game, we praised and thanked our Brazilian foes for the drubbing they duly gave us. We know a good party when we see one, so we were all quick to join in with the carnival atmosphere the Brazilian fans were laying on, in fact it was all swapping of football tops, caps and t-shirts. There were even a few south American revellers now dancing happily in kilts. It was getting hard to differentiate who was who, there had been so much clothes swapping going on, though of course the peeling noses and white spindly legs and guttural screams of Scotland kind of gave it away who was who in the end.

These were tremendous days; I was only nineteen so getting a two-week holiday and getting to experience the World Cup was a momentous occasion for one so young. The Scotland team were based in Malaga, so we had booked four apartments in Benalmadena which was just next to the resort of Torremolinos. Yes, eight brave young souls travelled from Kinghorn in Fife by train all the way to Manchester and from there flew to Malaga. As you can imagine, the resort was full of likeminded Scots with very little understanding of the dangers of mixing bright sunlight and copious amounts of alcohol. In our defence, we were all very courteous and the majority were sensible enough to relax and sunbathe during the day and leave all the other frivolities until later in the evening. Although I must admit I did witness some poor souls who hadn't followed the script being unceremoniously dumped into the swimming pool, still fast asleep, dead to the world from drinking a few too many beers in the afternoon. They didn't know anything about their ordeal till their sleeping bodies were rudely awakened by the cool waters of the swimming pool.

The best thing I saw was when four or five apartments were competing from four and five floors high and doing their best to hit some poor guy with buckets of water as he lay fast asleep on his sunbed. This managed to captivate an audience of two whole holiday complexes as people were out on their balconies enjoying this great spectacle. Luckily the onlooking crowd's oohhs and aahhs as each bucket of water missed didn't awaken the target. He was totally unaware of his predicament, paralysed by the blanket of late-afternoon sun that was keeping him locked into that deep unconscious sleep.

As the excitement was reaching fever pitch, the baying crowd were almost demanding a direct hit, so eventually one of the lads decided to climb from his apartment onto an empty balcony that was directly above our poor victim. There was little concern for the fact that the guy was actually taking his life in his own hands as he climbed from one balcony to the other, four storeys up. Had he fallen, it would have been certain death. A cheer went up from the watching crowd as he safely secured his position; now it was just a case of making sure he was passed a full bucket of water to complete the task. To everyone's despair, he threw the full bucket of water but still managed to miss. Even with water crashing onto the terrace close to the hapless victim's sunbed, he still didn't stir.

With no time to waste, the bucket had to be quickly passed back to the other balcony to be refilled. One of the other lads decided to make that dangerous balcony crossing as he obviously felt he was the man for the job. It didn't take long for the bucket to be refilled and passed to our new hitman; with outstretched arms, he tipped the water out carefully and the water crashed down onto the target below. It almost sounded like someone belly flopping into a swimming pool as the water smashed into his body with force – and let's remember, this wasn't pleasant warm water from the swimming pool, this was a full bucket of cold water straight from the tap. His body convulsed like he had just been hit with a bolt of electricity from a defibrillator and all around there was delighted cheering and screaming from the many onlookers. It must have taken our hapless victim a good few seconds to realise he was part of a very elaborate prank; he was obviously quite taken aback as he gazed around the many surrounding balconies that had joined in the fun. With all the cheering and shouting that was going on around him, he couldn't do anything else but smile and raise his arms above his head. He probably knew there and then that this would be a story that would do the rounds for many years to come.

Now it's not lost on me that for some people, turning up on holiday to find yourself camped out with twenty thousand football fans sounds like their worst nightmare, but in our defence, Scotland fans really go out of their way to be great ambassadors for their country. When they weren't buying ice-creams for all the kids or sending drinks to families' tables that may look a little shell-shocked at the commotions coming from the fans' boisterous celebrations, they would be making sure the waiters' tip jars were full to the brim with pesetas. The restaurant and bar bosses could afford a smile as their tills were red hot with constant opening and closing as the monies filled up their cash registers. Even the local police were enjoying getting in on the act as the Scotland fans were making sure they were the centrepiece of their holiday snaps; their faces must have been getting sore with all the smiling they were having to do.

The Brazilians who were sharing the same hotels seemed to be enjoying themselves too. Often, they could be seen playing keepy-up with a football around the poolside; even the girls who were with them had brilliant ball skills which would keep us all mesmerised. Being Scottish, seeing girls being brilliant at football while wearing bikinis wasn't something we saw very often.

Despite the language barriers, it didn't take us long to strike up friendships with our Brazilian counterparts who had travelled a massive distance to watch their beloved football team. Most of the Brazilian fans we met seemed to be very wealthy and had flown for nearly ten hours to Madrid then driven from Madrid all the way to Benalmadena. Most of the Brazilian fans were staying around Seville as that's where their team was playing most of its games, but the fans we met were cleverly treating it like a family holiday and had based themselves closer to the coastline; they could use the beautiful beaches during the day, then hire minibuses to travel the 120 miles to the games. Yup, it was fantastic. What more could a young man ask for – a fantastic holiday in Spain with all your friends and thrown into the mix getting to see Scotland playing in the World Cup. And of course, having a team like Brazil in our group was just a dream come true, they were undoubtedly one of the greatest footballing sides in the world. Personally, I always felt with their silky skills on the ball they were like the Harlem Globetrotters of international football.

As always, all good things must come to an end but unbeknown to us we were travelling home the same day as the Scotland squad. What a surprise when we walked into the departure lounge to find the players all sitting around chatting! Thankfully for us they were all very friendly and all seemed in a jovial mood. Being only nineteen years of age, it was a dream come true getting to meet the Scotland team. It wasn't long before we were sitting down talking to some of the players and getting photographs taken with the likes of Kenny Dalgleish and Jock Stein. To this day, I've still got a picture of Jock Stein wearing a sombrero and strumming a guitar we had taken with us on the trip. It's often been remarked that Scotland never get past the first group stages simply because we can only afford the two-week holiday.

It was hard to believe that had all happened nearly forty years ago. I found myself peering out of the van window desperately hoping I might see something I recognised from the last time I was there. But of course, there was no chance that somehow me sitting in a moving van on a road I'd never been on before I was going to spot anything that might jog my memory.

Seville was littered with historic buildings and ancient artifacts that had graced these same streets all those years ago. There was the great Gothic Cathedral, famous football grounds, royal palaces which have all been used as backdrops for several blockbuster movies and tv shows, but nothing in sight that might trigger some reaction from me. Sadly, I had been too young and stupid to appreciate the beauty that surrounded me at that time; now that I was older, I recognised that Seville would be a fantastic place to stay and spend some time, there was so much to see and do. It's reputed that Seville was the originator of the world-renowned tapas that has become a traveller's favourite around Spain; one theory is that a small farmers' bar in Seville would serve glasses of chilled beer with a small saucer on top to keep the flies away, eventually the bar started putting finger food on top of the saucers which must have been a real delight to the locals.

It's not just the beautiful architecture that Seville is famous for – it is probably one of the nicest smelling cities in Spain. Throughout the whole of Seville there are thousands of orange trees, and when they blossom every springtime, they give off a lovely perfume that wafts through the city's streets. When the oranges eventually ripen, they drop and litter the streets of Seville; unfortunately these oranges are very bitter and not palatable, so they are used for feeding some of the farm animals and of course much of the local wildlife takes advantage of this fruity feast. A lot of these bitter oranges are farmed and then shipped over to the UK and made into marmalade.

As much as Seville was beautiful and historic, it certainly couldn't be accused of being stuck in its ancient past, as the inhabitants certainly have a foot firmly placed in the future. As Jim and I were driving around the outskirts of the city, we couldn't miss a very futuristic-looking forty-storey concrete tower. This modern-day monolith stands proudly tall, surrounded by what looks like hundreds of shiny worshippers at its feet. What this huge tower is actually doing is collecting masses of reflected rays of sunlight from a surrounding field of 624 massive mirrors. When the light is really intense it can light up all the dust and water vapour in the air which makes it look like it's beaming out some form of strange energy. We could see it from a short distance from the roadside, and the best way I could describe it would be that it looked like something out of a sci-fi movie. This futuristic solar tower was sucking up so much power that it was creating enough energy to power nearly ten thousand homes. How does it work? I thought you might be wondering that. Okay, I'm not an expert but I'll try and do my best to explain.

The intense collection of the sun's rays is used to heat water pipes to incredibly hot temperatures; this thermal energy then produces steam which drives a turbine that then produces electricity. Even hours after dark, this extremely hot water is stored in thermally clad tanks where the water can reach temperatures of 250°c; paradoxically a lot of this extremely hot energy is used to power the air conditioners that cool the many buildings in and around Seville.

Anyway, this got me thinking. Imagine if you could put these towers around the perimeter of the equator, surely this would create enough energy to power the homes and lives of all the people in each of the northern and southern hemispheres. All these barren deserts could be put to good use, filling them with these fantastic towers that could bring so much more clean energy to the whole world. Yup, factually this could be a possibility, and it's more than probable that something similar will happen in the future. You could even go as far as to say that there is an inevitability about this sort of thing happening.

So what's stopping us sharing this great energy wealth around the world now I hear you ask? Money and lots of it initially. It needs investment – and the people and governments that have the power and money to do it will only invest if they're the recipients of huge profitable returns. And then there's the question of who will build and own these monolithic cash cows. You only need to look around the world today to see the problems we are having with the control and distribution of carbon-based fossil fuels. It could be argued that most of the wars going on today are related to energy and the control of these dwindling important resources, again all for the purpose of making money. And sadly, these wars are never paid for by the people that benefit from these conflicts. Oh no, that's all paid for by the taxpayer, our governments borrow money from our central banks on our behalf so they can pay for weapons and the military might that is needed. Yes, the military industrial complex makes an absolute fortune. Sadly our armies are not fighting for our benefit, they're actually fighting for the benefit of big business that then comes back to the taxpayers and sells us the resources that have been gained through war.

Now just a wee idea. Imagine if all the countries took even half of the taxes they spend on wars and energy supply security, and instead spent it on building projects that would lead to a worldwide energy system based on clean air technologies that could serve all our needs and possibly lead to clean air, less pollution and no more wars. Sorry if I make it sound so simplistic; changes of that magnitude would be globally seismic. If the world tried to make these changes overnight the world economy would crash leading to a worldwide depression, starvation and a panic that would lead to a total social breakdown in our cities and towns. But it could be done transitionally, as long as everyone was informed and on board, if people realised that these changes were exactly what was required to save the planet and make the world a better place to live.

I have a simple analogy for this, it's kind of like if you're on a bus travelling down the road at speed only to find out if you stay on this path, it'll eventually drive right off the edge of a cliff. You can't just automatically throw the bus into reverse as this would probably lead to a disastrous accident which would kill everyone on the bus and more. So, the correct thing to do is to slow the bus down and find a safe place so you can carefully turn the bus around and get back onto a safer road which is leading you and everyone else in a safer direction. So, obviously the point I'm trying to make here is that like most things you need to take everything into account, to make considerations and be assured of a safe transition. But before I totally discard my little badge and revolutionary beret, it's got to be said, sometimes you've got to crack a few eggs if you want to make an omelette.

7

As we started to leave Seville and its busier roads and intersections behind us, the van with Jim, me and the dogs in was now heading steadily northwards. My mind was drifting and feeling quite relaxed and I was beginning to feel very tired, but something inside me was refusing to allow me to fall asleep. "We're only a couple of minutes away from our next stop." These words from Jim helped me quickly come to my senses. Something I noticed was that the roads were never too busy, even when we were passing around Seville. I had thought the traffic would be a little more congested. I was about to pose the question to Jim when I realised he was pulling off the dual carriageway. I could see the service station; it seemed to be quite a new building with very few cars parked around it. If Jim hadn't known better, I would've thought it was closed.

The surrounding area was quite grassy with a tree and bushes close to the car park. This was fantastic I thought to myself, another environment that the dogs had never experienced before. I turned to look at the dogs and shouted, "We goin' walkies Harry!?" He started barking excitedly which soon got the attention of Evie and Charlie, who were both now sitting up watching Harry loudly barking at me.

It wasn't long before Jim had parked up and switched off the van engine. Straightaway I jumped out of the van and made my way round to the back of it. Things were so much easier as I was able to open both back doors, I hadn't forgotten how difficult a task this was when we were on the ferry. Now we were on solid ground with no sea breeze trying to blow the doors off.

First things first, I'd get Harry's lead on; not only was he the most excitable but I felt it was only fair that he should be first to stretch his legs on this lovely grassy surface. He caught me by surprise though as no sooner had I got his lead on than he jumped from the back of the van onto the soft grassy surface. "HARRY!!!" I shouted; I'd got a bit of a fright but the pleasing thing was that he seemed unfazed by the journey so far; he was full of beans, and it didn't take long for his nose to pick up all these new smells.

I could hear Evie now yelping from the back of the van as she was obviously panicking that Harry and I were walking off into the distance. Evie was besotted with Harry; it was one of the reasons we had got Charlie, just to get another dog in her life, we were worried how it would affect her if anything happened to Harry. In fact, it wasn't just Evie I was worried about, I was thinking of Nicky as well; Harry and Nicky were best of friends. They'd been in each other's back pockets for nearly fourteen years. And I hadn't forgotten how Nicky and Harry were when little Larry had died.

We had got Larry as a small pup back in 2017. It was a massive worry for us as we didn't know how Harry would react to a new dog in the house, it was bad enough out on the street as Harry was very reluctant to make friends with other dogs. Usually when we were out with Harry, he would pick up the smell of his furry foes and get really excited as he knew he'd be getting ready for a bark off. It didn't matter how cute or cuddly some of these other lovely dogs were, Harry was having none of it, and if the dogs were bigger than him that was just a greater challenge in his eyes.

Thankfully, and much to our surprise, Harry took to Larry fairly quickly and it was fantastic once we began to watch them playing together. It's just something we never imagined, Harry being nice and having a doggie friend and playing together. As Larry grew older, he was just a joy to take out; he loved meeting other dogs and their owners and was especially great with kids.

I remember one time as we were walking on the beach at the front of the five-star Bahia Real we decided we would take a chance and try letting him off the lead for the first time. Nicky was rather hesitant as there was quite a large society wedding under way at the front of the hotel. "Don't worry," I said to her, "he'll be fine, I'll watch him." As soon as we let him off the lead he was off through the gates and decided to run right into the heart of the wedding. Nicky was understandably fuming with me, and embarrassingly I had to make my way into the wedding to retrieve the pesky little mutt.

As I fumbled and mumbled a thousand apologies to everyone I encountered, Larry had become the star of the show as the bride and groom were all oohhs and aaahhs at this cute little guy that had crashed their wedding. Thankfully I had nothing to worry about as Larry had melted their hearts with his ears back, wagging little tail and lovely little googley eyes. Apologising profusely, I carefully picked him up and turned to leave, but everyone was full of smiles as they could see Larry was game for staying a little longer.

Many evenings we would walk the dogs along by Corralejo harbour; it was always beautiful as the sun began to sink in the west behind my favourite volcano, Bayuyo. One evening as we were walking past the Armas ferry, we came across a large party of fifty people waiting to board; they had all been to a wedding in Corralejo and were about to make their way back to Lanzarote. One of the party members happened to spot Larry and called over to him. This was music to Larry's ears, his little waggly tail and googley eyes went into action and before we knew it, we had to walk him through the whole entourage before we could get away. Now had this been just Harry, he would've barked at everyone and Nicky would've quickly jumped to his defence and suggested that the crowd should not have annoyed him. But as Larry was making his happy little way through the crowd, Nicky could only smile with pride at this little star, even Harry's ears were back in a friendly and welcoming manner. This was unheard of, Harry being nice to strangers, Larry was obviously having a great effect on Harry which in turn was making Nicky's life easier.

To be honest, Harry and Nicky were used to confrontation. Harry barked at bikes, runners, skateboards, helicopters, buses and other dogs, but Nicky's loyalty knew no bounds – whatever happened, she would fiercely defend Harry's honour. But things were beginning to change. Larry was helping make Harry's life happier, they had become good friends. And it wasn't just Harry – even our cats were enjoying Larry's company. Alex our tabby cat would often play and fight with Larry which would finish with them cuddled up and falling asleep together. Even Sophie our Siamese cat had been won over and they would chase each other backwards and forwards from room to room. This was unheard of as Sophie refused to mix with anyone, especially our other cats. It didn't matter where Nicky was in the house, you could be assured little Larry wouldn't be far behind.

Larry was half of Harry's size with a silvery grey coat which adorned his slight frame, whereas Harry's was much blacker and browner and slightly sun bleached from swimming in the sea; in fact I would sometimes refer to Harry by the nickname Rusty. It was around mid-January and Nicky had decided it was time for our scruffy little Larry to get a haircut; it was his first time and she had chosen a groomer we hadn't used before. Harry would just be taken along to our local vets where they had an inhouse groomer who seemed to cut Harry's hair with no fuss at all. So with that being the case, we never considered using anyone else – if Harry was going to allow someone to cut his hair without kicking off, that would do for us. But with Larry having a better temperament, we thought we'd give a specialised groomer a visit. It was a case of dropping him off at ten o'clock and collecting him at twelve o'clock.

It was the first time he had been out of the house on his own so we were keen to get there early to pick him up. On arrival we could see him through the window staring back up at us, all excited. His haircut looked great, he looked funny with his skinny little frame and longish legs but the most obvious of all were his really long ears. Getting him back into the house you could see Harry and Larry were glad to see each other after their short time apart. Harry was quite excited as he was sensing all these new smells coming from Larry.

Later in the evening we found Larry was shivering. Of course, with it being January it can get quite cool on a night, so we thought nothing of it and put on one of his little knitted tops. Over the next few days, we noticed the same thing, more shivering and he wasn't his usually chirpy self, in fact we noticed he seemed to be walking with difficulty. Without any hesitation, we rushed him up to our local vets. At first appearances the vet felt it was possibly an infection so the first thing he did was give him an antibiotic injection and booked him in for an x-ray.

For the first few days, everything seemed to be fine, but on the third day he was back to shivering and on the odd occasion he would make this very strange yelping noise. The following day it was time for his x-rays and, as an added precaution, the vet also gave him an anti-inflammatory injection. Once we eventually got the results of the x-rays, we found that Larry had an enlarged heart which isn't unusual for small dogs. But more concerning was that his spine was like a dog of eight years of age and had what is known as a parrot's beak, meaning there's a small hook at the bottom of the spine that begins to curl and is very brittle.

These results still didn't really explain most of his symptoms and further tests were required. Nicky was becoming quite concerned as we were not getting any closer to a proper diagnosis. I tried to allay her fears, saying, "Don't worry, you know Larry, he's full of life, he'll be fine." I was no vet, but Larry was only two years old, surely it couldn't be anything too serious.

For the next week he would be fine one moment then down the next; we were just praying the vet's next set of results would identify the problem and we could move forward and give him the proper treatment that he needed. A few days later the vet was back with a little better news – it wasn't a guaranteed prognosis as they were waiting on more info being sent through from the tests, but they were feeling relatively confident that they'd identified Larry's problem as Addison's disease. This was better news – we even afforded ourselves a chuckle as we realised this was the same problem that the late great President John F Kennedy had. Finally, some light at the end of the tunnel. Of course it was terrible that Larry was ill but with the right treatment he could lead a relatively normal life. All we had to do was take Larry into the vets on the Wednesday morning, hopefully they would do the relevant tests and we would have him back out again that afternoon. It was a big relief as we were starting to fear the worst, whatever that was.

Come Wednesday morning, we did our usual routine – both dogs were taken round by the harbour, obviously at quite a slow pace as little Larry was still struggling, not only was he not moving too well but the strong winds that had been forecast were making things that little bit more difficult for him. Eventually it was time to take him up to the vets. Nicky and I were confident that this would be the last time for a while and were prepared for our vet to give us a prescription for whatever drugs were needed for this Addison's disease.

On arriving at the vets, we were glad to see it wasn't too busy and we were attended to quite quickly. After a short conversation we left Larry having been told to expect a phone call around two o'clock where upon we would then have to go and pick him. That was all fine in our minds, we were now just looking forward to getting back to some normality as this had all been a bit of a worry for us.

After dropping Larry off it was time to visit our preferred supermarket at the time, which was Hyperdinos. It was all a bit of a rush as I would then have to quickly cycle up to my work at the Alisios Playa. This was a lovely small complex where I would be called upon to entertain our regular guests. The weather although windy was still very sunny so I knew that would help keep everyone happy and the complex was built in such a way that the pool area was sheltered from the wind. Having the same people coming back year after year really made my life so much easier – in fact, it was more like lots of old friends coming back for a visit. The guests all knew me very well and I had been telling them all about our little Larry, so

I knew they would understand if I was a little later than usual.

The Alisios wasn't a long way from the supermarket so before I knew it, I was back on the complex creating mayhem in my usual fashion, winding people up and just generally having fun in the sun. Being a lively person and trying to talk to as many people as possible, you really do lose track of time through all the excitement. I was quite surprised when I looked down at my ringing phone to see it was Nicky calling, the time on my phone said ten past so obviously Nicky must be coming out of the vets with Larry.

Answering the phone, I could tell Nicky was far from happy. "What's wrong?" I asked. "It's the vet, they've just rung to ask if we can come and get him at eight o'clock," she said in a soft voice. I could tell she was worried. "Don't worry, it's probably just because they are busy, they're probably waiting on Larry's results," I said, trying to reassure her. "Yeah, I suppose." She didn't sound too convinced. "At least we will both be able to go up together," I said, but in the back of my own mind there was a definite concern.

After I had finished the phone call with Nicky, my mind was going through all the scenarios, trying to work out if it wasn't so bad that we were having to pick up Larry a little later than planned. I kept telling myself that if it had been something serious, they would have told Nicky straight away, and certainly over the last few years, with the town growing so rapidly, the vets had been getting so much busier. They had even taken on more staff to deal with the increased number of cats and dogs in town. Laws had changed as well and now everyone was supposed to make sure their pets were chipped. So I tried to stay positive.

Once I started running around the complex talking my usual rubbish while at the same time trying to entertain the guests it wasn't long before I was lost in my own little world of nonsense. All my worries about Larry and Nicky slipped to the back of my mind for the present, but once I'd climbed onto my bike and started heading homewards, right at the forefront of my mind was Larry. I could only hope that after tonight we would be on the right road to making things better for our little furry friend.

Getting back to the house I could see Nicky was doing her best to disguise the fact that she was carrying the world on her shoulders. I gave her a hug and told her, "Try not to worry, we will soon be walking the little guy back down to the house." It wasn't long till we were both ready and leaving the apartment. Nicky was laughing as she had picked out one of little Larry's funny jerseys. I always made out that I found some of their little clothes to be silly, but underneath I quite enjoyed it. Especially all the cracking photos Nicky managed to have of both the dogs dressed up, she had even gone as far as to make these cracking Christmas cards with Harry and Larry dressed up as Santa's little helpers.

It wasn't long before we reached the vets. The door was open and the place seemed quiet; even the girl who worked at the serving counter was nowhere to be seen. Of course, at eight o'clock, it was just about closing time, so they were all probably cleaning up, I thought to myself. Suddenly one of the vets came out from the back room. She saw us, nodded her head and said she would be with us shortly. Nicky and I looked at each other, we were both aware that wasn't the usual greeting when we arrived at the vets. We stared at each other and shrugged our shoulders, but already I had that cold feeling running down the back of my spine. I had this overpowering sense something wasn't right. Just at that moment, the girl came back out and asked us if we could accompany her into one of the treatment rooms.

We both knew the room well, we'd had lots of our cats in there at one time or another; everything was familiar — the computer, the pictures on the wall, I'd even go so far as to say we knew which cupboards had what in them. I wasn't sure if I was focusing on the familiarity just to make me feel I was in a good place. As the young vet re-entered the room her eyes danced between Nicky's and my own as she gave us the grave news that Larry was very ill. He had been convulsing and having bad diarrhoea, and they were very sure that he was suffering from a brain tumour. At this point, everything was just a blur; I was thinking of everything and nothing at the same time, there was just a droning sound going through my head as I tried to deal with the oncoming shock.

Nicky and I weren't looking at each other as we both tried to be as pragmatic as possible and to ask the relevant questions. The little conversations that we were having with the two vets were meaningless to me. I knew exactly what they were saying to us, and I knew exactly where they were going with it.

When they brought Larry through we could see he was in a bad way, there was a terrible little moaning sound he was making, a sound I'd never heard him make before. It wasn't long till we were presented with the papers to sign. I pushed myself forward, it wasn't something I wanted Nicky to have to do. I was angry with myself, angry with the world as I put pen to paper. I can't think of a polite way of putting it – I was signing little Larry's death warrant. I tried to ask Nicky to leave the room but she was going nowhere, she was going to stay with her little friend right to the end. Little Larry had brought her so much happiness and there was no way she was walking out on him now...

A few minutes later and it was all over. I took a few snippets of Larry's hair, fighting back the tears. I was angry with myself – why hadn't I just grabbed little Larry and run out of the door? My mind was searching for that something that I might have been able to do. I know many people reading this will have been in the same terrible situation and will understand the many days you go through, missing your furry little friends. They're loyal and trusted members of your family, you are the most important things in their life, it doesn't matter how angry you get with them, they will always be pleased to see you as they patiently wait on you coming home.

It was a little easier for me as I was able to escape to my place of work where there were lots of people around me, asking me questions, wanting to know places to visit, or places to eat, and even just having people around to chat to. It was way more difficult for Nicky. Larry never left her side, unless he was running around with Harry or annoying Sophie or Alex, our two cats. It was even hard for Nicky taking Harry out, she knew everyone would see that Larry wasn't there and she would have to go through the motions of explaining what had happened. I remember phoning Nicky from work, I had been busy and was asking her how she was doing; there was a little silence and then she said, fighting through the tears, "I just see him everywhere." To this day, it's one of the saddest things I've ever heard Nicky say, it hurt me so much to hear her talking like that. I had been used to pain and disappointments over the years, but I just never wanted Nicky to feel like that. For a small dog, he had a massive character and left a gaping hole in our hearts and in our apartment.

In the beginning, we were almost embarrassed at the way we were struggling to deal with his loss. But it wasn't long till we started to hear from likeminded people who had suffered the same heartbreak, and it was them who said to us you've just lost a close member of your family. We had Larry cremated and his ashes were given back to us in a lovely little urn. And to get back to our journey, it wasn't just Harry, Evie and Charlie that were in the van, no, of course I'd brought little Larry along for the ride too. He was in his little urn, safely wrapped up and tucked away in the big hold-all in the back of the van; the mission was to get us all back to Nicky and all in one piece.

8

Three months later, Nicky and I were already discussing the idea of getting another little doggie but getting the right one was important, it had to be a dog that was going to be acceptable to Harry not just to us. We certainly didn't want to go down the road of looking at specific breeders as there were too many dogs that had been dumped or dropped off at the dog centre in Fuerteventura; we felt it was important to get another rescue dog. It's sad that so many people take on dogs as pets and then as soon as things begin to get difficult, they dump the dogs. The people at the rescue centre do fantastic work but it always seems to be an uphill struggle as they get left with more and more dogs and can only rely on their own hard work and other people's charity to save these dogs' lives.

One day Nicky and I were sitting on the beach looking out to sea while eating a sandwich; we had been playing in the waves and were now really hungry. Suddenly Nicky's phone started ringing. She had been helping out an estate agent and was expecting a call from a client, but I could tell by the way she was looking at me that this was something more serious. "Is everything alright?" I mouthed to her. She raised her hand in front of her face which I could only take as a sign she was asking me not to hassle her. Then I heard her mention Larry so I stood up and walked away to give her a little space. I couldn't hear what she was saying but I could tell the conversation was fairly intense and she seemed excited.

As soon as the call was finished, she called over to me. "You're not gonna believe it," she exclaimed excitedly. It was great news: Nicky started telling me that it was who we had originally got Larry from, and she had asked Nicky if she knew of anyone who would be able to take care of Larry's sister. The owners were moving back to South America and were not able to take this little female Yorkshire terrier called Luna back with them. It was a no-brainer, straightaway Nicky had told the girl not to worry, that we would take her. Nicky and I briefly discussed who in their right mind could abandon their little dog, but this conversation quickly changed into us jumping up and down with excitement. We would have to give her a new name. How would Harry get on with her? What food would she eat? So many different questions but there was one thing for sure – she was definitely coming to live with us.

It only took a few days to arrange a time and a place to meet up. It was all planned for the following Tuesday at five o'clock. Nicky would go and meet the girl with the little dog, and I would hang around a few streets away with Harry. Both Harry and I can't stand still for more than a minute, so we just kept on the move. It was still very warm, so we were doing our best to stay in the shade. Harry was walking with his usual swagger but obviously had no idea he was about to gain a new little sister. I did keep mentioning Larry to him so he would glance back at me; I'm sure it was only familiarity as he would have heard that name so many times in the past.

Feeling quite excited, I kept checking my watch. I could see it was now after five. Surely Nicky would have met up with the girl by now I thought; hopefully she would be phoning me soon to arrange to meet up with Harry. Everything was racing through my mind. What would she be like? Would she have the same temperament as Larry? Would she be the same size and colour? And why hasn't Nicky phoned yet!!?

Eventually, ten minutes later, the phone rang and I saw it was Nicky. "Hi, is everything okay?" I asked. "Yeah fine, she's the same size as Harry." ... I paused, then shouted out, "That can't be Larry's sister!!?" I could hear Nicky laughing down the phone – she had been joking and I had fallen for it. I heaved a massive sigh of relief – as much as I would've loved whatever dog she had turned up with, the thing that felt really special about this was that it was going to be like getting a little bit of Larry back, so I really felt like this was a bit of magic.

We arranged to meet in the middle of Corralejo high street and just really hoped that Harry and little Luna would get on. I finally caught sight of Nicky; she was carrying a bag with what looked like a little doggie bed in it and down by her other side I could see this little Yorkshire terrier trundling along beside her. I could see the smile on Nicky's face which was enough to tell me everything. The wee dog was a tiny little bit smaller than Larry and had really long hair. She had a cute little bow on the top of her head, but her colouring was exactly the same as Larry's. As we all gathered together, Harry jumped at Nicky as he was obviously excited to see her, not really noticing his new little friend – mind you, she didn't pay any attention to Harry either.

Nicky and I had a brief conversation about how the meeting had gone with the girl and laughed our heads off when we talked about how she had managed to wind me up. It was now just a case of walking the dogs home together and looking forward to getting back to the apartment. Still not really taking any notice of each other, they both walked along together fine. Harry's always at his happiest when he's out walking with both of us and obviously didn't mind his new little friend. Little Luna wasn't giving much away, you just couldn't tell what she was thinking, but again she just seemed to trot along with us nicely.

The little doggie took to us like a fish to water. We had her cleaned, got her a little haircut and renamed her Evie. Okay, she's a little different from Larry, she's fussier who she makes friends with, loves Harry to bits and gets extremely jealous when other dogs come sniffing around, but most importantly, she's our little Evie and has helped mend our broken hearts.

Harry didn't seem fazed by this long journey at all. As soon as I got him out of the back of the van he was on the ground and pulling on his lead as he wanted to get out and explore all these new smells around him. There wasn't much space and obviously we couldn't go too far anyway, and I still had the other two to get out for a walk, but we did try to run a little. It made such a change to be outside the service station and to have Harry walking on real grass – in all his nearly fourteen years that was something he'd never done before, he was so used to hard rocky sun-drenched surfaces.

After five minutes I took him back so I had time to get the other two out and about. It was so much easier being on firm ground, so different from the noisy, rocking ferry with the strong breeze threatening to blow the van doors off. Evie had been my biggest concern as she didn't seem to handle the boat journey very well, so I made sure she was the one I took for a walk next. As soon as I got her on the ground, she picked up on Harry's scent; this was the same tactic I had used back on the ferry, but this was so much easier as Evie too had picked up on the new smells and the change of surface and environment. She appeared to be back to her usual self which gave me great peace of mind as I was quite concerned with her not eating properly. But her whole demeanour had improved, her ears were back alert and she was very aware of everything going on around her.

It wasn't long before she was trying to drag me back to the van to be with her beloved Harry. Charlie seemed to be in fine fettle and quickly picked up on Harry and Evie's trail as he too pulled me along. This was great news. I could now get back to the van and send Nicky a nice positive message about the journey. All was well and I was feeling upbeat.

As soon as I had the three dogs safely back in the van and had made sure their dishes were topped up with food and water, I got myself into the service station. Feasting my eyes over the prepacked sandwiches, I was reminded how hungry I had become. Without a second thought I grabbed two packets of chicken and sweetcorn sandwiches. I knew once I'd eaten them it would leave me feeling very sleepy, so I grabbed a bottle of water and ordered the largest coffee that they had. Now I'm not the biggest fan of coffee as it doesn't usually agree with me – yup, too much coffee can leave me feeling jittery, anxious and really out of sorts. In fact the only time I drink coffee is when I'm ready to dunk nearly a whole packet of digestive biscuits in it. But for some reason there was just no way I could allow myself to fall asleep while the van was moving, I felt like it would be some kind of dereliction of duty. Jim was a great driver, that had been fairly evident, but for some mad reason I just had to stay awake. The coffee I ordered came in a large paper cup with a plastic cover for the top; it was massive, literally a pint and a half of coffee, but for some reason I knew it had to be done.

Pulling out of the service station I must admit I was feeling really positive. Although it still felt like I was thousands of miles from home, or let's say our final destination, it was good to know we were moving forward in the right direction. Outside the van there was a beautiful cloudless sky and thankfully the air conditioning in the van was working perfectly. Obviously, I didn't know exactly what roads we were taking but I did know we were heading in the direction of Merida. The roads were still a lot quieter than I expected but this was just making the journey even easier.

My next big concern was getting across the French border, but I tried not to think about it as it was still a long way off. Jim had the radio on so we could keep up to date with the news; we had it on BBC Radio 2 so we were being updated every half hour. The journey would have been a challenge in itself, having the three dogs, but now we also had all the pressures of Brexit and the biggest concern of all, of course, the pandemic. The rule changes because of Covid 19 were happening on a daily basis so every time the news came on, we were just praying that there had been no new legislation for crossing borders. Thankfully every time I mentioned these concerns to Jim he would always say in a very reassuring voice, "Don't worry, we will be fine."

The coffee had really kicked in now, fortunately without any adverse effects, no jittery feelings of anguish; my thinking was clear and I felt quite sharp, so I was well aware of the beautiful countryside we were driving through. Being so tired, the large strong coffee seemed to be balancing me out and sitting quite comfortably. I was enjoying lots of recognisable music coming from the radio and the roads were now beginning to take a few twists and turns as we sped through this very scenic route.

As I looked out to my left-hand side I could see a long line of very large pylons not far from the roadside, but what was really grabbing my attention was that there were huge nests on the top of these pylons. I'm not exaggerating in saying these nests were the size of a small car; my first impression when looking at them was that it looked like the pylons had developed some sort of horrific growths. I'd never seen anything like it; of course I'd seen many birds' nests in my time but nothing like this. When I looked up to the sky I was almost expecting to see prehistoric pterodactyls flying around making hellish shrieking noises while carrying live prey in their talons – or worse, human beings that they had managed to swoop down on and catch. Excitedly I turned to Jim, hoping he would have the answers I was looking for.

My first more realistic thought was that they had to belong to some sort of large eagle. Without a blink or a turn of the head, Jim was able to reel off all the information I needed. Yes, they were big birds right enough, but they were not eagles but large black and white storks. Unfortunately for me, the nests were now all empty as the storks that had been living there had probably not long migrated to North Africa for the winter.

Every pylon we went past seemed to have these massive nests built on top of them. I couldn't help wondering how long it took these huge birds to build these humungous things. After a little research I found it actually doesn't take that long as these big birds can carry quite a lot of sticks and twigs all at once. They go to a lot of bother making sure these twigs and branches are all cleverly intertwined, then as more are piled on the top, the weight of the nest begins to compress it all together, intertwining all the twigs and branches even more. The final part of this operation sees the birds bedding out the nests with long grass and other small plants. The same birds can revisit the same nests year on year, which means they can repair or even build the same nest up even bigger. Incredibly some of these nests can eventually weigh up to a ton. The nests soon become a real ecosystem of their own as they become a habitat for all sorts of little creatures. Lots of smaller birds begin using these gigantic strong structures to house their own little nests, and certain insects even use these large nests for the purpose of hibernating during the winter months. It's not just Spain that's home to these large migrating birds – places like Portugal, France and Germany are but a few of the other European nations they use. They used to fly as far as the UK, but for some reason that all seemed to end over six hundred years ago, although there are people working hard to try and reintroduce these birds.

9

Before starting this journey, I was concerned that it would be very long and laborious, just miles of dual carriageways with a constant stream of cars and lorries, endless road signs pointing us in the direction north, and finally me having to fidget through piles of paperwork every time we stopped. But so far, the journey had been fantastic, there were so many new things I'd never seen before, and whenever I wasn't sure about something I always found Jim would have all the answers, the knowledge just seemed to fall from his mouth with a confident ease. This whole experience was becoming an education. Now looking out of the front of the van into the vast distance I was starting to realise that it was becoming quite an adventure and this really lifted my spirits; I was now beginning to look forward with relish to all the other surprises that would pop up along the way.

Just as my mind was beginning to drift back through all the stages of the journey so far, my attention was drawn back to the radio as I heard a well-spoken BBC presenter announce that they were about to do a show talking to people who had adult forms of ADHD. And it wasn't just people that suffered from it, but they would be interviewing specialists on the subject. Straightaway I was all ears, although with a little apprehension, but I couldn't wait to hear what they had to say. With no explanation, I just blurted out to Jim, "This is what I have." I felt I must have said it like it was some badge of honour as Jim barely raised an eyebrow. There was still another song playing and once that had finished it would then cut to the news. Impatiently I just wanted it to fast forward to the next show, this was a programme that could hold all the answers to my whole life, I hoped so anyway. My focus was balanced out as I knew the news was important for all of us, there was always the potential that some new law could be quickly drafted that could affect the whole journey, even the volcano on Las Palmas was a concern.

The main headlines didn't touch on Covid or even the ongoing situation with the active volcano, they were more interested in a story about the Chinese being concerned with American and Canadian warships sailing close to the Taiwan strait. The next story was about former President Clinton being released from hospital after having an infection, finally they decided to talk about Covid although it wasn't what we were expecting. The Prime Minster and Carrie Johnson were accused of breaking lockdown rules the previous Christmas; despite the Government's strict social distancing rules it was claimed they had met friends at Downing Street. There were all the usual accusations and denials.

This story was then followed by a new report about the pandemic causing a psychosis surge, it said the condition could cause hallucinations and delusional thinking. At first the story sounded a little sensationalised and almost amusing but then thinking back to Corralejo I began to realise this story had legs. When the lockdown started in Corralejo it was certainly no laughing matter. The only people allowed out on the streets were essential workers, meaning local government staff and officials, maintenance guys keeping the hotels ticking over, supermarket staff, petrol station attendants and police officers, such as the local police and of course the Guardia Seville. But just to make sure everyone understood the severity of the situation and everyone was obeying the rules, they had even drafted in the help of the army.

It wasn't long till everyone had fallen into line and the streets became empty, all the bars, hotels and shops were deserted. The place being so deadly quiet was very eerie and unprecedented – scorching hot days and all of Corralejo's local inhabitants were behind closed doors. Yes, people were allowed out to do their shopping, but it could only be from the supermarket closest to your home, and it should be only one member of the family. You were only supposed to be buying essential items – food, toiletries, medicines and such like, but the beer was flying off the shelves. We were very lucky, not once did we have our bags searched, but rumours abounded that customers shopping at the farther end of the town at a supermarket called Mercadona were not so lucky. Not only were they constantly having their bags searched but they were having things like alcohol confiscated and being given hefty fines.

Nicky and I were lucky – because we had the two dogs, we had the chance to get out and about. Law determined that if you had dogs, you were able to take them out for walks, which was fantastic as it allowed us to often walk right along the front of the coastline. Hot sunny days, beautiful clean sandy beaches but not a single person in view, the Corralejo bay was always an incredible sight at the best of times, but with no one around it just looked so serene. We were so used to seeing those beaches being crowded with people, either lying sunbathing or swimming in the warm sea, and let's not forget the constant stream of surfers coming in and out of the water. Even the harbour had fallen silent with the many small boats that would take people back and forth to the small island of Lobos all moored up with nowhere to go. Yes, strange days indeed. And all the frontside cafes and bars that were usually busy and buzzing with the sounds of people talking and laughing, music playing in the background or being played by local musicians, the whole place was usually a happy hive of tranquil activity, but now nothing. It was just a beautiful ghost town.

But underneath that beauty there was a lot of serious worry and concern – people's lives had instantly been turned upside down. With no tourism there was no money and swathes of people were just unprepared for this unmitigated disaster. Within the first month lots of people were struggling to pay the rent and their usual bills; some of the lucky ones could contact their families and have money wired out to them using the internet. But quite a few didn't have that luxury and could only rely on close friends helping them out. And let's not forget that during the worst of our lockdown there was almost no way to get on and off the island.

Only a year earlier people couldn't have imagined this real-life nightmare that had befallen all of us. Most of the local police recognised me and Nicky so we didn't have any problems when we were walking the dogs, and would always nod and say hello as they passed. But one evening we did get a bit of a fright as we were walking past the Bristol Playa; the most northerly hotel in Corralejo, it faced onto the north shore and had fantastic views over to Lanzarote. As we were slowly walking by with our two dogs, we came across two Guardia Seville who were just standing beside their jeep. Unafraid of attracting their attention, I confidently shouted out "hello" in my usual cheery fashion. I suppose it was late, but we weren't too far away from our apartment so had no concerns that we were in any sort of trouble; suddenly the older and obviously more senior officer called us over.

At first, I wasn't too worried as we were very close to our home. But straightaway I could tell by his demeanour he wasn't in the mood for any friendly chit chat and was quick to demand we show him some identification. We had gone out walking the dogs so the last thing on our minds had been to remember to carry identification with us (sadly, by law in Spain you should always carry some sort of identification). I tried to explain in my really bad and now flustered Spanish that we had none on us but told him if he could wait, we were not too far from the house. "We actually just live over there," I said, pointing my finger, but he was having none of it.

Even Harry had noticed this conversation wasn't going well and he started barking at the Guardia Seville. For a small dog, Harry still manages to have a stout chested bark that is very loud. Not wanting to miss out on all the fun, Evie started to join in. This was starting to turn into quite a commotion. Through the din of Nicky shouting at the dogs to stop barking, the senior member of the Guardia was demanding Nicky and I pay 1500 euros each. This as a matter of principle just sounded ridiculous to me, I was only a minute away from my house where I'd been living for nearly twenty years.

Harry was quick to pick up on my excitement and was now barking twice as loud as when he first started which was winding little Evie up even more. Nicky had also joined in and was shouting her disapproval of this rather extortionate demand at the Guardia. The other Guardia officer who we had seen many times before didn't seem to be on board with his superior, and seemed rather reluctant to get involved in this now farcical situation. But he did place his hand on the other officer's arm and mentioned something about knowing us. We couldn't pick up exactly what he was saying but it did seem to have the desired effect as the older officer raised both his arms and said, "Okay, we will let you off this time," then mumbled something else that I couldn't really hear through the melee.

As we began to walk away with Harry still barking like mad, I looked the young officer in the eye and nodded my head as a gesture of thanks, he reciprocated by nodding back. As Nicky and I were walking back to the apartment we were both shaking with anger and could hardly believe what had just nearly happened to us – 3000 euros just because we were out walking our dogs. In all my twenty-five years on the island of Fuerteventura that was the first time I'd ever had a negative situation with the Guardia. One thing was for sure – I didn't want to ever go through that again.

Even at the height of lockdown, whenever I was stopped by the police or army, they were always very friendly and cordial; in fact sometimes they would just chat for five or ten minutes, they were probably quite happy just to kill some time, looking forward to the end of their shift.

Now admittedly most days I was taking a bit of a chance as I would climb on to my bike and zigzag my way through the quiet streets, carefully peering round street corners just to make sure the coast was clear; as soon as I could see there was no police or army,

I'd cycle as fast as I could up to the hotel complex. Once successfully at the hotel I'd make my way down to the hotel gym, where I'd start off by doing a little of the weights and finish off with five kilometres on the running machine. This was usually enough to have me sweating buckets as I'd be constantly guzzling lots of water to keep me hydrated. I felt really lucky as I knew there were lots of people who didn't have this lucky escape I'd managed to create for myself.

After finishing in the gym I'd make my way up to the swimming pool on my bike. The pool area had been cleared of all the sunbeds, so the terrace looked spacious and clean. The pool would be glimmering in the sun, the water settled and looking like a mill pond. After parking my bike up it was just a case of kicking off my training shoes and diving into the lovely warm pool. Normally I'd do about forty lengths, I'd front crawl in one direction then breaststroke the other. Although very enjoyable I would always be thinking about what the hell was going on in the world. What would happen if this pandemic never went away? When would people return to the island? And ultimately, how would we survive if things never got back to normal? Yup, it was a lot to think about.

Once I'd finished my swim the adventure would start all over again, I'd have to try and get back down to the house without being stopped. I knew once I got so far, I could then make out I was only making my way to my nearest supermarket. Yes, I was one of the fortunate ones. We were lucky to have two large terraces, the south facing terrace got the sun all day and the other had a table tennis table, so I was always pestering Nicky to play table tennis.

Another little highlight of the day was our regular visit to our local supermarket, Hyperdinos. As I said before, it was only supposed to be one member of each household, but Nicky and I would always go up together; all the staff there knew we were a couple, but it wasn't any hassle. In the beginning, just to make sure you weren't showing signs of Covid, the security guard would take your temperature. Then the law changed and when you were walking around the shop everyone had to wear thin rubber gloves. Then the rules changed again and the thin gloves disappeared, now everyone had to wear a mask and use hand gel on the way in.

These were just minor inconveniences that we had to put up with at that time, and they didn't really bother me, but it was more than obvious lots of people were not having a great time of it. People walking around the shops were not their usual happy relaxed selves, some people were very quiet, faces looked drawn, almost tired looking, some people didn't want to look you in the eye. It was obvious a lot of people were very worried. Not being able to get out into the fantastic weather was massively disappointing, people were literally imprisoned in their own homes, and remember it wasn't their fault, they hadn't done anything wrong.

People were extremely confused by it all – some were terrified of catching Covid, while others thought it was some kind of day of reckoning. Some people felt it was all some incredible conspiracy theory, part of a great plan to control the population, leading to a reduction in the world's population. Then there were the young who would sneak around and have parties on the rooftops. A lot of these parties would end in police arrests and the people who were caught would receive heavy fines. Some days surfers would head along to the north shore to try and catch some waves only to find the Guardia were out in their jeeps and would be waiting on these guys coming out of the water. Personally, I felt it was all very unfair; while these strict rules were in place, we only had about eight infected people with only two of them in hospital. So it was incredibly frustrating that we had all these wide-open spaces, and we couldn't even use them, especially with the infection rate being so low.

And looking back you can't help wondering what the hell it was all about. The day and the dogs and I set sail there were actually over 350 people infected across the island. In fairness I did have a great deal of sympathy for all the different governments across the globe – trying to get it right in these unprecedented times was not easy. The job of trying to keep the infection rate down while trying to keep their economies moving was obviously very challenging for them.

I'm sure lots of people felt the social distancing rules just didn't make a lot of sense. This was certainly the case around the bars and restaurants of Corralejo, and with the rules and regulations changing from week to week it became very frustrating – having to wear a mask as you entered a restaurant, then taking it off once you had sat down; the opening and closing times of bars always changing; as the infections began to climb, they put limits on how many people you could have in the bars and restaurants. Getting into banks could only be done by appointment, in fact getting anything official done could only be done by appointment. It was all very annoying.

One thing that did become very noticeable as the island began to open up again was the amount of young people we had on the island. Families and our usual tourist base were still being put off with all the added costs relating to tests before you flew, then having to be tested again before you left. For a family of four to go through all these different checks was a very expensive business, then there was the worry of catching Covid while you were on holiday, so most people just didn't feel it was worth the hassle and of course the money. But lots of savvy youngsters were beginning to appear on the island; every bar and restaurant you passed was full of these young professionals from all over Europe. (I include the UK when I say this, we are still geographically part of Europe.) These young people were making full use of the advantages of the internet, even students were coming out and doing their course work online. All the surf schools were fully booked, the excursion shops were doing a great trade, some of the bars and restaurants had never had it so good. Yup, these kids were having a great time. Even trying to rent accommodation was getting difficult as these digital nomads (as they were called) were flooding the market and having a great time. It really helped pick the place up and it was nice to see lots of young happy faces around.

I must admit it left me feeling pretty old, and it had me thinking wow, what a great time to be young – and let's be honest, you don't hear people saying that very often. It wasn't long before they started linking up with each other and some of the younger residents of the island began getting in on the act as they would help organise parties and other events. Mind you, not everyone on the island was happy with this as social distancing rules seemed to just fly out of the window with these "going to live forever" youngsters. One story I heard was that the owner of an apartment had received a ridiculously high fine because the people he rented it out to had decided to have a massive party, which unfortunately left the apartment in a pretty bad state. The owner also had to fork out a lot of money to sort out all the damage they had left, and even though he had no knowledge of the illegal party, it was him that got hit with the hefty fine. A tad unfair I thought.

10

Things slowly started to crawl back to what was now known as the new normal. This was assisted by the roll out of the new vaccines, but this was another hugely divisive opinion splitter. On the face of things, there seemed to be a lot of ambivalence on the subject, especially in Corralejo and around the rest of the island of Fuerteventura. One thing was for sure, our infection rate had been very low for most of the time on the island and we were certainly not seeing the devastating effects that were happening around the rest of the world. The weather was always warm, people with happy smiling faces were enjoying our luxurious beaches, getting in and out of that fantastically warm sea with that glorious volcanic backdrop; we had clear blue skies and that fresh clean air blowing in off the sea. It just seemed a million miles away from this horrible pandemic. So it was almost understandable that some people on the island had become very sceptical, and many people hadn't bothered to book themselves in for the vaccination jabs, and as time moved on, people's opposition regarding the vaccines began to grow, in fact many people were becoming what was known as anti-vaxxers.

Now with so many people being vaccinated, there had been some stories of people suffering bad side effects, even stories of young fit healthy people dropping dead. Some people felt it was an infringement of their human rights, others felt it was a massive money-making scam by big business. Then there was the odd few who believed it was part of a wider conspiracy to control the world's population, and of course some of the more extremely religious who thought it was the mark of the devil. If I've got to be honest, I know my beloved social media was sadly helping fill people's heads with misinformation. Sometimes it's just people being rather economical with the truth. But other times it can be certain people deliberately using little bits of data that suited their agenda, and worse people falsifying facts in their studies. And last but not least you have the people playing the devil's advocate, and they just seem to revel in provoking controversy.

My own personal opinion on this was much the same as a lot of my friends – when you're feeling fit and healthy there is a train of thought that goes through your head that if it's working why fix it!? It was just that niggling little idea that your body maybe doesn't need that vaccine stuff in your body, I mean what the hell is in it anyway? And maybe I was just hiding the fact I'm a complete softy when it comes to getting needles stuck into my arm. Had it been a case of just popping a small tablet into my mouth with a glass of water, my attitude would probably have been far more relaxed on the subject.

Just in case you're wondering, yes, I did eventually get vaccinated, unintentionally, but yes, both jabs done. Most people in town had been vaccinated, I just never managed to find the time to get it done, sort of thing. My dad was forever getting on at me to go and get it done. "Naw, don't worry Dad, I'll get it done eventually," I'd always say down the phone.

Nicky was having a small health issue and was having no luck with the local doctors in Fuerteventura. We were just never getting to the bottom of things; even after using private health insurance and seeing different specialists, no one could seem to put their finger on exactly what the problem was. This understandably was beginning to really grind Nicky down, it even got to the point she was just dreading getting out of bed in the morning knowing she would keep having this same problem but never being able to find a solution.

There was nothing else to do but get Nicky back to the UK to see if someone could help her there. Like me, Nicky hadn't yet been vaccinated, and like I said, we were honestly not against it, we just never got round to doing it. Like I said earlier, we had never really met anyone on the island who had ever had Covid, so you never felt there was any rush. But now that Nicky was going to be flying back to the UK, if she wanted to be on that plane, she was going to have to be vaccinated. It didn't take long to arrange; we went up to the local health centre and organised a time and a place for her to receive her vaccination.

On the day of the appointment, I said I'd cycle up with her, it was right on the other side of town. It wasn't really a health centre but a newly built council building that they would sometimes use for cultural events and council meetings, but ideal for a few doctors to use as a vaccination centre. It was another typical hot sunny day as we left the apartment. I was glad to get on to my bike and get a bit of fresh air. The night before I'd had a few beers with my good friend Drew. The idea was to just pop round to his house for a few beers and a blether. Drew's house was only a stone's throw away from mine, so I didn't have far to travel, but as usual it ended up going into the wee small hours of the night. Once I got cycling though I felt fine.

The plan was to leave Nicky to get her injection and I would then travel a little farther and get some shopping from the supermarket Mercadona. Once we finally got to the centre, we could see that there were a few people hanging around so I decided, instead of just cycling off and leaving Nicky on her own, I would do the honourable thing and wait with her. Like I said earlier, it was a beautiful day, and I was feeling much better for being out in the fresh air. It didn't take me long to find a place to lock the bikes. As we approached the building, we could see there were a few people outside who we both knew, they were just standing quite happily chatting. As I locked the bikes up, Nicky went over and started talking with the couple who were standing close to the entrance. We were in no rush as Nicky was about ten minutes early.

Once I finally got the bikes locked up, I went over and was just about to join in the conversation when a young doctor came to the door. Nicky was still busy chatting with her two friends when the young doctor just happened to look directly at me and said, "Are you here for your vaccination?" Before I answered I grabbed Nicky's attention. "Nicky, that's one of the doctors". She quickly pulled out her appointment card to show him. As he looked at the appointment card, he briefly looked at his watch and could see that she was early, so his eyes turned back to me and he asked, "Have you got your appointment card?" I quickly said, "No I haven't got one." I was smiling and hoped he'd return his attention to Nicky, but no such luck, he now looked at me a little more sternly and with one of his fingers pointing at me he asked, "Have you had your vaccination?" With a somewhat guilty look on my face I could only answer, "No I haven't." Without any hesitation he said, "Ahhh, you better come with me then."

I couldn't believe it. I could see Nicky smiling at me as she could see the look on my panic-stricken face, but there was no way back as he was standing holding the door open for me. Well, you've got to give these folks their due, they were not hanging about, they were obviously doing their best to get everyone vaccinated.

It only took me a minute or so to fill out the form with my address and my NIE (your NIE is your proof of residency on the island). My mind was racing, I had been caught off guard and my hangover had now come back full tilt. I felt as if as soon as I got this injection I'd pass out or even worse die. How did I get here? One minute I was cycling up the road happy as Larry, the next minute I was in a position of near death! Yup, a typical over reaction from me in my state of panic.

Thankfully it was all over really quickly, and I didn't feel a thing. I was still slightly worried after I had my vaccination as they had a large room where they asked everyone to wait for fifteen minutes after they'd had their vaccination, just to make sure there were no side effects. I didn't fully know what these side effects could be, and I certainly wasn't going to ask. After the fifteen minutes were over, I got up and walked out, feeling quite relieved – I was still alive, which

I thought was a good sign. Secretly I'd been hoping that Covid would eventually come to an end, that it would die out on its own steam, and that I'd slip through the net and not need to get vaccinated, but alas it wasn't to be, they'd got me bang to rights.

Once we had got back out into the fresh air, I could hear Nicky still chuckling away to herself at my misfortune. I didn't mind, I could now see the funny side, but I was still a little shocked by it all. Just for a moment in there I'd felt like a caged animal, but I was out now, free at last.

We hadn't long unlocked the bikes when a car drew up to where we were standing. "Aye aye." I recognised those dulcet tones coming from the now lowered window. As I peered in, I could see it was a friend who we hadn't seen in a little while; he had two surf boards fastened to the roof of the car. "Hey, how you doin?" I replied. That was me now gone full circle, from looking like a rabbit frozen in the headlights to being the coolest guy in Corralejo, or trying to be anyway.

"Long time no see, how are you?" he shouted back. It was Yan, a German lad I'd known all the years I'd been living on the island. "Good thanks, we're just on the way up to Mercadona, just thought we'd cycle up here and grab a bit of fresh air," I said, now fully back to my reassuring self. "Ahhh so you haven't been sucked into that place, getting jabbed with all the other little sheep," he said casually, pointing back down to the makeshift health centre. I quickly turned my head round and looked at the place like I hadn't even noticed it on the way up the hill. With a puzzled look on my face I said, "Ahh, so that's what it is," quickly looking back at Nicky. I was hoping she would play along with my momentous lie.

"Yeah I watch them going in and out of there all day," Yan said in a sneering voice. Yup, Yan was a fully signed-up all-knowing anti-vaxxer. "There's no way I'd put that shit in my arm." That was it, he was off on one; we had to stand and take a lecture about drugs companies making shit loads of money, and how the "sheep" didn't have a clue what they were getting pumped into them. "Geez, terrible," I said, nodding in agreement. I was now looking at Nicky as if to say, you can't spill the beans on me now. I could see her rolling her eyes in disgust.

Yan wasn't finished yet – he proceeded to talk about the people he knew, and stories he'd heard about terrible cases of people who were having mysterious side effects and, in some cases, even dying. He even got onto footballers who were dropping stone dead of heart failures in the middle of football matches. I knew a bit about that, but I wasn't going to let on that I knew as it would obviously only prolong the conversation on this subject which I was desperately trying to change.

Thankfully we got back on to the subject of surfing and tide times as Yan was hoping to catch some waves along our very rocky north shore. The swells had been massive of late, and the North shore was certainly not the place for beginners, or the faint hearted. I wasn't so sure about his Covid stories, but I knew one thing for sure – there had certainly been a few surfing fatalities along Fuerteventura's famous North shore.

At that, our conversation drew to a close. "Hey, nice to catch up." He said it like it had been a two-way conversation; in truth I'd just stood there and given him a good listening to. "Take care Yan," I said, giving him a wave as his car pulled away. Not once had he acknowledged Nicky, but why would he have talked to her? She wasn't a surfer, she was just a normal human being. Anyway Nicky should know better that Yan doesn't do normal. She now fully understood why I'd gone to great lengths not to mention my vaccination, it just wasn't worth the hassle. We were both laughing as we climbed back on to our bikes and headed for the supermarket. I reassured Nicky that Yan actually had a heart of gold, which he did. He had about five dogs which he'd got from the rescue centre, and they were all very well looked after; he was just different I told her. And everyone knows, if you're going to be a shit hot surfer, you've got to be cool man.

Patiently sitting in the van listening to the news my mind was still fixating on the next programme to come on the radio. I'd never spoken to anyone professional about my ADHD, and although I had done bags of research on the subject, I was still desperate to hear what these people were going to say about it. Maybe I'd learn something new, they might have some good advice on how to deal with all the little problems the ADHD brings along.

Listening to the news can obviously be quite depressing, and it was made worse today as we were listening out for more Covid stories, and we also needed to keep up to date with what was happening with the volcano in Las Palmas. Looking back round to the dogs I could see they seemed quite happy, they were just staring back at me with their ears alert, probably just waiting on me saying, "C'mon, let's go for a walk."

Harry was used to the car, he'd been taken round many times to Cotillo which was a small fishing village on the northwest coast. Once there he would swim around in the lovely clear water, these were gorgeous lagoons where the reefs would protect him from the large Atlantic waves. For all I knew, that's maybe what he was thinking about, he might believe he was going to Cotillo, and it's just taking a hell of a long time to get there! Even Evie looked better now; she certainly didn't look well back on the boat. Hopefully she was beginning to settle down, and was now becoming a little more used to her surroundings. Charlie also seemed to be looking well. He had done a few journeys in the car, but not the luxury of travelling twenty minutes to Cotillo for a romp on the beach – his were more stressful visits to the vets in Rosario where he had to have an operation on his cruciate ligament. Then there were the check-ups and physiotherapy, and this all happening in his first year; he was always really well behaved in the car, but sadly it was probably down to his fear of the vets.

Whatever was going through their minds they certainly had no idea that they had another gruelling 1500 miles and three customs posts to go through. But luckily for them they didn't have to worry about all these terrible scenarios that could potentially befall us during the journey, and of course they wouldn't make head nor tail of all the terrible news that was coming out of the radio, it was all just babbledegook to them. What a simple life they led.

As Jim and I patiently listened out for any stories on the pandemic, the news reader trawled through a different array of stories. Sadly twenty-five people had died due to floods in Kerala in western India. This was difficult for us to process as we were staring out of the van and up above us were clear blue skies. One of the big stories which made us laugh was the news that the Chinese economy had slowed down from 7.9% in the first quarter to the now devastating 4.9% in the latest quarter. Now obviously that was quite a drop, but could you imagine if the UK economy was growing at 4.9%? Our banks and investors would be cock a hoop. The closest we got to any important developments regarding Covid was a story about the Royal College of Paediatrics calling for an end to Covid testing in schools.

Another major concern for Jim and I was the volcano in Las Palmas. The last we had heard was that a new powerful vent had opened up on the island and that the molten lava was now reaching the sea. Once the lava hit the sea it could become potentially very dangerous. Thankfully where the lava was falling into the sea was an uninhabited area so if there were any reactionary explosions nobody would be hurt by the flying molten lava or shards of volcanic glass. Another side effect from this can be clouds of very acidic steam which is called lava haze or just "laze". It contains chlorine which can be very corrosive. So people living not too far away from this can be hit with acid rain which can result in health problems like skin and eye irritation and possibly breathing problems.

Another major concern for me was the worry that airports could be closed due to dangerous ash clouds high up in the air that can cause disruptive flight cancellations. It was less alarming for Jim as he would be making exactly the same journey back by road and sea. But I had already got my flight booked to return from Manchester directly to Fuerteventura in two weeks. Jim and I remembered when flights were cancelled due to the eruption of a volcano called Eyjafjallajökull in Iceland. I couldn't forget the mix of panic and excitement as the news that their flights had been cancelled came through to the guests staying in our hotel. Some people were understandably concerned, some were even in tears, people worrying about jobs, commitments and arrangements that they had to rearrange. And of course, people were worried about their finances – our hotel hadn't long changed to all-inclusive, so people had only brought so much spending money.

Thankfully people's worries and concerns were allayed very quickly as the insurance people, holiday companies and our hotel, the wonderful Dunas Caleta, seemed to get it all sorted out very efficiently. All of a sudden, the atmosphere in our hotel changed completely; what had been tears of woe had now turned into tears of joy as the recipients of this volcanic disaster realised they'd just got themselves an extended holiday all paid for thanks to an angry volcano. And although I'm probably a little biased, the Dunas Caleta was a fantastic place to end up having an extended holiday. All our staff had worked there for years and most of them were on first name terms with our many repeat guests, so it was really a home from home for these lucky holiday makers, a lovely home without all the stresses and strains and of course the weather was always fantastic.

After it was all done and dusted, and these people were eventually able to make their way home, it was understandable that there were a few more tears of sadness as people had grown really close with each other. Many of the same faces had spent time round the pool chatting and really getting to know each other, and it wasn't just the guests, the staff were always encouraged to chat with the guests so inevitably a close bond developed between the guests and the staff. It was so nice to watch them all hugging and holding each other with so much affection at the end of what was supposed to be a terrible ordeal, which in actual fact turned out to be one of the best holidays they ever had.

11

Yes, I had been very fortunate to spend so many years happily working in a very friendly hotel that would, over the years, see many of the same faces coming in and out of the complex. This was something we put a lot of effort into, making sure we built up a strong repeat guest base, it just made life so much easier for everyone across the board. First and foremost our repeat guests fell in love with the Dunas Caleta. It was their go-to place, their very special home in the sun, which affectionally became known as "The Pleasure Dome". My bosses were kept happy as we managed to stay really busy at a time when the island was really suffering, and of course the holiday companies gained as well because they had a unit (hotel) that wasn't expensive but was full of very happy customers. It was a simple formula of making sure you kept everyone happy, and thankfully it seemed to work.

But in the back of my mind, I knew that the whole situation could become volatile very quickly, there were a whole array of factors that could turn this gorgeous sunny holiday island into a dark nightmare. The most important thing to the economy of Fuerteventura was tourism, although quite a service industry has also built up over the years due to more people deciding to relocate and come to live in its beautiful sunny climate. You could say the island has had a massive influx of immigrants from northern Europe and some from farther afield, including people moving over to retire in a sunnier climate or even moving the whole family over to start afresh, either working for the businesses on the island or even starting up a business of their own.

So real estate has done well as people have invested in apartments and opened new bars and restaurants. There's been a massive increase in surf schools, mountain bike hire, dive schools, island excursions – lots more daytrips on boats either just around the island or over to the little island of Lobos which is not too far away from the harbour of Corralejo. Most of the musicians and other types of entertainers have travelled from afar and some of the larger hotels could afford to bring in very expensive and exotic acts from all over the globe.

There had also been a growth in supermarkets and shopping malls, all the big names in fashion and fast food were getting a foothold on the island. It's funny, when I first moved to the island in 1995, there weren't any real clothes shops to talk of, only surf shops, so everyone in town wore surf gear. Everyone was very brown with sun-bleached hair and dressed in much the same clothes, so it was quite refreshing, especially for the girls, when some of the bigger named shops moved in.

Other industries were moving in as well like the textile industry, which was growing, as well as kitchen design and home improvements in general which were springing up everywhere, and finally, the new modern-day entrepreneurs, the digital nomads, these guys and girls were the most versatile of the lot. It didn't matter how things were doing on the island, these people were taking full advantage of the worldwide web. They could be operating their own online business while simultaneously studying another beneficial course which helps keep them a head of the game. Yes, they had destroyed the old mantra "work hard, play hard" and turned it into "work a little, play hard anywhere in the world". Yes, if I had my time over again, spookily enough that's the life that would suit me.

But my main bone of contention here is that life out on an island in the Atlantic Ocean can change drastically when we are directly affected by a natural disaster. Again working in a popular hotel in Fuerteventura when the volcano erupted in Iceland wasn't a disaster for us. In fact, at the time, we were really lucky, but it was a setback for the smaller businesses like the bars and restaurants and all the people that they employ. Luckily for everyone on the island this only affected us for two weeks before everything went back to normal, but the warning signs were there for all to see – we were most certainly an island that desperately relied on tourism. It's difficult to not make this sound crude or cynical, but holiday destinations rely on plane loads of people landing in their airports, enjoying themselves while relieving themselves of all their cash and then flying off again. So of course, things become very competitive. Just before and after the Icelandic volcano eruption, Fuerteventura in particular was feeling the pinch as there were so many cheap flights to places like Greece, Egypt and Turkey. Yes, we were lucky, we had our hardcore regulars who had fallen in love with our island, but it wasn't enough to satisfy all the businesses that had begun to grow on Fuerteventura. Again, Dunas Caleta was very lucky through the lean years as we had such a large number of guests who wanted to return to our hotel, but some of the other complexes were really suffering, some unfortunately closed down, and some tried to reinvent themselves as residential complexes.

My concerns for the island started years before. Being something of a news junkie I was always keeping up to date with world affairs, especially all the large and small wars that seemed to be based around securing carbon-based resources, namely crude oil. It didn't take too much research to realise that this black gold was the life blood of any successful growing economy, but the major problem was that a great deal of scientific research was beginning to show that this invaluable resource was close to running out. So, as you can imagine as economies around the world begin to grow, so does the demand for oil, as the demand goes up so does the price, but then throw into the mix that this resource is beginning to run out all of a sudden, the price of oil can then begin to go through the roof. Everything then begins to crash around our ears as production costs for businesses begin to become too expensive – plastics alone takes eight to ten percent of oil production, the rest is used for manufacturing and of course fuel. This collision course that we were on with the resources eventually beginning to run out is called peak oil. One thing is for sure, cheap flights would have disappeared very quickly, leaving us all stranded on Fuerteventura with no holidaymakers and literally no money.

Although peak oil hasn't gone away it has been sort of "kicked into the long grass" for a while thanks to clean air technologies such as wind turbines, hydro energy, solar power, wave and tidal energy and geo-thermal, and a massive effort from governments around the world reinforcing recycling. But still many scientists around the world would argue that we haven't gone nearly far enough. And of course, nuclear power has played its part also, although I must admit I'm not a fan of nuclear power as it's far more dangerous than all the other renewables. For instance, as long as the earth survives any major wars or large asteroids crashing into us, we can safely rely on the moon and the sun to look after us for millions of years to come. We only have to go back a short amount of time to be reminded of a few nuclear accidents that still affect the planet to this day. And we still have to concern ourselves with nuclear waste – believe it or not, it stays very active for up to half a billion years, so it's a very costly business trying to dispose of any of its waste. Sadly, in my home county of Fife in Scotland we have lots of decommissioned nuclear submarines rotting away in bays in Rosyth Dockyard, and no one really wants to talk about it as the cost of cleaning all this up is astronomical. As people choose to ignore this problem that's not going to go away, these ships are leaking nuclear waste that seeps into the River Forth and ultimately into people's lives.

There were so many volatile situations going on in the world and I knew my safe little life in Fuerteventura could be ended by any of these global happenings; no one anywhere was safe from its grasps. On a smaller scale, Morocco had voiced an opinion that the Canary Islands should really still belong to them, and this call became louder when it was discovered that there was oil not far from Lanzarote and

Fuerteventura. Thankfully the oil price dropped enough to make it a bad investment to bring all that oil to the surface as the profits would all be swallowed up by the production costs, but sadly it's "in the post" as they say. There had been small protests from environmental groups as they were concerned that the health of the islands' marine life could be seriously damaged – in fact one bad oil spill could be enough to put these beautiful islands out of action for at least a few years. Ironically you would see large four-wheel-drive trucks and jeeps with "Fuerteventura says no to oil" stickers on them.

And last but not least, there was always the possibility of that tsunami hitting us from Las Palmas. I'd always imagined if it had happened many years earlier that I'd find a way to get Nicky and our then four cats to the top of our volcano, Bayuyo, as quick as possible. It was wishful thinking, but I'd certainly have tried had the situation arisen.

One last point I want to make about my worries for the survival of the island – I always wanted to find a solution, especially for the most realistic problem the island could face and that of course was flights coming on and off the island. We had already suffered because of a volcano thousands of miles aways, and our economy did suffer because there were cheaper flights taking people to other destinations, and there was always the possibility that flights could become so expensive that there could be a further drop in tourism to the island.

Yes, transportation and oil were a very real problem to the survival to the island and the only long-term solution I could find was in the form of Maglev technology. I still to this day believe that it will be the future and the answer to most of the world's transportation problems. I'll do my best to explain it as best I can, but if any of you reading this just don't get it, I suppose you can always use the internet to find more detailed information. Who knows, years from now someone might actually be sitting on a Maglev train reading this, thinking, "Wow, this guy really knew his shit."

Anyway, at the time of writing this, China, South Korea and Japan are the only countries using this system, despite already having spent over a century on research. I would've thought that we would have seen more countries moving towards this fantastically safe speedy system. Again, at the time of writing, China has the fastest of these Maglev trains which can reach speeds of up to 600 kilometres an hour which is nearly 380 miles an hour – that would have cut our journey in the van with the dogs down to just over six hours, not the five days that we expected. Maglev trains travel on magnets which are electrically charged. If you've ever played around with magnets, you'll have noticed that if they are strong, it's difficult to pull them apart, but when you turn them around it's very difficult to get them close to each other as the magnetic force field is working in reverse. Once you put an electrical charge into these magnets it massively increases their strength in both directions. So, that's how these trains work – they are sitting on large magnets that are electrically charged which then has them levitating above the track. This means that their movement is completely frictionless and they can move at incredible speeds.

There are specific companies working on a tube-based system which will be able to travel at speeds of up to four thousand miles an hour, which will travel on land or underwater and again using a fraction of the amount of energy we use now. No stopping at petrol stations to refuel or having to recharge batteries as the power will be transferred through the magnetic system. Now not all Maglev trains will need to travel at these speeds – only trains that are travelling through countries and continents, these would be the mainlines; you'd have branch line services to get us from the cities to towns.

So, to get back to our present-day form of travelling, it's all really outdated and incredibly bad for the atmosphere and the general health of the planet as we still massively rely on fossil fuels. This new revolutionary system will be powered by electricity which will be supplied at source. Electricity, wherever it has been produced in the world, will eventually be linked up, for instance, wave or tidal power produced in the north of Scotland or geo-thermal power generated in Iceland. And let's not forget my previous idea about the possibility of solar towers which can be built in sunnier climates closer to the equator.

To some this might all begin to sound quite utopian, but I think it'll be the only direction we will be able to move in if we are to survive. To put something like this in place will be momentous, it will need cooperation from governments around the globe, it'll probably be the end of the international car industry, there more than likely will be an end to mass production of commercial aircraft. I would imagine it will even affect the freight that is carried many miles across the sea. But on the upside these great shipping ports will become docking stations for Maglev transportation, even airports might eventually be called Magports, the possibilities will be endless. Realistically the costs of starting the project in this monetary based economy would be staggering, but I'm sure it will be a mouth-watering prospect for all those adventurous investors. And you never know – it might even put an end to global warming and all those continual oil wars that have plagued us over the last century.

Just as the news was finishing, I turned to look back at the dogs, particularly Harry, he was the whole reason we were on this long and wonderful journey. Every time he caught me looking at him, he would stand up in his cage and bark at me in usual loud way, his tailless small stump waggling away. We didn't dock Harry's tail, we would never dock any dogs' tails, that's just the way we got him. Thankfully in the UK that's all stopped now. It's the worst thing you can do for a dog, it's the wagging of their tails that helps keep their spine in line.

As I looked down in front of Harry's cage I could see the bag with all the dogs' essentials in it. I was reminded that Harry had a box of Valium tucked away in the side pocket. What would I do if he started having a fit in the van, I thought to myself, I couldn't just pick him up and pop him into the bedroom till he settled down. In fact, we hadn't given him any Valium for over a year. I wasn't going to worry about it, for some reason, I was confident he wasn't going to have a fit, he was too lively – more than that, he seemed really happy, like he was enjoying the journey.

Charlie and Evie on the other hand seemed very subdued, Charlie wasn't too bad, but Evie hadn't been the same since that first day we had got onto the ferry. Although she had improved since we had got off the boat and back onto the road, she was still sitting with her ears drooping at the side of her head and she was panting a lot which was telling me she was still stressed out. Charlie seemed fine but was just sitting very quietly staring back at me – usually when Harry barked that would be a great excuse for him to join in. But since the journey had started, Harry was mostly barking solo, although that might have not of been a such bad thing.

The afternoon sun was shining in through the van's windscreen; it helped light up Harry's face and you could clearly see that mad doggie smile of his with this strange glint coming from his eyes. Sadly that was coming from the cataracts that were slowly building up.

Poor Harry, I thought. It's hard to imagine what life will be like without him. He was now in his fourteenth year and still seemed to be going strong. Yes, he had obviously slowed down a little but not that anyone who didn't know him would notice. When anyone of late had just met Harry for the first time, they were always very surprised when we told them how old he was, especially if he had just had a haircut. He looked big for a Yorkshire terrier and had a very muscular body; he was like a little lion inside a Yorkshire terrier's body and completely fearless.

He is always at his happiest when he is walking with Nicky and me. He proudly walks just in front of us but bang in the middle and ready to bark at anything that crosses our path. Annoyingly he has no patience if we meet friends and stop to chat – after a minute he will start to bark at us very loudly, obviously it's his way of telling us to shut up and get walking. Most people probably saw Harry as a noisy, badly behaved little dog who probably got all his bad habits from me. Although I can understand why people would believe that, as if my hyperactive vibe travelled down his lead, but in honesty I would have to disagree with that idea, it's just the way Harry is. Larry was totally different, he was far more patient and loved everyone, and not once did I hear anyone say, "Aww Gary, that must be down to you." It didn't help that when Harry kicked off, Nicky would use me as an excuse, it was so unfair, always having to carry the blame for Harry being a mad wee dog.

If I was to be honest though I was proud as punch of Harry – the wee guy walked with a swagger, and you couldn't get a more loyal friend. I looked at Harry just a little bit longer, I was hoping he could read my mind. "C'mon little guy, you hold it together, getting you back to Nicky in Bridlington is gonna be a great day."

Suddenly, my attention was drawn back to the radio – here it was, the show all about adult ADHD. I knew the presenter was going to be talking to some professional person who had ADHD, so I was sure the programme was going to be a more positive look at how people live with it. I wasn't going into this blind, hoping there was going to be some great revelation that would be the answer to all my problems. But you never know, they might bring up some new techniques that I hadn't heard of before, there might have been some new research that offers a better and easier way of dealing with it.

My own research had been extensive. I knew that people who had ADHD had to deal with it in their own way and that ADHD came in many different levels, some people needed medication, whereas some people didn't. Now I know I've already touched on this subject earlier, but this is really just to clarify it a bit better so please bear with me. As I babbled on about earlier, realising I had ADHD was really a great relief, but it's not just as easy as that because in fact, it's far more complicated than most people understand. Quite simply, people's life experiences are so different that everyday tasks for one person are completely different for another. Can I just say from the offset, if anyone reading this thinks they might have ADHD, then please get yourself diagnosed, it might really help you. I sadly don't always practise what I preach and can only write what is my opinion and try to help by highlighting my own experiences and difficulties, but hopefully I'll touch on a lot of things that will hopefully be of interest to everyone and maybe help enlighten some.

First of all, the programme wasn't really all that informative. It highlighted that there are lots of people out there who suffer from ADHD and included a light-hearted discussion with two professional adults on how they deal with their ADHD. Both had been diagnosed later in life and were getting through life quite happily. From what I could tell, their problems weren't too severe and both of them were eating healthily and getting lots of regular exercise, only one of them was on some form of medication. To me they just sounded like a couple of normal human beings who seemed to have stumbled upon some sort of malfunctions in their daily lives and their prognosis was helping to get them back to normal.

Even though there wasn't much to be gained from the programme it was nice to hear it being spoken about in the open. It was something I could now freely admit to suffering from without feeling any embarrassment. But ADHD is not as simple as that, and it certainly hadn't been for me. I'd been crashing my way through life from a very young age, and it certainly hadn't been a barrel of laughs. The problem was that no one around me noticed that I was struggling, and in fairness it would've been hard to pin me down and discuss with me that I might be having problems.

My home life was far from perfect, in fact there was absolutely no rational to be had there. It was beyond my dad's thinking and his words of wisdom would come in the form of "Just get yer bloody finger out ya dope" and that's when he wasn't shouting at my mother for drinking too much. Yup, home life could be a living hell when things were bad. I used to dread coming home from school, especially if my mum was off work because of her troubles. It was a mixture of anti-depressants and alcohol which would leave my mother in a pretty bad way, and she could be nasty with it as well, so the best thing for me to do was to get out of the house as soon as possible.

It was a double-edged sword: I couldn't discuss with my mother that school wasn't going too well, and then once I'd escaped the hell which was my home life, I couldn't then discuss the problems I was having at home with my friends. So I was constantly covering up and bottling up my emotions with absolutely nobody to turn to. My close friends knew things weren't right at home, but it wasn't something that could ever be discussed, the idea of that was way too embarrassing. It just felt like it was a lifetime of making excuses. So eventually when anyone did ask me "How's school Gary?" I would just say, "Yeah it's fine" then quickly change the subject.

Obviously, I'm not a doctor and I can only give my opinion on this subject, but I'm sure my ADHD might have been offset by trauma. Now before I go any further, it wasn't always like that. I was very fortunate to have two fantastic grandmothers who really helped me, and to be honest, we did have fantastic family holidays with my mum and dad, so I can recall lots of fabulous times we had together.

But when it was bad, it was bad. For instance, to read two of your mother's suicide notes at a young age is going to have a very profound effect. Thankfully she failed both times. I don't mean to sound flippant in revealing this, I just couldn't find another way of bringing this into the story. I've only ever spoken with a couple of people about this, so to be here writing about it is no small matter. What I'm hoping to do here is to make people aware of my emotional state when I was a child. I was going through these horrible emotional explosions and I had to control myself, there was just no one to turn to.

If you have a large dog, people will advise you not to break its temper, not to get it too over-excited, the reason being is once they reach these emotional heights it becomes harder to control the dog, especially if it's been pushed over the emotional edge. It becomes far easier for the dog to reach that same mental state. You sometimes find this with rescue dogs that have been mistreated and suffered some sort of abuse. They can be very nervous to loud noises or people shouting and it can take a long time before they begin to trust you and settle down. This is much the same with human beings – disappointment, pain and hurt are emotions that are never too far away from the back of your mind. When things start to go wrong you can sense these emotions bubbling back up to the surface. Yes, a lot of times it's an overreaction but the connections to these emotions are very close and very real. Time is a great healer as they say, so the more you're able to stay away from these emotions, the weaker the connection becomes, and the more you understand this the easier it becomes to deal with.

The problem with my mother was they were trying to deal with her problems medically, but the underlying problems were never being dealt with at home so her mental state was slipping further into a place of helplessness and self-pity, and as anyone who's suffered depression knows, your self-esteem begins to hit rock bottom. You begin to hate yourself, your self-loathing grows, you feel that you bring misery to everyone else's life, and you genuinely begin to feel that it would be much better for everyone else if you just weren't around anymore. Then you have moments of clarity leaving you feeling scared and very lonely which then again only exacerbates the whole situation. That's when people begin to become reckless and the self-harm begins, whether it becomes substance abuse or attempts of a more physical nature.

Thankfully these many years of turmoil seemed to pass, and we all began to find some normality, whatever that is. Many years after, my parents would happily visit me almost every year in Corralejo, so that side of things did thankfully improve. But sadly, I feel it probably left a lot of lingering emotional scars, although I was fortunate to be very resilient and am now very philosophical when looking back over my childhood. The downsides of ADHD are very well documented and sadly I can relate to a lot of these very confusing emotions and now find myself constantly apologising to people and friends for my previous disruptive behaviour. But I'm now so much more at peace because I have a better understanding of what was actually wrong with me.

For most of my life I felt that I was different from other people, like I was slightly abnormal and didn't really fit in, and even though I understand the ADHD better, I still get these same feelings. It's just that now I'm learning to deal with it better, I've learned to accept that everyone's different, we don't all think the same, and when it comes down to it, the word normal is very overrated. Sadly, with ADHD you think so fast, and you try and think of everything at once, which eventually gets you nowhere, that is until you can find some balance where everything starts to slow down and make sense.

You see, ADHD is a paradox of opposite abilities and behaviours that resonate at more intense levels than in those who do not have ADHD. For instance, I love astrology, I can rattle off all sorts of information about how large the known universe is, and stuff about the trillions of galaxies within the universe. But I really don't understand it at all, so everything sounds very contradictory, so a paradox is the coexistence of seemingly contradictory qualities or phases I go through.

If this is beginning to sound very complicated, it is simple really. Even though I have a higher-than-average IQ, the learning difficulties are holding me back from demonstrating my true intelligence in daily achievements. So my problems are brought about because I'm easily distracted, I have problems focusing on the matters at hand, and my impulsiveness and general restlessness can sometimes be on fire; this then manifests itself into what they call executive functioning disorder. At its worst I would describe it like an old-fashioned radio when you're turning the dial really fast through the stations, a mixture of fuzz, chat and music all comes at you in an incoherent fashion. While in that state of mind, the best place for me to be is in a swimming pool or out on my bike with my earphones on, that soon helps to clear the fog. You can imagine my excitement when years later, after I found out I have ADHD, I realised I had inadvertently been doing everything a doctor would advise me to do to deal with my condition. And of course, I had been incredibly lucky that I ended up working in a job that would be best placed for my boundless energy.

I was happy working in the bar at Dunas Caleta. It was a long bar so there was plenty of space to move around and with it being a happy holiday atmosphere I was generally dealing with smiling and laughing people. This made it a great place for me to exercise my pranks and silly sense of humour. Maybe it was something from my past that inspired me, but I enjoyed making people laugh and as my old grandmother used to say, it's nice to be nice. Yes, there's no point disguising it, this interpersonal intuition could only have been helped by my ADHD, people felt like I was getting away with murder with my strange and highly provocative pranks, but it just came down to knowing the people and knowing what you could get away with.

I had a lot of life experience behind me. I came from a small town where all different ages and professions would mix, whether it be the local townsfolk chatting in pubs or being involved with local football teams, there were so many people I grew up around who fortunately had a great sense of humour. Then there were all the different environments I had worked in. As a youngster I had worked in a bakery, eventually moving to a butchers; these were cold even hard environments to work in. The people there were used to working long hours and I must admit I was very relieved to move away from that line of work.

I eventually ended up working in a factory which was much better as I was mixing with lots of different people from all different backgrounds. One thing about the ADHD is while someone was talking to me I might eventually zone out it into my own little world but it didn't stop me from watching them, their little mannerisms, the way they spoke. I could spot in older people how their characteristics had obviously built up over time; lots of people without realising it begin to blend in with their environment, the way they talk, their attitudes, all borrowed from their peers.

Even once I moved into the world of advertising in the busy streets of London it was still very noticeable, they had trends to follow, there was a way of doing things and if you were to succeed you had to fall in line. I'm not trying to be facetious here, I went into these jobs wanting to be successful and I'm not having a go at the people who were around me, the vast majority of them were fantastic people, but there was a train of thought, a road to be followed that I just couldn't seem to grasp. Something inside me would start to rebel, something in my head would just refuse to let me move forward. I warmed to the idea of money and visions of splendour but there was no way I was focused enough to achieve it through these channels.

Some of the people in positions of power within these organisations did little to inspire, there was nothing about them, the way they lived or what they believed in. In fact even after smiling my way through their usual professional advice, I was always left with that feeling of dread. Often my dad's words of advice would go through my head: "Look, just get your bloody finger out." But no, it just wasn't to be, it would always end up another failure.

It wasn't the dizzy heights of success but getting a job as an advertising salesperson for the Sunday Observer sounded pretty impressive for me – in fact that was one of the papers my dad would buy every Sunday. But even that turned out to be a failure, my badly wired brain put paid to that. But the one thing I did take away from it was the memories, the people, how they acted, how they spoke, what they aspired to, what made them tick. This was completely invaluable by the time I got to working at the bar. I could mimic people's accents, their attitudes, and really put it all to good use. Nothing was ever done with malice. I enjoyed being with people and ultimately and genuinely enjoyed putting a smile on their faces, this inadvertently came from a weakness, all stemming from my ADHD. I never enjoy it when people are angry, so this is what really drove me to work hard at keeping people happy, nothing can ever be that bad if you can create laughter. Whatever I did, it worked, and it was fantastic seeing the same faces walking back through our reception doors the following year.

It wasn't long till I was offered the entertainment job, they felt I would be better up on the stage as I was attracting a lot of attention at the bar because of my antics. It was nice of them to offer, but it was a suggestion that initially had me wanting to run to the hills. There's a big difference between what I thought was clowning around at the bar and going up on stage to entertain kids, mums and dads and all the other holiday makers. I had this idea in my head that it just wasn't for me, it was something else that just didn't inspire me. While I'd been working at the bar I'd had time to watch some of the other entertainers and they'd failed to impress – it wasn't the entertainers themselves, it was more the type of work they had to do. And anyway, working at the bar, I only had to work on an evening, which gave me the day to myself which meant time out on the bike or down at the beach and spending time in the sea.

After nearly two years of avoiding doing the entertainment, I eventually relented. I'd bitten the bullet and decided to jump in with both feet. It caught everyone off guard especially the manageress. I'd been avoiding the entertainment for so long that Neives had given up hope and had even stopped asking me. When I walked into her office, pushed the door closed gently behind me and sat down in front of her desk, Neives could tell there was something on my mind. "What's wrong Gary?" she asked inquisitively. "Okay, I'll do it," I said quietly. Neives knew just by the look on my face what I meant and burst out laughing. There was no need to explain why I'd had a change of heart, she was just glad that I was going to do it; she knew things weren't going well with the entertainment as the main entertainer had just left to go and open a bar of his own, which left two youngsters on their own and to say they were struggling was putting it mildly.

Over the last few months, the bar environment had changed, there had been a lot of changes of bar staff which for me had really taken the shine off the job; a lot of the staff I had previously worked with were great and some of them I'm still in contact with to this day. But the new bar manager kept bringing in these people who just didn't seem to get it, they were all very friendly amongst themselves but just lacked when it came to dealing with the customers.

I'd been watching the entertainment long enough to know what was working and what wasn't, I could see where it was all going wrong. I'd been working at the complex for four years now and had taken a bit of pride in the place, so it didn't please me to watch the entertainment going downhill. This is where the benefits of my ADHD were once again kicking in without me realising it, you see ADHD doesn't always mean a lack of attention. It can actually mean paying attention to everything, even things others might miss. You see, us ADHDers have a variety of skills and abilities beyond those of our neurotypical counterparts, and with a little creativity, my usual spontaneity and loads of my abundant energy, I just knew I could turn the entertainment situation around. It wasn't like I had anyone's boots to fill, there was absolutely no pressure there, in fact the entertainment programme had more or less hit rock bottom. So, I knew I could start afresh, it was like starting with a blank canvas. I couldn't have picked a better time to jump ship and move into entertainment. There was an excitement building inside me, I knew this was the right move for me to make.

The hardest part would be the kids' discos, this was my greatest challenge, I just didn't get it, the whole kids' disco thing for me was just nonsense. Now don't get me wrong, I've nothing against music, in fact it was part of my mental therapy, I loved my music, I wore it like a badge of honour, but my personal preference was loud and hard, my music was too cool for school. (Or so I thought at the time.) The kids' disco music was way at the other end of the spectrum; as far as I was concerned, it was just complete nonsense, it was the worst part of the whole entertainment programme. Even if you didn't have any children, you still had to put up with a half hour of this excruciating drivel. Of course, the mums and dads were always glad to see their small children beginning to interact with other children, it was a special moment for them, standing together as they watched their little ankle biters make their first formative steps into dancing at a disco. I understood that – but something had to change.

For the first couple of weeks, I avoided doing the disco, I left it to Adam and Claire, the two youngsters I'd inherited with the job. In their defence, they were lovely – their only crime was that they were young and lacked a little life experience. But thankfully they had no qualms about standing on that stage and dancing along to some of the worst tunes ever written. But there was no escaping it... I was going to have to swallow my pride and eventually get up there and join in with the disco. I couldn't procrastinate any longer.

A massive flaw in many people with ADHD is putting things off, always running away from situations that make us feel uncomfortable. We can go to very strange and difficult lengths just to avoid these unwanted moments; ironically it is sometimes easier just to get on and do what needs to be done. On a more serious note, procrastination can be a real struggle for people with ADHD. Looking back over my life I can pick out the glaringly obvious moments when I ducked and ran, but there was no escaping this moment. I was going to have to get up on to that stage and get on with it.

Thankfully young Claire and I had gone along to the hotel gym and she had put me through my paces – come hell or high water I was going to learn those moves. It was much to her credit that she had the patience to persevere despite my nonstop grumbling as I stumbled my way through this most painstaking of experiences. Miraculously it wasn't long before I was standing between Adam and Claire and leading the disco from the front – I seemed to excel in charging it with a new burst of energy. In between the dances I was constantly talking on the microphone to the kids and the adults; at first it was all a massive release of nervous energy, but slowly but surely it was becoming like a well-oiled machine. Even people who didn't have kids were stopping to enjoy the show as I would drive the kids' excitement to fever pitch whilst lambasting the parents at the same time.

I'm obviously telling this in hindsight; I didn't really realise at the time that I was doing a good job. For one thing, I didn't aspire to what I was doing, it was something that I'd avoided for years, and although I was always being praised by the guests for my efforts and for the job I was doing in bringing people together, I just couldn't see it; as far as I was concerned, I was just being me. I would find it hard to accept praise, I mean it just flew in the face of all the negative feedback I'd been receiving over the years. Although it was really nice of them to offer such kind words, I just felt if they really knew me, they'd know I was just an idiot. Sadly I had this overactive inner critic that would haunt me, it would remind me of all my many past failures, and my dad's words would echo in my ear: "You're a bloody dope."

Even trying to stay focused when someone was speaking to me was incredibly difficult. Once they started talking I would begin to analyse what they were saying. I'd start playing out the scenarios in my head, but then I'd realise they were still talking and because I was overthinking I'd missed a lot of the important conversation. Then of course I didn't want to embarrass myself, so I'd just keep nodding my head like I was fully comprehending everything they were saying when really I wasn't. You'll often hear people say, "you never listen to a bloody word I'm saying", and they're right, but it's not intentional.

Yup there's a horrible sadness, feeling that you're different, never feeling like you properly fit in, knowing it's going to go wrong somewhere along the line. Don't get me wrong, I can be very philosophical at times and can be very understanding to other people who are struggling and feeling down and need help. Even on the world stage I can't seem to ignore some of the horrific injustices that are going on around the world, it angers me to know that people are starving and suffering all for the purpose of protecting our own way of life. Many times, I would let my opinions slip into my volcano walk but again I would try to persuade and discuss things in a very philosophical manner, doing my best not to offend anyone.

In my defence, I was always trying to be honest, I didn't want to lie or deceive, it was important for me to be as informative as possible as I needed these people to trust me. Maybe it's just a case of I know full well the system is broken and I'm actually angry with myself because I don't seem to be doing anything at all to help, and spreading the message to others helps to clear my conscience a little. And even though I know that it doesn't really do any good to worry about things you have no control over, it's something that I still foolishly do. Being in people's faces all the time always helped me keep my head above water, constantly laughing and cracking ridiculously bad jokes, but I'd be lying if I said everything in the garden was rosy. There's always that self-doubt bubbling away not too far from the surface.

But the job was fantastic for me and of course for my ADHD that I didn't know I had, it was putting my incessant talking to good use. If people needed to find something out, I was the guy to go to. But no matter how hard I tried to be informative, I couldn't help myself when it came to talking absolute nonsense, my sense of humour wouldn't allow me to be too serious for too long. I was literally being paid to make people happy while thoroughly enjoying myself at the same time. Pulling people together and helping make lifelong friendships was something I enjoyed immensely. Making families feel good about each other was another thing I would work very hard at, in fact there was no real surprise when all the same faces would come walking through the door the following year. And yes, it was nice when people would say "You made our holiday."

Part of me wishes I'd known earlier in my life that I had ADHD so I could have understood where all that self-doubt was coming from, but on the other hand maybe if I'd known about it, that might just have poured a little cold water over my creative magic. Now after years of self-study I have built up a great deal of knowledge regarding this strange phenomenon that is ADHD. Yes, I've had my problems, some of which are ongoing, especially the procrastination part. I need to drink less, it would really help if I improved my diet, these things I keep promising myself I'm going to start tomorrow but I always seem to put off, but on the upside, I do a lot to keep myself fit. My bike and my swimming are part of my everyday life, and finally my writing, it helped me express myself in ways I never thought I could.

A lot of this may have been coming over as very negative, but all I was doing was giving a little background to how my head sometimes works and obviously a little bit of background as to why my mind might at times have been thinking like that. But the energy that builds inside me strives to be happy and I'm at my best when I'm laughing and being happy, and hopefully that'll never change. Again, paradoxically I still zone out at the wrong times but can burst into moments of hyperfocus, for all my weaknesses I'm still very resilient and do my best to keep myself happy. If you make the effort and work at it, and if you can defeat the procrastination, ADHD can be turned into a superpower.

Sitting in the van looking out as we sped along the road at a steady pace, everything seemed to be going very smoothly. Although extremely tired, I was still feeling upbeat after listening to the radio programme about ADHD. I knew we still had loads of challenges up ahead but for the moment everything seemed to be going well. One of the main things that struck me was that at no time had I noticed the roads getting very busy; yes, there was a bit of traffic on the roads as we left Cadiz but since then the traffic seemed to be thin on the ground. Now that we were driving not far from Merida there had still not been any increase in the traffic. It was early afternoon with the sun still very high in the sky. Our views were very clear and bright and although the temperatures were obviously very hot outside, inside the van the air conditioning was keeping us nice and cool. Looking back at the dogs I could see they were all very comfortable and settled. I wasn't going to disturb them as it was nice to see them at peace. I knew Jim was planning on another stop once we passed Merida so I would disturb them from their slumbers then. I was doing my best not to chat too much as I know once I get started, I don't shut up, but I couldn't help myself, I had to ask Jim why the roads seemed so quiet.

I was quite confident that Jim wouldn't mind as he had already been a wealth of knowledge so far. As far as I could tell he was quite enjoying keeping me informed, it was probably helping him stay focused on the job at hand. Jim explained that he had planned the route carefully, knowing that the roads he had chosen would be a lot quieter; had we been passing close to any of the major cities things might have been a lot different, especially if he had chosen to drive closer to Madrid. Jim told me there were a few other factors for the roads being a little quieter, one reason was that there is actually a lower-than-average amount of drivers in Spain than in other European countries. But Jim was quick to add that the road system is also very well organised and had been well planned out over previous years when the government had decided to make improvements to the infrastructure.

Also, a lot of the roads in Spain have tolls which has put a lot of pressure on the Spanish Government to make sure the roads are well maintained. They were first introduced as a way of creating alternative routes in particularly congested areas of the country. So motorists could choose to pay for a quicker way to get to their destination, while also providing a sustainable source of revenue for ongoing road maintenance and improvements. Another important point Jim made was that it was easier to police these roads with a toll system, with the tolls having cameras it helped keep unnecessary traffic off the roads and made it all a lot safer for many of the decent drivers out there.

I asked Jim if he thought it was worth it, did he think it was too expensive? He said the costs vary on different roads, but he reckoned it averaged out to about a euro every ten kilometres. When he told me that, it had me scratching my head. I thought for the distance we are travelling that worked out to be quite expensive, but Jim quickly reminded me that there were only tolls on some routes. Not that I was an expert, but the roads seemed to be fantastic, all very new looking and all very smooth and well-marked out. Again Jim reminded me that this was thanks to the traffic not being so heavy and not having to endure the UK's diverse weather conditions. Yes, in the UK there were more drivers than ever, and with the rain, sleet, snow and ice it was a never-ending battle to maintain the roads.

We were now by-passing Merida and still there was no heavy traffic to talk of. I was certainly happy that we were not seeing a lot of other vehicles, it was making the journey easier. With less traffic on the roads, it just felt a bit more relaxed. Even though it wasn't me who was driving I was keeping an eye on everything that was going on. Now that the excitement from my radio programme was starting to wane my mind was beginning to drift again. I was certainly in need of one of those large powerful coffees to keep me going.

As the roads were beginning to take long upwards bends away from Merida, I was doing my best to see if I could view any of the sights. I knew Merida was an ancient place and another that the Romans had made good use of, in fact the city preserves more ancient structures than any other city in Spain. And remember there were Roman buildings and artifacts to be found all over Spain so that was no mean feat.

An important factor was that the city is on the banks of the River Guardiana, which was a massively important lifeline as the river ran just over eight hundred kilometres, coming through parts of Portugal and all the way down to Cadiz. Merida was used as a place where Augustus Caesar could rest his soldiers, safely tucked in the hills away from danger; in fact, back in those days it was called Emerita Augusta. Obviously, you had to be important to be able to stumble upon somewhere you like and then rename it after yourself. Of course, this was all a very long time ago, in fact I think Merida was founded in 25 BC.

Looking around, I could see the attraction of hanging out in Merida. I could imagine back in those days this would have been a great place to live. Some of the hills were reminding me of Scotland and of course it had that beautiful river, but unlike Scotland there was no really cold weather to worry about. The trees were always bountiful with fruit and the river full of fish. Yup, if it was good enough for Augustus, it was certainly good enough for me. Okay I'm obviously never going to be as important as him in history, but we clearly share the same good tastes.

Just to give you a little more info on Augustus, he was the first Roman emperor, reigning from 27 BC until his death in 14 AD, and his status as the founder of the Roman Principate has consolidated his legacy as one of the greatest leaders in history. Now I don't want to cast any aspersions on the guy, but he just happened to be the dude who came to power right after the assassination of a certain Julius Caesar. Now I'm not saying he was one of the eight senators who stabbed poor Julius, and I think he was even involved in trying to avenge poor Julius's death, but it was Augustus who restored the republic of Rome with the help of many of the senators who had planned the murder. In his defence, regardless of my suspicious opinions, he was responsible for restoring peace and prosperity to the Roman state, and on top of all that he managed to change nearly every aspect of Roman life.

And just on a final note, if you're lucky enough to go travelling around Spain, Merida is a must, it's not a big place but it's well worth spending a couple of days there just to go and explore some of the extensive and impressive Roman ruins that are sprinkled around the town. It even has a Roman theatre that is still operating after two thousand years, you can watch classical theatre in the summer months with an absolutely fantastic backdrop. To be honest I haven't done it myself but from what I've researched it looks spectacular. Maybe one day I'll get there to watch it.

12

We were now driving deep into the Iberian Peninsula, not far from the Portuguese border; in fact we were sort of driving parallel to the border and heading close to Caceres. But before going any farther it was time for our next stop. Jim informed me that he knew of somewhere we could stop for refreshments and more importantly let the dogs out so they could stretch their legs. It didn't take long for Harry to pick up on the conversation as he was now back sitting up and barking, which seemed to be the rallying call as Evie and Charlie were quick to join in. I apologised to Jim for all the commotion; I think he found it quite amusing as I was failing miserably to restore some order and was probably just adding to the noise as I was shouting to the dogs to be quiet.

As Jim pulled off the dual carriageway, we climbed the slip road and crossed an overpass; down below I could see what looked like a brand-new service station. At first sight it looked like it wasn't even open as there were hardly any cars parked, and through its large glass windows it seemed like there were no lights on and certainly no people roaming around.

Fortunately, as Jim pulled up to the main entrance, we could see that it was open and thankfully a few people came out carrying what looked like food and drinks. This raised my spirits – for some reason when I'm travelling, I'm permanently hungry. I think eating brings me some sort of comfort, and there was one thing for sure, I was desperate for another of those strong coffees.

But first things first, it was time to get the dogs out for some exercise. As usual I got Harry out first and he literally bounced out of his cage with his ears pricked up. I could tell he was still in fine fettle.

There was a lot of grass and some surrounding bushes that were really grabbing his attention, these were smells that he had never experienced before. I think he was picking up the scents of other dogs that had obviously passed through this service station of late, and of course he had to leave his mark, a sort of doggie version of "I was here". I let him sniff a little bit longer and then started to run with him a short time. Although it was still warm there was a little breeze just taking the edge off it, so I wasn't too worried about him overheating and anyway the van had the air conditioning on which was keeping them all at a comfortable temperature.

On getting Harry back to the van, I could see that Evie was in a panic because her beloved Harry had gone without her. As I bent down to pick Harry up to put him in his cage, he suddenly jumped past me and right into his cage. As much as it gave me a fright, I was over the moon to see him so lively and still with so much energy. He was really taking this journey in his stride, although it was early days and I couldn't take anything for granted, we still had a long way to go, but it was so pleasing to see him handling this all so well.

I filled his dish with water and poured more biscuits out for him. The bottom of his cage was a complete mess so I just made sure he had somewhere comfortable to lie. Once again I promised Jim that I would clean it all out eventually. Jim didn't seem concerned in the slightest, I think he'd had far more difficult customers than my mob, and I'm sure he was just as relieved as I was that things with the dogs so far were going so smoothly. I had pre-warned Jim that the whole reason for this journey was Harry's infrequent bouts of epilepsy so I'm sure he understood my relief at Harry's seeming well-being.

So as to not panic Evie any further I took Charlie next knowing she would settle down again now that Harry was with her. It was quite a good system I had going, all I had to do was take Charlie the exact same route I'd taken Harry, and like clockwork I knew he'd pee and stop exactly where Harry had, they even did their business in the same place. Charlie certainly wasn't as frisky or as alert as he usually was, he seemed a little out of sorts and I could tell he was unsure of his surroundings and was only sniffing when he recognised where Harry had stopped. The most important thing was he was still drinking and eating so I wasn't too concerned. Charlie was just over a year old so he still had a long future ahead of him – well that's if he doesn't kill himself chasing motorbikes or choking on something he's not supposed to be eating. We could only hope he would grow out of these bad habits as he got older.

Once we got back to the van Charlie actually allowed me to pick him up and place him into his cage. Charlie's cage was so much tidier, his water and food were still in his dishes where it was supposed to be. Not like Harry's where he had kicked everything over; in fact Harry still had that pink mark on his nose where he'd scraped it trying to get to the biscuits that he'd spilled onto the outside of his cage.

Then it was Evie's turn. She was so much more difficult to deal with – all she was interested in doing was turning her head and trying to drag me back to the van so she could be with Harry. Thankfully after a minute or so she started to pay more attention to her surroundings, and it wasn't long before she picked up on Harry and Charlie's trail. Once again Evie peed in exactly the same place; there was no number two to deal with but that didn't really surprise me as I knew she hadn't been eating much. I knew I'd have to try and find something for her to eat as she was just refusing to touch her biscuits.

Again, Jim tried to allay my fears and reminded me that this happens a lot with some dogs when they're travelling. "Once you get her home, she'll be fine," he said reassuringly. Once I got Evie back to the van, I could see her cage was still immaculate. I did have to refill her water dish, but it was fairly obvious she hadn't touched any of her biscuits. I knew I'd have to make a point of finding something for her to eat, just anything to keep her going. I was hoping they would have some plain chicken sandwiches or even a simple pasta dish where I could suck off any sauce that might be on it.

I shouted to Jim, "I'm heading off into the service station, I'll try not to be too long." Jim was busy sorting out some of his paperwork and shouted, "No worries, we're in no rush, we are making good time." Those words echoed in my head: "We are making good time." What did he mean by that? I had assumed we would be making a stop somewhere for the night, but during the journey this hadn't been discussed.

Before the journey had got underway, I was sure the plan was to find a hotel for the Monday and Tuesday nights, but I didn't have a clue where we would be stopping, never mind the name of the hotels we would be stopping at. This was obviously a big worry for me. Would these be dog-friendly hotels, or were they just expected to sleep in the back of the van? Again, my head started to work overtime as the same worries started plaguing my mind again. What if I'm sleeping comfortably in my hotel room and someone breaks into the van and steals the dogs? Could you imagine me trying to explain that one to Nicky? Maybe they would be safe in the hotel car park, maybe it would be a hotel in the middle of nowhere. Either way, I knew in my heart of hearts that wherever it was I'd never be able to get to sleep knowing they were out on the street alone in the back of the van. Whatever happened, wherever we stayed, there was only one thing for it – unless it was a pet-friendly hotel that would let me have all three of them in the room, I'd have to sleep in the back of the van with them, there was just no other way.

I must admit the idea of me and the three dogs all sharing a hotel room did really amuse me, but I could also imagine them all kicking off as people passed our room at night, so it was a real possibility we could all end up getting kicked out. But then again, the idea of us all getting kicked out seemed to amuse me as well – what a great story that would be to tell Nicky, it sounded a little bit rock'n'roll to me. The thing was, we were not a rock'n'roll band – I was in my late fifties and the rest of my gang were three crazy Yorkshire terriers. I was still slightly surprised that someone at my age could have such silly, immature thoughts.

There was another issue that needed to be addressed – we were supposed to do another Covid test somewhere before we crossed the French border. I could feel another little bit of panic setting in – not only had I the worry of the dogs behaving themselves as we crossed the French border, but I was now reminded that there was always the possibility that one of us could test positive for Covid. That would be an almighty spanner to throw in the works, it didn't bear thinking about – stuck in North Spain with a lot of out-of-date paperwork on our hands. I was starting to feel like I didn't have a clue what was going on. I could hear Nicky telling me this, that and the next, I even remembered her saying, "You'll forget everything I've told you" and me adamantly replying, "No I won't." But here I was, extremely tired, in a sort of confused panic mode and yes, I'd forgotten everything.

There was no point in getting angry with myself. I'd do what I always do in these situations, just shut my mouth, and at worst, change the conversation and just see what happens along the way. Now that my mind had made the executive decision to bury all the serious questions I needed answered, it was time to get on with the job at hand. I was bloody hungry, but first I was bursting for the toilet.

Walking into the service station I could see it was quiet. There was no one apart from a few employees moving around behind the food counters; there was one other customer did pass me coming out of the toilet, but that was it. The place was large enough to sit hundreds of people, but it was like a ghost town. The whole place was surrounded by tinted glass windows which would help keep it cool on these regularly hot days, it was all very clean and looked brand new. Standing at the toilet I could see the marble cistern had been freshly cleaned as my mind began to wander again.

I was feeling relaxed now, but it all seemed quite strange. What was I doing here? It was amazing – only a week ago we were all lounging around the apartment together, now here I was, slap bang in the middle of this great adventure. As I washed my hands, I quickly reminded myself that I must find something suitable for Evie to eat. My head felt heavy but there was no surprise there – since the beginning of the journey I'd hardly slept a wink. I had to put these thoughts right to the back of my mind as I didn't have a clue when I was next going to feel the comfort of a nice cosy bed.

Getting to the food counter my prayers were answered straight away as I could see there were quite a few packets of chicken salad sandwiches. There was no point looking at anything else, they would do I thought. I was about to buy three packets, two for me to eat then I would dissect the other packet so Evie would get the chicken, but no, I decided I'd only buy two packs.

I remembered back to when I was working at Systems Reliability in Dunfermline in Fife selling computers. In the mornings this lady used to come round selling sandwiches. I was young and energetic and always ridiculously hungry. So I'd order two chicken salad sandwiches with mayonnaise and sweetcorn and two cheese, ham and peach rolls; they were some of the nicest rolls I've ever had. But once it got closer to twelve o'clock, I would be struggling to stay awake, my head would literally be rolling about my shoulders. So one day I said to my dad, "I don't know what's wrong with me but every day as it gets close to twelve o'clock, I'm struggling to stay awake?" My dad, straight to the point, said, "Look, you silly bugger, don't eat so many sandwiches. When you eat so much, all the blood runs to your stomach, that's what makes you so tired." So, with sadness in my heart, I cut it down to two sandwiches, but my dad was right, I felt much more awake. This was a memory I couldn't forget, and the real bone of contention here was I just couldn't allow myself to fall asleep while we were driving along in the van. So this was what inspired me to only buy two packs of sandwiches.

Looking around I was still amazed at how large but quiet the place was. At the far end of the big room, it was like a mini market that sold just about anything you needed, from earphones to gardening equipment. One of the only things they didn't have was dog food.

This wasn't a problem as there was enough plain white chicken in this sandwich, which I knew Evie would eat. I'd just have to be careful Harry didn't notice as chicken was one of his favourite things.

Looking past the clean orange Formica tabletops and plastic chairs and out through the big tinted glass windows of the service station I could see Jim sitting on a bench just across from the van, which was sitting in solitary splendour in this spacious carpark. I must admit the van looked great, all smooth contours, even the colour, which was shadow black, made it look very sporty. Yup, if you were going to go on an adventure covering thousands of miles, this looked like the vehicle you would want to travel in. Still looking at the van, it was amazing to think that Harry, Evie and Charlie were in there too, sitting patiently in their cages waiting on me getting served. Yup, I'm definitely not going to hassle Jim about where we might be staying for the evening, let's just see where the journey takes us, I thought to myself.

While I was staring out at the van, I heard the woman behind the counter asking "Algo mas?", so I turned and said, "Yes, could I have one of your large coffees please." I never thought I'd drink such large coffees – the cups were like the containers you'd get a large soft drink in at a cinema or a fast-food place like McDonalds. Usually, the idea of drinking a coffee that size would be enough to make my heart explode, but for some reason they were working perfectly for me. The woman had put my sandwiches and my large coffee in a paper bag so I grabbed a few extra serviettes as I knew I would need them if I was going to be pulling one of these sandwiches apart for Evie. At the last minute, I couldn't help myself, I turned and asked the woman for another chicken sandwich; there was no way I could sneakily give Evie chicken and miss out Harry, especially with it being his favourite.

Just so there wasn't too much fuss and barking I pulled the sandwiches apart at the side of the van so the dogs couldn't see. I made sure Evie got the most as she hadn't been eating any of her biscuits. I fed Evie first and then gave a few bits to Harry and Charlie which I threw into their biscuit dishes to disguise the fact that Evie had had a little more. Once that was sorted, I climbed back into the van and we were off, back on the road and heading north.

13

We were now heading North past Caceres and the views were beginning to change dramatically, the landscape was becoming more rugged and mountainous. I wasn't sure if it was the coffee, but what I was seeing from the front of the van was very uplifting, this was made so much easier with the roads being so quiet, it allowed my eyes to drift towards the mountain ranges far off in the distance. This was a part of Spain I'd never experienced before and it was easy to see why so many of these places were used for filming "Game of Thrones". We seemed to be passing most of the locations they used. It was no wonder they had filmed in Seville and the still very medieval and mysterious Caceres with its cobbled streets and high stone walls, these provinces were a far cry from the now very modern cities of Madrid and Barcelona.

As we headed closer to Palencia, we were brushing past the edges of the Monfrague National Park. Even from the van you could see this was a place of sheer beauty. One thing Fuerteventura shares with Monfrague National Park is that we also had our share of Egyptian vultures, though that's where the similarities end. Monfrague is a green mountainous place that is full of all sorts of different wildlife; lots of tourists and bird watchers flock to the park just to watch the migratory birds such as the vultures and the black storks. The park is home to the griffon vulture, the black vulture, the Spanish eagle, the Bonelli's eagle, the peregrine falcon and the eagle owl – how all the other little animals survive there with that lot running the skies is anyone's guess. Especially the rabbits – they must be right at the top of these predators' hist lists, everyday must be like running the gauntlet for these poor little animals. And it doesn't end there, lurking in these dense forests is the Iberian lynx, a wildcat cat species endemic to the Iberian Peninsula, though sadly this lovely animal is on the endangered species list.

At the other end of the scale, the deer and wild boar numbers are going through the roof. Hunting was banned in the park in 2020 so they are at pains to find a decent way of keeping the numbers down. A few contentious methods have been used which has rightly had environmentalists up in arms. Ironically with the wild boar and deer numbers being so high they do a lot of damage to the surrounding forests which has an ecological knock-on effect. Personally, I'm too much of a softy and I certainly wouldn't like to be the one having to make the decisions on how to keep these animal numbers down, I would just leave them all to die of old age or try and find a way of expanding the forest so there was more room for them all.

Running through the thick oak forests are the clean-flowing rivers and the deep fish-laden reservoirs. These crystal-clear waters are full of all sorts, from carp and trout to the more predatory pike and zander. The pike is one of my favourite freshwater fish; it's known as the freshwater shark, and for good reason – it can take frogs and even unsuspecting small birds. The zander is actually a cross between a pike and a perch, goodness knows how that cross breeding came about, the one thing I do know is that the spikey dorsal fin on the perch was the one thing that stopped it being eaten by the pike.

The perch is another fish that's close to my heart. At the tender age of only eight years old, it was the first fish I ever caught. At that age one of my favourite things to do was to go and visit my cousin Rab who lived at the Pitliver estate near Dunfermline in Fife. To me this was just one massive adventure playground in the lovely countryside. But one of Rab's favourite hobbies was fishing, and if it was good enough for my favourite cousin at the time, it was most certainly good enough for me. I became fascinated with the whole thing, the different types of rods and reels, the different strains of fishing gut, hook sizes, all the different types of skilfully handmade flies you could get. These were all made on a vice with special thread and feathers; a good eye and a steady hand were the order of the day. Even the fancy boxes that all this equipment was kept in was something I would check out in all the sports shops.

I loved rivers and lochs anyway, especially if they were surrounded by woodland, it was just so serene and peaceful, but I couldn't ever look at them without wondering what size of fish would be lurking under the waters. This was all fuelled by that special day when I caught my first proper fish with my own first rod and reel. Rab had decided to take me fishing, I can't even remember the exact location, but it was a small loch somewhere in the hills at the back of Dunfermline. There were no trees, it was quite a lonely quiet place with a barren landscape; the grass was long and windswept and it was obviously not used by many people.

Now I'm not one who's known for sitting still but when it came to fishing, I could quite happily sit for hours staring over the water and watching for any slight twitching at the end of my rod that might suggest a possible fish on the end of my line. I was even careful enough to put new hooks on and thankfully never once did I get a hook stuck in my finger. Sometimes when people are putting a new hook on, the rod can slip and as it falls it drags the fine line through your fingers and the only thing that stops it is when that catches into your hand or finger. If the barb on the end of your hook goes all the way through your skin, it's almost impossible to get it to come out the same way. It's obviously made that way so when it catches into a fish's mouth there's no way that the fish can escape. (Sorry to any fish lovers if this all sounds a bit cruel.) Usually if a hook goes through a person's finger you have to make sure the hook goes all the way through and then you need a set of plyers to snap off the end of the barb. Yup, after many years as a kid fishing, I was lucky enough for that to never happen, which looking back is very surprising.

Anyway, we set up close to the water's edge and Rab had given me my very own rod and reel. I'd been a few times before, so I had a little knowledge of tying on hooks and small lead weights and even putting bait on the end of the hooks. Whether it be maggots, worms or even little bits of bread, it all had to be placed on the hook very carefully. The rod he had given me was quite small and it had an Abu reel on it, which means it had a little metal casing over the reel which should've made it easier to use.

We must have only been there half an hour when I noticed that there were little bits of movement at the end of my rod. I tried to quietly signal over to Rab, but he was a little farther away and I wasn't close enough to really get his attention. I had to act, this was my big moment, I quickly jumped into action, grabbed the rod and yanked it into the air, hoping that if there was a fish, I would manage to catch that hook in its mouth. Yup, I felt something there, so I started reeling in the line as fast as I could; within seconds I realised that the rod was now bending over at the front, and whatever was on the end of my line wasn't coming in without a fight. There was only one thing for it, try and keep the front of the rod up and reel in as fast as possible.

All my excitement had managed to catch Rab's attention and he was hurriedly making his way over to join me. I was so happy, I couldn't believe it; I was bringing in my very own fish! All of a sudden, just as I was reeling in as fast as my hands could move, something gave way. It was like my rod had just fallen apart. I couldn't believe it – not now, how could this happen? Through my panic as I looked down to my hands, I could see that my reel had come away from the rod. Not wanting to lose any momentum I just dropped the rod and held onto the reel and ran as fast as I could from the water's edge. I don't think Rab could believe his eyes as I kept running, but now we could see the fish coming to the top of the water. I couldn't stop till I got it safely on land. It worked, I managed to land the fish – okay, in a very unorthodox fashion but I got there! In all the years I'd known Rab, I'd never seen him laugh so much.

After all the excitement, we managed to get the fish off the hook and onto Rab's set of scales to find out how heavy it was. It was only ten and a half ounces which made the whole situation seem even funnier – all that fuss for a ten-and-a-half-ounce perch. But to me that was a fantastic moment – that was it, pardon the pun, but I was hooked and fishing became an important hobby in my early life. I loved freshwater fishing, it was always more scenic; I loved when we went to rivers or lochs hidden away in beautiful countryside, out of the wind on a sunny day. I could literally just stay there for hours, and obviously it was a total bonus when you actually caught something. I don't think that's a fisherman's tale that will be passed down through the generations, mind you that fish might just get bigger over the years, just like the one that got away.

Realistically that small loch in Fife probably never had fish much bigger than that ten-and-a-half-ounce perch – it was a small loch which must have been quite shallow; only having a small volume of water would determine the size of the fish. Certainly, the Monfrague rivers and reservoirs wouldn't have that trouble – with the deep reservoirs and the long-running rivers, the fish would have so much room to grow. It must be fantastic watching the eagles swooping down from a great height and pulling out a large unsuspecting fish with their large sharp talons.

It wasn't all left to nature though, some of the reservoirs were stocked with fish from different parts of the world. Quite a few companies had paid for permits which allowed them to organise fishing trips for people, whether it be fishing from the land or from boats. It wasn't just fishing either, with there being so many different birds, there were also organised bird-watching groups and organised treks through the forests, whether it be the more strenuous, steep mountain climbs over the rugged mountain tops or the more relaxed walks close to the riverbanks. And of course, my favourite, mountain biking. I'm too old for down-hilling through dense woodlands, I'd prefer a safer cycle along some of the tracks, so I could stop and gaze across the rivers and possibly watch the wildlife in action. I remember sitting looking out of the van window at all that beautiful landscape, saying to myself, "I hope I come back here one day." Maybe if I become successful and wealthy, I'll have a week here with my trusty mountain bike.

The van was now driving round the east side of the city of Palencia, although we couldn't see much of the city, again another beautiful place that was renowned for its thirteenth-century cathedral. Right next to it was one that they had built in the fifteenth century, this new one had more gothic and Renaissance elements and was surrounded by more of these big stone medieval walls. This isn't your usual holiday destination, it is more favoured by the discerning wealthy travellers who can afford the expensive hotel rooms with their fabulous views over the old city. And there are plenty of high-end restaurants to match the splendour of it all, especially with their abundance of fresh quality foods, I mean they have it all right on their doorstep, even down to the wine that is produced from their historic vineyards. Yes, most of these local high-end restaurants have their very own well-stocked wine cellars. Geez, if the van did break down here, it would be like breaking down in paradise. This dream was short lived as I was reminded that Harry, Evie and Charlie were in the back of the van. Mind you, as I looked round, they all seemed to be curled up sleeping. I knew that wouldn't last for long; sometimes individually they can be well behaved, as long as there are no bikes, skateboards, runners, buses, lorries, other dogs or even helicopters to set them off barking. Why couldn't I have three normal dogs like some other people? Why must my three have very strange characteristics? Truth beknown, I loved them to bits, and I wouldn't have them any other way.

Leaving Palencia behind us we were now heading in the direction of Salamanca; the roads were long and winding. Jim was being quite talkative, and his interest in and knowledge of the place seemed second to none. He was quick to remind me that we had probably followed the same route as the Romans had used so many years ago all the way from Cadiz up to Salamanca. You could almost smell the history as Jim waxed lyrical with his extensive knowledge of the area; he obviously enjoyed driving through these beautiful places.

Jim was also interested in what they hadn't found over the years. He believed that if there weren't lots of unfound treasures hidden in amongst the hills there must surely be a wealth of undiscovered Roman artifacts; and it wasn't just the Romans – the whole place was steeped in Spanish history, with small monasteries and castles at every turn. There were so many small rivers coming off the hills with clear fresh water, this must have been a source of refreshment for so many travellers over the years.

There was still no real traffic to hinder our journey and the only cars we did pass were obviously tourists out exploring this beautiful landscape. Sadly, up until now my knowledge of Spain had been fairly thin on the ground. I always associated Spain with the Costa del Sol and people flocking to their sun-drenched holiday resorts, but I was now beginning to realise there was so much more to this fantastic country. I kept saying to myself, "I must make a point of returning to these places one day," but I knew it would be hard as I don't have a driving license and I imagine it's imperative to have the use of a car to cover all these beautiful cities we had just driven past.

Salamanca was no different, it was even referred to as the Golden City because of its honey-coloured sandstone; in the early evening, as the sun goes down, it gives off this golden hue. What a magnificent sight that must have been hundreds of years ago as weary travellers first set eyes on this incredible sight. They must have felt as though they had stumbled upon a magical golden city. This famous sedimentary stone of Salamanca was also referred to as the Piedra Franca of Villamayor.

It'll come as no surprise that Salamanca is arguably one of the most beautiful cities in all of Spain. It's actually one of the smaller cities, but boasts some of the richest architecture in all of Spain. Right in the centre you have the Plaza Mayor where you can join the holiday crowds enjoying the hustle and bustle of the fabulous cafes and restaurants, renowned for their world-famous Iberian hams. Sadly this beautiful square was actually built for the purpose of bullfighting of which I'm not a fan.

With it being a small city, it means that all the historic sites are neatly packed together so everything's within walking distance. It's not only Plasencia that can boast of having two cathedrals, Salamanca also has two fantastic cathedrals that stand side by side. The first is the Vieja de Santa Maria and the newer one, another Gothic masterpiece, is simply called Catedral Nueva.

Salamanca is also one of the most important university cities in Spain and attracts thousands of international students from over fifty different countries. Not only that, but the University of Salamanca is the oldest university in Spain. This ancient university was founded way back in 1218. If I'd been lucky enough to go to university that's one of the places I'd have liked to have studied – not only being able to live in such a beautiful place but to study in buildings that carried so much history must be so inspiring in itself. Okay, maybe I never made it there, but I know someone who did. Yes, Gary and Mandy who own the very successful Rock Island bar in Corralejo have a son called Aydan, and this lucky young chap managed to get a place in this ancient university, not only that but managed to pass his degree in history with flying colours. As you can imagine, Gary and Mandy were rightly very proud of his achievements; not only that, but it just came so easy to him, nothing's ever too much trouble, he's always very pleasant and always stops for a chat, a nicer lad you won't meet.

Yup, the contrast between myself and Aydan couldn't be any bigger – he's a well-balanced, nice young lad with a good future well mapped out in front of him, and rightly so as it was all down to him through all his own hard work. Then there's me – an ADHD-fuelled lunatic who has literally stumbled through life, bouncing from pillar to post, still with no sense of where I'll end up, but similarly all down to my own efforts.

Now leaving the vicinity of Salamanca we were heading in the direction of Valladolid. It was still really bright and sunny outside. I wasn't sure, but I had thought with it being late in October the temperature would start to dip a little, the farther north we travelled. But no, it felt like the temperature had just stayed the same for the whole journey so far, and we were now over a thousand miles away from Fuerteventura.

When I was younger and fortunate enough to be taken on holidays to Spain by my parents, I thought it just never rains there. The first holiday was way back in 1970 and we stayed in a place called Sitges. We even had my grandmother and my Auntie Rose with us. Every day we were on the beach and like clockwork the same time every afternoon this guy would come round selling ice-creams. The sea was always warm with lovely clean beaches and never a single cloud in the sky. The narrow streets were always filled with the warm smell of chickens roasting on a spit and I remember drinking bottles of the best chocolate milk in the world.

As I got a little older, my dad had a friend who had this four-bedroom apartment at the very top of a thirteen-storey building in Alicante, it had a massive terrace with panoramic views as far as the eye could see. At the bottom of the apartment block was this amazing swimming pool, and it was only a minute from this gloriously long beach. And again, every day the sun would shine. Yup, I certainly got to learn about sunburn from a very young age.

There was this one time, it must have been just after six o'clock, and we had not long come off the beach. Now remember this was mid-September and the weather is always fantastic at that time of year in Spain. Another little bonus was that only two weeks before we had returned to school from our summer holidays – my dad would always book our holidays for mid-September which meant I got another two weeks off school. Anyway, we were all getting ready after being on the beach. As usual we were all having showers and putting fresh clothes on (luckily there were two bathrooms so there wasn't too much hassle with everyone getting showered) when suddenly I heard my dad shouting, "Quick, come and see this!!" So my brother Michael and I went running through to join my dad who was gazing out of this massive sliding patio door. The views were fantastic – the main road was directly outside our apartment block and from there it was straight onto the beach, we were so high up we could see the full stretch of the beach. But not this time, something very strange was happening. As we looked out of the large sliding door, just off the water's edge it was like a cloudy mist had befallen us. All across the top of the water it looked like it was boiling. "That must be some really heavy rain coming in," my dad said. We could see it was coming towards us really fast – the last stragglers on the beach were making a mad dash for cover.

At first it seemed quite funny, watching these last few people running from this really heavy rain. Then it was upon us, and it wasn't rain, it was hail stones, the biggest hail stones I'd ever seen. Quickly my dad pushed us back and closed the sliding door, the noise was almost deafening, this crash bang wallop was all around us. In fact, it reminded me of one of those films where a guy is holding a machine gun and he spins around and lets the whole bar room have it, with broken glass everywhere and bullets making that pinging noise as they rebound off bits of metal.

This may sound like a bit of an exaggeration but after five minutes, when it stopped, we went back out onto the large terrace and the place was a mess, my mum's ashtray and two glasses were all smashed. The clothes horse had been turned over and was broken, and then my dad noticed the small table the glasses and ashtray had been sitting on. "Look at that," he said, and when we looked closer, we could see that the metal table was covered in small dents. "I wonder how we're going to explain that to Bob," my dad joked. Bob was one of the company directors who owned the apartment.

Then my dad panicked. "Christ, I hope the bloody car's alright." We all ran to the balcony and looked down – as far as we could see it looked alright, the windscreen hadn't shattered and the back window seemed fine as well. It was a white Opel Rekord with a two-litre engine. Not leaving anything to chance, my dad, Michael and I jumped into the lift to go down and give the car a better inspection. As we left the lift and went outside the car seemed to be fine, but as we got closer, once again my dad shouted, "Jesus Christ, look at that." The car was covered in small indentations. By now, most of the ice had melted and steam was rising from the ground as the sun was again beating down on us. The hailstone storm had disappeared like it had never happened in the first place. It wasn't too much of a problem for my dad as it was a company car and it could always be replaced, but the one lasting memory I have of that day was the frightening clamour and noise of those heavy hailstones clattering around us.

14

Now, after over twenty-six years in Fuerteventura, I've managed to experience all sorts of strange weather fronts, and boy o boy when it rains, it's incredible. The worst rainstorm I ever experienced was early one evening while out on my bike. Usually before I started my work as an entertainer at the now defunct Dunas Caleta, I would quickly rush through to our buffet restaurant and try to inform the guests what entertainment we had on for that evening. This would probably involve me being loud and messing about and acting the clown. Once I'd finished doing that, I would grab some food and eat it ridiculously quickly, people were forever telling me that I'd get indigestion, but thankfully I never did.

The reason I was eating so quickly was that I always liked to stick my earphones on and go out for a good cycle just before I started work, a sort of pre-work warm-up if you like. So I used to rush my food down quickly which would allow me that little longer out on the bike. I would usually do around ten miles with my music blasting loudly into my ears; this cycle ride would take me a way out of the main part of Corralejo and out round the back of the town. It was great fun, back in these days this part of Corralejo was quiet, with very few people and hardly any traffic.

Cycling out to this part of town was quite a steady climb and would eventually see me parked by a roundabout at the end of a street that was just over from the Volcano Bayuyo. This was the volcano that I would take thousands of guests round over the many years. I liked to think I had a real connection with this volcano as I don't think anyone else has been round it as many times as I have. Just before turning round, I'd always look up to the volcano, maybe check my phone and possibly enjoy the view that I had back down over the town. I'd done this cycle so many times and would stop at the same location, it was just a nice place to just stop and reflect.

But as I looked up towards the volcano, I noticed two quick lightning flashes and that unmistakable rumble of thunder that always follows. Looking up towards the sky I could see it was strangely grey and dull, and the air seemed really still. When I had first started out it had seemed like a normal evening, and I hadn't heard any weather reports that had told me any different. My first thoughts were of Harry as I knew electrical storms could have an adverse effect regarding his epilepsy, so just to be on the safe side, I got my phone out to send Nicky a message so that she was aware that there was a little bit of a lightning storm around.

Once I'd sent the message, I decided to hang about a little longer and watch a few more flashes. I loved thunder and lightning, it was one of those strange phenomena I just couldn't fully understand. Foolishly I kept saying to myself, "Right, after the next one I'll get going," but for some silly reason I kept hanging on. Realising time was moving on, I knew I had no option but to turn the bike round and start heading back. It had got very dark all of a sudden, and I realised that it was probably going to rain but I knew the ride back was always a lot quicker with more downhills than up, so hopefully I'd be back at the complex before it started.

No sooner had I turned the bike around than it started to rain. Had I not been in a hurry, I might have looked for a place to grab a little shelter till it past, but I was confident if I got my head down and really went for it, I could be back in the complex in fifteen minutes. As I climbed out of my saddle and started throwing my body weight down into each pedal to gather speed, I realised this was no normal rain shower. Within seconds the heavens had opened, even the stillness of the wind had changed. I could feel the rain pummelling my back as the rain hit me like it was coming from a power shower. I was lucky that it was coming from behind as the wind and rain were pushing me in the direction I needed to go – had it been head on, I might have chosen to seek refuge.

It wasn't long before I was completely drenched, soaked through to the skin which put paid to any ideas of stopping, there was just no point. Not only was my visibility poor but there was so much rain coming down that you couldn't tell the difference between the road and the pavement. As I approached a busier stretch of road, I saw that the few cars on the road had come to a halt, the rain was coming down so hard that their wipers were not able to clear the amount of water that was hitting their windscreens. This actually helped me realise the difference between the road and the pavement as I weaved my way between the stranded vehicles. I could see their headlights on full beam but none of them could see me. It was the weirdest cycle I'd ever been on, and still in my ears I could hear the muffled sound of music playing into my ears as I fought my way through this watery Armageddon.

Taking a left at the bottom of the road, I headed up towards the Oasis Village and past the Campanaro; to the right of me, up a long stretch of road, was the Atlantic Gardens and then the Oasis Dunas. All around me, cars were just stuck in their tracks as they had no visibility to move forward. Why I'd chosen this route I'll never know, as there was almost a river of water now running against me. Finally, when I got to the top of the road, I took a right at the Oasis Dunas and eventually made my way back to the hotel.

As I walked into our reception, pushing my bike and soaked through, everyone was laughing and cheering at my drowned rat appearance. Not to be outdone, I put my bike down, went into my DJ unit and grabbed my microphone. As I walked out onto the stage with a big smile on my face, I said, "If anyone's thinking about going out, please be careful, it's raining out there." Honestly, from our hotel down to the bottom of the high street it was like a running river, you'd have been better travelling down there in a canoe. The only good thing was that it was still warm.

I think that was the worst rainfall I witnessed over the years, but we certainly had our moments when it came to rainstorms. The majority of the time it was very dry and hot, but we always seemed to get caught out when the rain decided to turn up. No one was ever really prepared – many locals didn't even own a brolly or wellington boots, although most of us living on the island enjoyed a good rainstorm. The only downside was that it wasn't exactly what the holidaymakers were looking for.

Even though Fuerteventura is part of a group of islands sitting out in the Atlantic, we never had to concern ourselves with the very destructive hurricanes that the Americas had to endure. Fortunately for us, the trade winds would always push them from east to west, and of course the cooler winds that blow down from the north also helped our cause. But back in 2005 we were visited by an unusual tropical storm. We didn't have smart phones in those days so most of our weather reports would come from the news or local surfers in the know, especially the windsurfers as the wind is their bread and butter so to speak. I remember the rumours building up from the day before, there seemed to be a lot of excitement building. As is the way with these things, there's always a few people around who you just know to take everything they say with a pinch of salt. And yeah, I knew a few of these guys.

One of the young lads working in our bar at the time was a young and very enthusiastic lad called Frazer, he was a good enough guy but could get a little carried away with his excitement. He wasn't one for telling stories, but sometimes he could get carried away with the "ifs and buts" – the realities were always possible, just maybe a little improbable. So as he excitedly told me about this incoming storm, I lost a little of his enthusiasm knowing there was a good chance this wasn't going to amount to much. I'd been here before and had to listen to the excuses the day after when things didn't materialise.

So, on the big day, as I expected, things seemed to be pretty settled, although we were getting a strange warm wind blowing in from the southwest. As the day went on, this strange wind kept building and quite a few people gave up using their sunbeds as it was just uncomfortable trying to settle as these winds steadily grew stronger. As usual, I travelled home in the afternoon with the wind at my back. Once home, we were beginning to hear stories that the other islands were getting hit bad and that we were next in line. I wasn't sure what to do – should I stay safely in the house and just wait till it had all blown over, or should I head to work where I might be needed? I knew there was only one thing for it, I had to go up to work, my conscience got the better of me, all the other members of staff would be there, and I just knew it was the right thing to do, plus I had to go and make sure all the cats were safe.

As I made my way up to work, I could see that many of the businesses had not even bothered to open, the streets were very quiet apart from the wind that was now whipping its way across the town. Nicky and I struggled to keep in a straight line as we fought our way through this head-on blustery wind; loud cracks could be heard as signs were breaking off and crashing to the ground. It began to dawn on Nicky and myself that this was getting very serious   for once, Frazer had been right on the button and this was a proper storm, and it was still building in strength.

We finally got to the complex a little earlier than we would usually be there, but we knew it had been safer to leave for work before the storm hit full pelt. As we made our way through the reception doors, we could hear that the wind was howling through the hotel. They had closed the big windows that faced poolside which made sense as that was the direction that the wind was blowing from. Lara our receptionist was on the phone, looking back at me with a very worried look on her face. I thought it best to hang around and see what she had to say once she put the phone down, but she began pointing towards Inma's office, signalling for me to go straight in.

As I walked in, Inma had just put the phone down and looked at me and said, "It's not good." From what I could tell no one knew how bad it was going to get, all we could do was head out to the poolside and talk to the very busy maintenance guys and see if we could be any help. The whole bar area was surrounded by large glass windows and doors that were rattling loudly with the force of the wind. There were large gaps where you could hear the wind whistling through, and this looked even worse as the long curtains flailed in the wind. Large gusts of blustery wind were blowing hard against these large panes of glass, causing them to rattle and creak; we were beginning to worry about them shattering and breaking. There was no way we could have anyone sitting around the bar area, it was way too dangerous.

Eventually making our way out to the poolside terrace, we could see sunbeds lifting and levitating across the terrace. William, one of the maintenance men, was frantically trying to tie them down. All around the complex you could see worried faces peering through the windows of their apartments. Luckily for our south-facing apartments, they seemed to be missing the worst of it, but once we got round to what we called C block, we realised they were really bearing the brunt.

As Inma and I walked round, trying to avoid the debris, we could see that two large palm trees had blown over. One of the trees had gone over with such force that some of the branches, thick with foliage, had crashed through a window and got themselves wedged into an apartment while the rest of the tree rocked back and forth in the wind. Luckily it was near the end of November and the apartment was empty. It was still a frightening situation though, as darkness had set in really quickly and the wind seemed to have intensified. All around, we could hear things crashing and breaking, the wind seemed to be taking advantage of any little weakness it could find.

Travelling around the outer parts of the hotel we came across a tree that had a massive sheet of plastic pinned around it by this ferocious wind. We could see it was a sign from a mini-market that must have blown off and got caught up with the tree. The biggest worry was if this large plastic sign broke free from the tree and went flying it could potentially cut someone in half, and to make things worse, it would've have blown in the direction of our reception. Inma managed to contact our head of maintenance via the radio handset, and it didn't take him long to sort it. With great difficulty, he and his team were able to ingeniously form a wind break which took the pressure off the plastic sheet and then they were able to move it to a safer location.

After we had done everything we could do to secure as much as possible Inma said, "I think you and Nicky should go home now before it gets worse, or would you both rather stay here?" It didn't take us long to decide we would rather get back to the apartment – we knew the cats were probably frightened as they'd never experienced anything like this either, although hiding out in the bar did seem like a safer option. Nicky and I grabbed the bikes from my DJ unit and made our way out into the storm. The one thing we had in our favour was that the wind was at our backs so there was no need to waste energy cycling as the wind would take us in exactly the direction we wanted to be going.

As we made our way onto the main road, heading down towards the high street, all we could see was carnage, it was like a scene from a disaster movie. The air was thick with dust as signs from bars and shops were being strewn across the street. We could see that some of the larger signs from across the tops of bars had completely disappeared and a few were flapping in the wind, just waiting to break off. This was our main worry as we tried to get home in one piece without being taken out by flying debris.

Luckily with the wind at our backs it didn't take us long to get off the high street and away from the worst of the flying debris. I chose to go round by the harbour where there were fewer buildings. As we looked out towards the sea and onto Lobos in the distance, we could see all the moored-up boats rocking backwards and forwards, we were sure a few of them would disappear through the night. The sea had this weird effect where it looked like the waves that usually crashed up against the harbour wall were now being blown back out to sea.

As we left the harbour area we were now not far away from the apartment. In all the journey down the road we hadn't seen another living soul. Everyone else must have been already safely tucked away inside their apartments so it was great to get through the entrance of our complex and quickly indoors.

The small lamp in the bedroom was still on and the cats were huddled together on the bed; they all looked unfazed by what had been happening around them. In fact, it looked like we had just woken them up. The noise outside was still incredibly loud as the powerful wind screamed across the front of our apartment, and we could still hear the odd crash and wallop of something being destroyed on other people's terraces. We had just managed to get the cats fed when all of a sudden, the electricity went off. It wasn't really a surprise, I had been expecting it and had quite a few candles and matches prepared for what seemed inevitable.

We sat a little longer, listening to the wind surging very powerfully now and again, just keeping our fingers crossed that nothing came crashing through our apartment windows. As we sat staring into the flickering candle I couldn't help but realise how fragile life can be at times. We were lucky that there hadn't been any rain with the storm as this would've made things much worse and caused a lot more damage. And to think this was only a tropical storm – how on earth did people put up with force eight hurricanes? I mean, at this time of year it was quite normal for some people to start boarding up their windows for the oncoming storms, for them it was just a way of life.

The following morning everything had gone back to normal, it was a lovely sunny day, and it didn't take long for everyone to muck in together and get the whole place knocked back into shape. If anything, it was going to be a great talking point for a few days and a cracking story for all the holidaymakers to take home with them.

Another weather front we sometimes have to endure is when we get hit with a Calima; this is basically a dust bowl that seems to pick itself up from the Sahara Desert then blow over the Canary Islands. At its worst it can last for a week. This horrible orange dust is almost as fine as flour and seems to find its way into everything. Not only does it cover all the outside tables and chairs, all the cars and vehicles, and your terraces and windows, but you can't really go cycling or running because it gets into your lungs. In fact, a lot of older people usually stay indoors, away from this hazardous dust as it can make them very ill. It even turns all our lovely swimming pools a horrible orange colour and plays havoc with the water pumping systems. Some of the shops have got really clever and put air conditioning units just above the doors which helps stop the dust getting into the shops. Your clothes, bed sheets, everything gets contaminated with this pesky orange dust; bike chains, car engines, miscellaneous machinery – nothing seems to escape. It's no wonder the army never enjoyed having to fight desert warfare as it just brings everything to a clunking standstill. These Calimas can travel thousands of miles as this dust is carried with the winds.

Yes, I was glad that the weather had been great so far on this journey as it just made things so much easier, and although it had been hot, with air conditioning in the van it was something we didn't have to worry about. The major elephant in the room, or I should say the van, was that we had still not spoken about when and where we were going to stop. If we just kept going, I'd be quite happy with that, but surely that would never happen. I was sure we would have to stop somewhere, and with being tired, I wasn't sure if we had to be tested again for Covid before we crossed the French border.

The more I thought about it, the more confusing it seemed. Yup, it's all well and good knowing you've got ADHD but that doesn't exactly cure it, so as per usual I decided to push my worries to the back of my mind. I'd heard Jim speaking earlier to his wife on the phone, and I'm sure she had asked him where and when he was going to stop, but for the life of me I couldn't remember what his reply had been. Maybe he thought I knew where we were going to stop, maybe he wanted me to decide, maybe I'd make myself sound stupid if I asked.

Being really tired, these questions and more were making me worry. Once again I turned and looked at the dogs. They were looking relaxed and at peace. As long as these van wheels kept on turning at least we were moving closer to our destination, I said to myself. I felt a bit more settled, so I calmly asked, "Where are we now Jim?" I could see he was looking in his wing mirror as we were just overtaking a lorry with a tractor on board. "We're just about to make our way around Valladolid," he replied. I'll be honest, I didn't really know where that was, but I still went ahead and answered him, "Awww, great stuff," like I knew where we were going.

The road had got a little busier and I could actually see into part of the city, and to the left of me on Jim's side I could see what looked like vineyards. At that moment, Jim pointed out that these were the vineyards that produced the Ribera del Duero wine, which struck a chord with me as many a time we had bought bottles of this from our supermarket Hyperdinos. Wow, we were actually driving through "the land of the great Spanish wines".

Valladolid is the capital city of the autonomous community of Castile and Leon, an area where the rivers Pisuerga and Esgueva meet, and the hills on each side produce a collection of great wines. There were at least five or six different types of grapes grown there, producing some of Spain's finest wines, whether it be white, red or rose, the names were synonymous with quality. Names such as Ribera del Duero, Cabernet Sauvignon, Malbec, Rueda, Viura, Sauvignon blanc, Tierra de Leon, Tempranillo and last but not least Garnacha. And with so much of this gorgeous wine being exported, this area around Valladolid was bringing nearly six billion euros a year into the Spanish economy – yes, the wealth wasn't in Valladolid's beauty alone.

I was beginning to really understand why each city on our route was steeped in so much history, it didn't just happen by chance, the land and the rivers were literally goldmines when it came to the riches that they had given over the many hundreds of years. Now I realised why there were so many castles and cathedrals that had been graced by kings and emperors alike, it was paradise on earth. And although you can't miss its sheer beauty, the true wealth of this region seemed to go unnoticed, it was like the whole place was trying to protect its best-kept secret. It was so uplifting to be made aware of this place's greatness that my worries about the journey seemed to pale into insignificance. Despite my tiredness, my eyes were gazing out of the van in wonderment.

The road had quietened down again and there wasn't much in the way of traffic. I was still amazed at how clean and new all these roads seemed to be. The road signs above us were showing turn-offs to Santander and Bilbao and my heart lifted as I knew we must have travelled some distance as these places were truly in the north of Spain. We were headed for Burgos, but my head was still trying to think back to the last time I was in Santander.

Obviously, I hadn't been on this road before, but I must have passed through this area at some point I thought. Yeah, it would've been over forty years ago when my dad drove us from Santander to Alicante, then at the end of the holiday all the way back to Santander again – only this time, the shiny new car was covered in lots of dents from the hail stones. The one major thing I remember was my mum agreeing for the first time ever not to smoke in the car. Can you imagine that now in this day and age? Quite rightly, adults are now banned from smoking in the car with children. When I was younger, I used to suffer badly from car sickness. You would've thought if they'd put two and two together they would've have sussed out that my mum's smoking was probably contributing to my puking up all over myself and the car. And to add insult to injury, my dad didn't even smoke and had the audacity to warn us of the pitfalls of this filthy habit while my mum puffed away with not a care in the world.

Eventually the penny dropped, and Mum reluctantly agreed not to smoke while I was in the car. I remember her giving me these long dirty looks as if I was just doing it out of spite. I mean I almost felt guilty, why was I such a stupid loser, puking up on myself at the merest whiff of a fag and almost ruining my mum's holiday through my selfishness? I'm still susceptible to travel sickness on the odd occasion, sometimes if we used the bus in Fuerteventura it could leave me feeling terrible, but if I'm in a car and up front it seems to be no problem at all, and it had certainly been the last thing on my mind during this journey.

Again, the views were becoming more scenic as we made our way around Burgos; it was strange but every city we approached seemed to be trying to outdo the previous one. Yup, this was the capital of the autonomous community of Castile and Leon and could boast that it had been selected as the 2013 "Spanish Gastronomy Capital" by UNESCO. Even its cathedral was a World Heritage Site, and wherever you go in Burgos you'll come across historic churches that have catered for the needs of many of the Spanish monarchs over the years. And of course, there's the Abbey of Santa Maria la Real de Las Huelgas, a monastery that had been the site of many royal weddings both Spanish and foreign, including that of Edward Longshanks and Eleanor of Castile.

I am certainly not a fan of Edward the first of England, but I suppose it is important to realise how powerful he was in Europe. I certainly would have preferred it if he hadn't been kicking his way around my country of Scotland, his power was so great that he was able to convince the pope to extradite Scotland. That was until Robert the Bruce was able to get us back on side with a piece of historic genius that came in the form of "The Declaration of Arbroath".

Don't worry, I won't bore everyone by diving too deeply into Scottish history, but when it comes to learning, the University of Burgos is another fine place of educational excellence. This fabulous university has over eight thousand students and is world-renowned for its research quality and relationship with business. It's incredible how much universities excite me, and ironic that my own efforts at education left a lot to be desired, although I now realise that my undiagnosed ADHD probably played a large part in my educational failings.

Having said that, I feel in the future universities will have revolving doors, where people of all ages will come and go as they look to stay focused and prepared for a continually changing world. Okay lots of people now work and study online, but I still feel we need these institutions where people can interact with each other, this interaction helps inspire creativity. What's the old saying – "Birds of a feather flock together", yeah, having lots of good people working together can only produce great things.

If I've not already blown Burgos's trumpet loud enough it's worth mentioning that it has over ten museums with the most important ones being the Museum of Burgos, which explores the incredible history of the Provence of Burgos, and the Museum of Human Evolution, which is based at the archaeological site of Atapuerca. This is located twenty kilometres east of Burgos and has been designated a UNESCO Heritage Site, so it'll be no surprise to find out that it's the tenth most visited museum in Spain.

I had never imagined this journey was going to be this interesting. I was beginning to realise that I knew so little about Spain. I'd always kept up to date with things that were going on in Madrid regarding their football teams and their politics. I knew all about the very controversial and powerful dictator General Franco and remembered when they removed his body from the Valley of the Fallen. And coming from Scotland I was always watching what was going on in Barcelona with regards to the Catalans looking to break away. And of course, I knew all the different holiday locations all the way down the east coast where it was all long beaches, sunshine, villas, Bodega bars, Flamenco dancing and siestas. I mean, what more was there to know? But what I hadn't realised was that I actually knew next to nothing about this fabulous country. This journey was turning out to be a real education and I was thankfully learning a great deal more about Spain's deeply rich history, this living, breathing tapestry of its beauty and cultural past were the pillars of its very being.

Because this wasn't a commercial journey, Jim was able to relax a bit more and was not only my driver but my tutor as well, and I don't think he could've picked out a more historic route if he had tried. And it wasn't finished yet, we were now heading deep into the mountainous region of the Basque country. This was an autonomous community that had very strong cultural traditions, and the region was full of feisty industrious natives who were very proud of their history, and rightly so.

We were now driving across the bypasses around Vitoria. As the road began to carve its way through the mountains, parts of these rocky hillsides were literally arching over the roads. To the left of us was the Park Natural de Gobeia. You could see there was just a little cloud gathering around the mountain's peak, but it looked so clean and fresh, almost like some huge painting that had just come to life. The feeling of tiredness had left me for the time being as I was overcome with that feeling of euphoria that had obviously been brought on by these stunning views.

Every now and then we would pass through these small tunnels that would be like another entry post to even more spectacular views. Without asking, Jim would give out the relevant information as my eyes gazed out of the windscreen at the sights around me. It was like he was reading my mind as he pointed out all the places of interest while at the same time keeping me posted as to where we were headed.

We were approaching another hillside and I could see we were about to enter another tunnel. This was the longest of all the tunnels we had passed through, the Isuskitza tunnel, and was over three kilometres long. An amazing feat of engineering to say the least, it seemed a lot longer than it was as it took us a few minutes to travel the full length of the tunnel. I can remember it playing with my head, the very extreme change of views in such a short space of time – one minute we were cruising through very beautiful scenery, then within seconds we were travelling through a long and winding never-ending tunnel. In the distance we could see the light at the end of the tunnel fast approaching. As we were flung back out into the daylight, it was like someone with the flick of a switch had turned the dream back on. I could now see steep grassy slopes with tall beech trees higher up on the hills and Swiss-styled houses with their very prominent alpine designed roofs. You'd have been forgiven for thinking you had reappeared from the Isuskitza tunnel in the Swiss alps.

I could see a wry smile on Jim's face as he knew that I'd be blown away with this very impressive view. This was all part of the Aizkorri Aratz Natural Park, which was the second largest of its kind. It was easy to see why it was so popular with the mountaineering community with its limestone ridge and valleys and even higher summits which were reaching up to over 1600 metres. These very prominent ridges that pierced the skyline are littered with caves which archaeologists still spend a lot of time exploring as they try to piece together a lot of the forgotten early history of the area.

According to Basque mythology, legend has it that the goddess Mari can be seen travelling through this spiritual environment, moving from cave to cave. Mari is often seen as a woman dressed in red and is very much associated with changes in the weather as she travels through the mountains. When she is coming from the Antobo mountain in the west she seems to bring rain, but when she's living in the caves on the Aitxuri summit to the east she always brings the dry weather. I was rather taken aback when Jim told me that no one from the Spanish meteorological department had ever been to pay her a visit. What do I know? But it definitely might have been a good opportunity missed.

Still weaving our way through the hills, we could see shadows now as the sun was beginning to sink a little in the west and was hiding behind some of the surrounding mountains. Checking my watch I saw it was nearly quarter to six, I couldn't believe we had been driving for so long. The sun-parched landscapes of the south of Spain was well and truly behind us. I briefly thought about where we might be thinking about having a longer stop, but these thoughts soon passed, I knew it was easier for me just to not think about it.

Turning to check on the dogs I could see they were all sitting with their ears alert, almost as if they were enjoying the journey. I could only imagine that the fresh mountain air and the smells of rivers and trees were attracting their attention. At that, Jim shouted out that we were passing a place called Altamira where there was a cave that was famous for its magnificent prehistoric paintings and engravings. Considering these were over 36,000 years old, archaeologists were amazed not just at the quantity but also the quality of this polychromatic art. These caves are so important that they can't be visited anymore for conservation reasons, but replicas of this prehistoric gallery are situated not far from the original site.

It's funny but just as my mind would begin to ponder the potential pitfalls of the journey Jim would break my train of thought with lots of interesting information on the surrounding areas. And just seeing everything in my view I seemed to not only be taking on board everything he said, but I was feeling so in tune with it all. There was some sort of clarity shining through that had me electrified to everything around me – the history, the mountainous landscape, the very fresh clean air that was coming in through my window, it was all so intoxicating.

I knew within myself I was going through another hyperfocus euphoria moment, but hey, moments like this don't come along very often. It felt like if I jumped out of my side window I would've just flown alongside the van like a bird. In a weird and strange sort of way I felt like I was already home, especially with that scenic masterpiece in front of me which was not dissimilar to the Trossachs in the west of Scotland. This was the most positive I had felt during the whole journey and even with all that I had still to endure regarding the rest of the journey, there was a feeling of hope that seemed to encase me like a suit of armour.

It was obvious Harry was now wide awake and trying to tell us something as he had started barking really loudly. For a biggish Yorkshire terrier his bark was loud and powerful. Before I could say anything, Jim shouted out to him, "Don't worry fella, we're going to be stopping shortly." It was now after six o'clock and it had been nearly three hours since we had last stopped. Thankfully Harry had decided to stop barking as Jim's good news seemed to have worked. I was looking forward to getting out and stretching my legs and feeling so tired, I knew I needed another of those large coffees.

"Is it far from here Jim?" I asked. "No, not far at all, we can get freshened up, and grab something to eat as we're not going to be too far from our next toll." I could tell by his answer that he knew exactly where we were, and it hadn't escaped me that he mentioned the word "toll". I knew we were in the very north of Spain and couldn't help thinking that we couldn't be too far from the border crossing. I was dying to ask him how far that was, but I let it slide – no doubt he would tell me as soon as we got close.

It was only a matter of minutes till Jim put on his indicator as we began to pull into a petrol station, not that there seemed to be much need for the indicator as the roads had really quietened down again. The service station was laid out very neatly as we pulled up in front of the café part; further to our left was the petrol station.

With it being early evening now the place looked very picturesque. We were still surrounded by hills and woodland and looking beyond the café I could see that we were just above a small town. With my spirits lifted I turned to tell Harry he was about to go for a walk. Jim suddenly interrupted me before I could speak. "Just be a little bit careful, there are sometimes a few dodgy people around here. They can steal stuff from the cars and there's even been a few muggings." Well I didn't expect that. I looked around me – all of a sudden, this picturesque little watering hole had turned into something else. Just to reassure myself Jim meant what he said, I said, "It seems really quiet here at the moment though Jim," hoping he might agree. "Yeah, they come up from the small town down below the petrol station so just keep your eyes on the van." Trying to remain cool I quicky said, "Yeah, no hassle Jim."

As usual I got out of the van and went straight round to get Harry out first. Although it was a little bit cooler, it still seemed warm with no breeze at all. You could hear the odd bits of traffic passing the petrol station but apart from that it was all very quiet. Had Jim not said anything I would've been really happy and settled but now, getting Harry out of the van, my eyes were suspiciously scouring the area for any possible assailants getting in and out of cars or doorways. Yes, I hadn't added this into the equation of things that could go wrong during the journey – the possibility of getting mugged or the van being robbed as we were parked up at a petrol station. From a picturesque leafy little service station it had now turned into a desperadoes' hang-out in the middle of bandit country.

None of this of course had affected Harry, who happily bounced out of the back of the van full of the joys of spring, ears up and ready to go. He was dragging me away from the van ready to go exploring this newfound land with its fresh exotic smells. Harry's enthusiasm certainly helped to take my mind off the imminent danger that could befall us at any time.

On getting Harry back to the van it was Charlie's turn. He too seemed in fine fettle and was enjoying his new surroundings as he kicked his way through some fallen leaves, sniffing at all these things he'd never experienced before, but always picking up on Harry's scent, peeing and pooing in the same place. Feeling much more relaxed, I got Charlie back to the van, refilled his dishes like I'd done with Harry before him and lifted him back into his cage.

Now I only had Evie to take for a walk. Once I had done that, I would go and get something to eat and grab one of those large coffees I so desperately needed to keep me awake. Just as I got Evie out of her cage, a white unmarked van pulled into the service station and decided to park right next to us. "Why so close?" I thought, it was quiet and there were loads of parking places. "Did you really need to park so close?"

Without thinking, I stared into the van. I could see there were around four blokes in there. "Shit!!" I thought. "If this goes wrong, I'm desperately outnumbered." To make things worse it was ages since I'd watched any action movies so I hadn't any memories of how to deal with two or more attackers. It was important I didn't react too quickly, hopefully my natural survival instincts would take over. Evie and I kept walking as they all left the van. Only two went into the café while the other two leaned against the van laughing and chatting. At that moment, I saw Jim coming out with his drink and what looked like sandwiches and climbing into the driver's seat. Well at least that was one less thing to worry about – they couldn't steal the van with Harry and Charlie as there was no way they'd get past Jim.

Evie and I took the same route as Harry and Charlie did and, like clockwork, she stopped in all the same places, so it was time to make our way back to the van. I could see all four of the occupants of the other van were all back outside again. From what I could see of the guys, I presumed they were locals who had just finished work by the way they were dressed, they certainly didn't look like tourists. As I got closer to the van, I could see they weren't paying too much attention to me or Evie. I mean I'm sure they wouldn't see us as much of a threat – me, five foot eight on a tall day, balding with grey hair holding on to a cute small Yorkshire terrier. Thankfully nothing transpired and I was able to get Evie's water dish filled and her safely back into her cage. These guys didn't know how lucky they were that nothing had kicked off – Evie and I might not have looked much of a force to be reckoned with, but little did they know that I could have swung Evie still attached to her lead around my head like a furry mace. It would've meant utter devastation for these guys. Without realising it, these four blokes had really dodged a bullet that day.

I was glad to eventually use the toilets in the service station, which were very clean and well maintained. Although it was only prepacked sandwiches I was buying, they seemed fresh enough considering the time of day. And of course, not forgetting Evie who had given up eating her biscuits and was costing me a fortune in extra sandwiches which I was having to peel apart and pull out the fresh chicken and throw the rest to the birds. And last but not least, the most important thing I could get my hands on – the extremely large coffee that I had now become so dependent on.

As we got moving again, I questioned Jim in more detail about some of the goings on at the service station and where these dodgy people were coming from. It turns out that the town at the back of the service station was Hernani; what we were seeing was just the outskirts of the town and some of the more undesirable elements found this isolated service station easy pickings. What Jim hadn't mentioned to me at the time was that this happened less frequently now, as a long, high fence had been erected just below the service station which stopped anyone entering from the back, while at the same time blocking any quick escape route. I suppose it's always better to be safe than sorry, but I'm sure I'd have been a little less excitable had I known about the fence at the back of the service station.

With Jim, me and the dogs all fed and watered we carried on down the road. I was still hanging onto my large coffee and trying to drink it as fast as I could, I knew we were not too far away from some big moments in this journey, and I certainly wanted to be wide awake for them. Our next stop would be to go through another toll and then I imagined our next one would be heading towards the border with France.

Because I was all psyched up and fully charged with that strong hit of caffeine running through my veins, I promised myself I'd ask Jim more about how far we were away from the border control post and what I needed to have prepared. I had my file with all the appropriate paperwork just under my seat, so I quickly grabbed it and had a check through. First of all, the three dogs' passports, all with their rabies jabs and wormer stamps; on top of that, their fit to travel form.

I quickly turned around to look at the back of the seat to make sure the muzzles were there. That was the bit I was dreading – it was less than three days ago I was dripping blood on the vet's floor after failing miserably to get Charlie's on. I kept visualising that being the part where it all goes horribly wrong, once one of them kicks off they all go. Again I'm thinking about *Butch Cassidy and the Sun Dance Kid* where our two hapless heroes are gunned down in a blaze of glory, or even *The Godfather* where Sonny is assassinated at the Long Beach Causeway toll and his car is peppered with bullets. I could imagine everyone talking about it in Corralejo as we make the headlines. I know Harry and Charlie can look quite ferocious when they're snarling at their worst, but Evie? Maybe her little photo in the papers would earn her the nickname Babyface.

"Enough," I thought to myself. I started checking my own paperwork was okay – my passport, my document to say I had been double jabbed, and my French entry form. We had been constantly listening to the news and as far as we could make out there hadn't been any changes, the only problem could be if the customs officers wanted us to show them an updated Covid test which had been required only weeks earlier. And how could we forget Brexit – would they look upon us differently now? I could always tell them I personally preferred being part of Europe, but I still imagined some French customs officer looking down on me, saying, "Yeah, we've heard that one before" as he refused to let me cross the border. Yup, I was doing a great job of winding myself up. I quickly tried to remind myself that not thinking about it at all was the best way forward – how did the song go? "Que sera, sera", "Whatever will be, will be".

It was not long after seven o'clock and the roads were very quiet. I was still surprised that during most of the journey we hadn't really seen much in the way of heavy traffic; the only time it had got busy was as we were pulling out of the port at Cadiz. With less traffic on the road, it must have made it so much easier for Jim and with it being that bit more of a relaxed journey it must have made it a little less tiring. One thing I did do was make sure Jim didn't have any of the hassles of looking after the dogs. I wanted him to only have to worry about himself with this long drive and that included me not talking incessantly. The only problem was that while I thought I'd been doing a good job of keeping quiet, Jim might be of a different opinion.

It wasn't long before Jim pointed out that we were coming to the next toll. I could see it up ahead, there were a lot of gates for lots of traffic going both ways but only two of them seemed to be open. This was no surprise as the traffic had been so light. As we pulled up to the toll, we could see no one was actually in the booth taking money so Jim had to just feed the money into the machine himself.

As I looked to the right of me, I could see what looked like four policemen standing chatting and having a laugh. I didn't recognise their uniforms, I could only surmise they were traffic cops. "Look ahead, don't stare at them," Jim said to me. At first, I thought that was a slight over reaction from Jim. I've seen police before and I can usually spot if they look menacing or not, and I could definitely tell these guys were quite relaxed.

Jim pulled away from the toll and as I looked back at the police officers it dawned on me that they weren't actually Spanish at all. As I quickly turned my head to look ahead of me, I could see the signs above were for French towns. Very slowly I said to Jim, "Have we just gone across the French border?" Not hearing anything coming from Jim, I turned my head again to see him grinning like a Cheshire cat. We had done it!! We had crossed the French border. I felt as though I'd just won the World Cup.

I turned to look at the dogs who were just sitting staring back at me. They obviously didn't have a clue, but to me it was massive. It was one of the biggest worries I'd had about the whole journey. The money we'd had to spend on bits of silly paper had all been for nothing, but I didn't care – we were over the border and that was all that mattered. The countless times I'd gone through the paperwork just to make sure we had everything we needed. I could still hear Nicky's voice in my head saying, "Make sure you've got everything you need."

I turned to Jim again and it was then that I realised that he'd known we were coming not only to a toll gate, but to the border crossing as well. The four what I thought were police officers were actually customs officers, and Jim had known all along. I was smiling from ear to ear – it was a massive weight off my mind. Jim told me that he had decided a while back not to keep me posted on the border crossing, he knew there was a good chance we would get through quite smoothly so he thought he would surprise me. Well surprise wasn't the word for it – I was ecstatic. All the mad visions of border shootouts had thankfully been a complete waste of time. I hadn't told Jim about my worries about the border crossings, but he could tell I wasn't looking forward to it. One thing was for sure, no one would hear my mad ideas about the dogs possibly ending up in a shootout, thankfully, as I don't think anyone would believe me.

Yes, things were going really well, and I was still cock-a-hoop and feeling a great deal more relaxed after the very successful border crossing. Things couldn't have gone any better. And on top of that, I was still feeling awake from that strong coffee I'd only finished about twenty minutes earlier. Not being able to contain my excitement I had to phone Nicky and let her know we had crossed the border with no hassle whatsoever.

Nicky was over the moon but sounded concerned at the same time. "I can't believe you've crossed the border already, haven't you stopped anywhere?" she asked. "Yeah, I had the dogs out of the van not long before we crossed the border." I knew that wasn't exactly what she was asking and that I was using my tried and tested avoidance tactics. I was nervously looking over at Jim and smiling, hoping he couldn't hear what Nicky was asking. The truth was, I didn't know what to say to Nicky. I know there had been earlier discussions about spending a night in a hotel in Spain, but that plan seemed to have got lost during the duration of the journey.

Before that could become the main part of our conversation, I excitedly told Nicky how good Harry had been and that I was happy to report that all the dogs were fine. I didn't mention about me having to dissect sandwiches for Evie – the last thing I wanted to do was to worry her. I did manage to turn the phone towards Harry and asked him to say hello to Nicky. "Harry, Harry, say hello to Nicky," I said, and thankfully he obliged by starting to bark loudly. Because of all the noise this was a good cue for me to end the call. I promised I'd message her later and keep her posted about our progress. Even though the call was quite brief, Nicky would've been able to tell by the way I was speaking that things were going well, and on top of that, hearing Harry barking in his usual excitable fashion would really have given her peace of mind.

Yes, I definitely felt more positive. Crossing that border in the way we did was a real milestone in the journey; now that was out of the way we could really focus on the road ahead. Realistically we still had over a thousand miles before we came to the end of this incredible adventure. With still loads of pit stops to make, dual carriageways and motorways to cross, another ferry journey and more customs officers to meet there was still a lot that could go wrong. But even the thought of all this couldn't dampen my spirits and I was once again quizzing Jim as to our whereabouts, and as always, Jim was happy to oblige.

Even though we were still in Basque country we were now in part of the Pyrenees, or the Pyrenees Atlantiques to be precise. To the west of us was the Bay of Biscay, and although it was beginning to get slightly dark you could still see these glorious mountain tops off to the east. It was over sixty-five million years ago that the Iberian and Eurasian plates collided to create the Pyrenees mountains, a range containing just over 19,000 named mountains, the highest of which was just over 3400 metres.

Straddling the border of France and Spain this incredible mountain range covers nearly five hundred kilometres between the Mediterranean coast and the area we had recently travelled through, the Cantabrian mountains. The Pyrenees is also renowned for having a diverse biosphere and this was being cleverly protected by designating most of the area as natural parks and reserves. Very much like the Swiss Alps, Andorra is a very popular resort for skiing and has become even busier with the growing popularity of snowboarding. Quite a few people I know sometimes choose to escape the sunnier climes of Fuerteventura for some hardcore downhill snowboarding during the wintertime, and rather than spend a fortune travelling all the way to the Alps, there's a far more affordable option in travelling to Andorra. Not only is it closer, which helps reduce their travel costs, but the very high standard of accommodation is better priced. Also, being a landlocked sovereign microstate in the heart of the Pyrenees, it has tax haven status which is great for duty free. I didn't get this little bit of information from Jim but from my good friends Shaun and Sally. Yeah, I must admit these guys have it pretty good. When they're not mountain biking round some of the most beautiful parts of the island they're taking advantage of some of the world's best beaches. Shaun was always a very keen windsurfer and surfer; Sally is slightly different, although she does enjoy swimming, she much prefers basking in the sun while lying down on her beach towel so it doesn't blow away.

But the Pyrenees is not just about lofty snow-covered peaks and skiing, with such an extensive area to explore there's a network of hiking trails that can lead you around some of the extinct volcanoes. Some of the walks will take you through long stretches of forests that may be broken up by waterfalls with such clear water that it can sparkle in the sunlight, or long fast-flowing rivers that carve their way through the beautiful mountainsides. And for people like me who love their bikes, there are cycling tours that can take you the full length of the Pyrenees from the Mediterranean Sea to the Atlantic Ocean. Although personally, I'd prefer to be off road using my mountain bike to hurtle along the narrow paths that cut their way through the breath-taking beauty, an endless journey through paradise that I imagine must go on for miles.

With the Pyrenees being such a vast area, there are also quite a few small medieval towns tucked away that have charming boutique hotels or log cabins that offer self-catering accommodation. Most of these villages have wonderful restaurants that not only have fantastic views from their tables but menus that reflect the warmth and the culture of the Pyrenees, whether it be fresh fish from the many rivers or the sumptuous meaty dishes.

I don't know if it was just the excitement of getting through that border crossing so easily, but my head was filled with the notion that I'd have to return to some of the areas we had just driven through and of course somehow I'd have to bring my trusty mountain bike. I couldn't just spend a few weeks either, it would probably take months to visit all these historic cities, staying in their prestigious hotels and sampling all that fabulous food they had to offer in their many restaurants. And then there was the cycling through the Europa mountains, all the national parks we had crossed and let's not forget losing myself somewhere happily in the Pyrenees mountains. Yeah, although I was obviously getting carried away, it was helping me get through this long journey and I must admit I genuinely hoped that I might do it all one day.

15

We were now heading along France's famous A63, affectionally known as the "French wild west". This was a lengthy stretch of motorway that was the main heavy goods artery between Portugal and western Spain, taking lots of containers filled with all sorts into France and the rest of northern Europe. Lorries are no longer meant to drive on autoroutes during the weekend, which is a bonus for holidaymakers as they are making their way back and forth between destinations. However, it does mean that on Mondays it can become a little more congested with even more HGVs catching up on their enforced weekend stop.

I didn't like the sound of this; although we were on a three-lane motorway, the idea of us becoming bogged down in heavy traffic due to the increased amount of large artic lorries made my heart sink a little. I think Jim could sense my disappointment. "Don't worry," he said. "It doesn't look too bad to be honest, and remember, most of it will have passed through earlier this morning." Even better I thought. "Yeah, these guys would've been up and at it at the crack of dawn." I then realised that we had been getting off the ferry at Cadiz on Monday morning and it was now Monday evening – it suddenly dawned on me how long we had been travelling and how far we had come. Because of the tiredness, my perception of time had certainly become jaded to say the least. Saturday morning's loading of the van with bags and dogs seemed a lifetime ago, but in the same breath, paradoxically it only felt like it was five minutes ago. I couldn't get my head round it all, but as far as I could remember, we should be rolling into Bridlington sometime on Wednesday afternoon.

The more I thought about it, the more confused I became.

Obviously the only way I could get the answer to my conundrum was to ask Jim but I couldn't as I'd only make myself sound stupid, and sure as fate, I wouldn't understand what he was trying to explain to me anyway. Having ADHD and being extremely tired was as bad a mix as you could get, so I opted for my usual tried and tested option – let it slide, forget about it, think about something else.

We were still travelling along the A63 at a steady pace but now drawing closer to the capital of the southwest of France, Bordeaux; with its exceptional eighteenth-century architecture it had acquired the nickname little Paris. For once this was a place Jim didn't have to tell me about as I had been here way back in 1981. It was the last family holiday we all had together. Yup, me, Mum and Dad, Michael and Kenneth; it was strange really, as I was still living with my parents at the time but was at the age where I was hardly ever at home. I can't even remember why I decided to go on holiday with them as I was eighteen and fairly independent in my thinking; maybe even back then I had the foresight to realise it would probably be the last thing we would do collectively as a family.

My dad had booked the holiday through an advert placed in the *Sunday Observer*; some minister had a house for rent in a small but picturesque village called Cadouin very near to the Dordogne River. I didn't have a clue why my dad had chosen this place, in fact I didn't know anything about the area at all, so I obviously didn't have a clue what to expect, and it's worth remembering there was no world wide web to help you check places out in those days. But my dad knew exactly where he was going; he loved French food and was becoming a self-proclaimed connoisseur of all the best French wines.

Once the car was all packed up, we were off, from Kinghorn all the way down to Plymouth, then the ferry over to Le Havre; once at Le Havre we had to drive by where a lot of the D-Day landings were. I remember that as we passed this spot, I had my Sony Walkman on and was listening to "Here Comes the Sun" by the Beatles. No free

Wi-Fi, Apple Music or Spotify in these days, no iPods or MP3 players either, it was just my trusty battery-run Sony Walkman.

Having five of us in the car plus all our cases and stuff meant there wasn't a lot of room for much else. As nice and spacious as the car was, a lovely metallic blue Rover, there was certainly no room for any more clutter. So I decided to only take three double-sided tapes, and cleverly only two boxes as there would always be one tape in the Walkman. So I had Rush "Farewell to Kings" (even to this day probably one of my favourite albums) and on the other side another highly acclaimed Rush album called "Moving Pictures", next it was the Beatles "Help!" and "Abbey Road" and the other tape was Hawkwind's "Quark, Strangeness and Charm" and on the other side "Hawklords Twenty-Five Years On". I can imagine some of you will probably only recognise the Beatles.

On top of this small but weird eclectic collection of music I also had JRR Tolkien's classic *Lord of the Rings* to read. As I mentioned earlier, I suffered from car sickness so there was no way I could read anything till we finally arrived at our destination. In honesty, my memories of the journey are not great, I just remember fantastic views and the music, especially "Hawklords Twenty-Five Years On". It's certainly not an album that would ever get into my top one hundred, but I still play it every now and again and I'm sure I still feel the same weird emotions I had when I was sitting in the car all those years ago. Even though I can't remember exactly what I was thinking about at the time, I can still remember how I was feeling, another ADHD fuelled paradox I suspect.

Sitting in a car with my dad was great – wherever we went, he'd either been there many years before or he had read up on it. So if we were driving along and we pointed something out, more times than not my dad would have an answer for it. I always trusted him because if he didn't know about something I pointed out he'd always say, "Sorry, I'm not so sure about that son, I'll need to look that up." He wasn't interested in making things up, it was always important for him to find out the facts.

My dad wasn't just a member of one library, he was a member of about three or four, so there were always piles of books next to his side of the couch or bed and of course he would always bring about three with him on holiday so our trip to the Dordogne had been meticulously planned out. His love of French cuisine had been reinforced by his admiration for the Roux brothers Michel and Albert, and it wasn't long till my dad started trying his own hand at cooking and became quite adapt; the only downside was I'd always get the job of cleaning up behind him – words like, "here take this", "get me a spoon", "watch out, that's bloody hot" and "here, wash this for me" still echo around my head to this day.

So it was no surprise that he picked this quaint little village that was tucked away at the bottom of a valley right in the heart of the Bessede Forest and of course in the middle of all the greatest wine regions. Cadouin itself was beautiful; right in the heart of the village was a masterpiece of religious architecture, the Cistercian Medieval Abbey. For such a diminutive town, the abbey had some incredible stories to tell; at some point in its early history, it actually came into possession of what was believed to have been the facecloth from the tomb of Christ. So, as you can imagine this made Cadouin Abbey an important place of pilgrimage and wealth, but the wars of the thirteenth and fourteenth centuries brought about a dramatic collapse in the number of pilgrimages. Then what really finished it off was the French Revolution when all its rich possessions were looted, and its library burnt to the ground. Spookily enough, when we were there the new library stood in the square where the original had been so maybe not all was lost.

The countryside was just gorgeous – very green and surrounded by forests. Being so low in the valley, there was never any cool breeze to talk of but thankfully, a short walk from where we were staying was the Chabrol lake, so most days, if we were not out in the car, we would be off swimming. Now, usually in Scotland, our lochs (lakes) would be freezing cold as the water that kept replenishing them would run down from the hills. But this lake was very sheltered from any breeze and was caught in a sun trap which seemed to keep the water very warm. The Chabrol was also a popular spot for the locals to go fishing but being just a quiet village not once did we come across anyone else using it for swimming or for fishing. We had an open grass bank to sit on and bask in the sun with the other three sides of the lake covered with trees.

All the houses in town seemed to be built with the local stone so everything just blended in nicely together, whether it be the town square or the Cistercian Abbey. The streets were never busy, it was always so quiet. Yes, we would see the odd tourist visiting the abbey or strolling around taking pictures but I'm sure we were the only people on holiday actually staying in the town.

The house in Cadouin that we had rented had three different floors and although on three different levels, the rooms were very small with low, beamed ceilings. You could tell by just looking at the house that it was hundreds of years old. As you entered the front door you were welcomed by this huge boar's head; we all found it really amusing and used to hang the door keys on one of its large tusks. It was no wonder these animals were regarded as being fiercely dangerous as that massive head was just full of strong teeth; if it had come charging out of the woods at you when you weren't expecting it, it could knock you clean over then just rip you to bits. In fairness to the boar, it's not something you hear of happening very often. In fact, they are only really dangerous when they're protecting their young but looking up at that old boar head it was certainly not something you'd like to meet on a dark night. Running at full pelt, these gruesome looking creatures can reach speeds of up to twenty-five miles an hour – imagine hearing something like that moving at speed through the forest, grunting loudly as the noise of it crashing through the forest drew ever nearer.

The house smelled a little musty with small windows set into really thick walls, all adorned with long curtains made from thick material. All the furniture was made from solid wood, with the couches covered in fabric that had seen better days. My dad was quick to point out (jokingly) that he was sure he had seen similar things going for a fortune on *The Antiques Roadshow*. Although doubles, the beds in each of the rooms were very short in length and were probably at least a few hundred years old. The shared bathroom was great – it was the same size as the bedrooms and had a bath which was almost big enough to swim in.

The most modern thing in the house was the old gas stove in the kitchen although that too had seen better days. Right next to it was one of those deep old sinks which had an old-fashioned wringer attached to it. But most importantly, everything was functional, everything worked, the house, although extremely old, was spotlessly clean and felt really homely, even down to the bed linen – white sheets with heavy feather-filled quilts and large comfortable pillows.

The back garden was just outside the kitchen and was a masterpiece, all handmade rockeries with flowerbeds and trees. At the very bottom of the garden was a very comfortable swinging chair which was suspended by thick strong ropes and hung close to a small waterfall that led down to a little river that ran all the way through the town.

This became my favourite spot and I spent most of my time there reading my book; I could hardly believe it when I actually managed to read all of *The Lord of the Rings*, but it was such a perfect setting for it. This was a massive achievement for me, not only to actually complete reading a whole book but *The Lord of the Rings* which had well over a thousand pages, and to do it in under three weeks. Admittedly, I became engrossed in it, whether late at night in that ancient old bedroom, or sat in that idyllic spot in the garden, I felt I was almost there in the shires with them. If you've never read the book, it's a classic – a group of strange people, elves and hobbits, who are reluctantly thrown together and take on a task of epic proportions where failure is just not an option, no less they have to save their world from consummate evil. Most people will be familiar with the films that smashed box office records at the time of release, but the book is so much darker and more frightening at times, especially on your own in such a perfect setting and with me in a fully charged ADHD hyperfocus state of mind I just couldn't put it down.

One early evening my brother Michael and I decided to go outside at the front of the house to have a little kick about with a football; the house was tucked in off the main road which to be honest was never busy anyway. It was like an old courtyard with old but smaller houses to the opposite side of ours, so there was plenty of room for us to kick a ball around; it was very quiet, and it didn't seem like we had any neighbours to annoy so we were not causing any trouble. It was only just after half past six in the evening when we began to notice flashes in the sky just to the south of us behind the hills. There did seem to be a bit of cloud coming over which was helping to darken the sky, and there was no breeze at all.

Michael and I decided to stop kicking the ball as we were more interested in watching what was obviously lightning. "Brilliant," I excitedly shouted to Michael, "it's definitely getting closer." Slowly but surely the sky got even darker, then all of a sudden, a bright flash happened right above our heads and straightaway there was the loudest roar of thunder I've ever heard. Without any hesitation both Michael and I ran into the house. Michael got in first as I had gone back to pick up the ball; just as I was approaching the door the rain started and massive droplets of water bounced off my head. As I rushed into the house laughing I could see my mum also rushing in, only she was coming in from the back door; she had been a little less fortunate than me and she was shaking the water from her head as she had been caught in the rainfall trying to do her best to gather up the clothes that had been left airing outside.

Both Michael and I ran past the boar's head and bolted up the stairs, quickly racing into the bedroom. We both dived towards the small window, this was a lightning show we were certainly not going to miss. Michael and I could both see it was really dark as we were relying on the old lamppost where we had just been playing football to keep us focused on the street outside. With it getting so dark I put on the little lamp at the side of my bed that I used for reading and repositioned myself at the window with Michael so we could both enjoy the lightning storm.

Well, it certainly didn't disappoint! Simultaneously there was a double flash and deafening bangs that seemed to light up the whole sky. As bright as it was, everything seemed to be in black and white; it was so loud and bright that Michael and I were frozen to the spot in shock. As the flash which had gone on for ages disappeared, we were left in darkness, and all we could hear was the rain lashing the ground and trees outside.

There was another double flash with an almighty rumble of thunder that sounded like a plane was crashing into the house; you could almost feel the whole building shake. The lamppost outside went out and the lights in the house were all off. In the background we could hear my youngest brother Kenneth crying as the rain lashed even harder outside. It was becoming noticeably clear that this wasn't fun anymore. Michael and I were scared witless. We could hear my mum and dad down the stairs but there was no way we were going into that dark hallway to go down the stairs. This quaint old house had just turned into the creepiest old building you could ever imagine. It was like something out a horror movie – every time another flash went off you just didn't want to look around for fear of what you might see.

Thankfully my mum and dad came shuffling up the stairs with Kenneth. Being on the ball as usual, my dad had managed to find a stash of candles and we all huddled in the one room. Now that everyone was together our anxiety started to ease up as my dad stated the obvious: "Christ, that's some bloody storm." But he did point out that because we were in the bottom of a valley the thunder would sound so much louder as the noise would reverberate off the surrounding hills and literally roll along the valley like an echo chamber.

As usual, my dad took it all in his stride, he was always so philosophical about everything, there was always a logical reason as to why things happened the way they did, and in fairness he did actually help to calm us all down. But I must admit it was a really frightening experience, not only do I have an ADHD-fuelled vivid imagination, but I'd been reading my *Lord of the Rings* book which I'm sure contributed to my panic.

Next morning I woke up in my bed, the sun shining in through my bedroom window – yes, I'd woken up in my quaint little house again. It was almost like the night before had just been a bad dream. I didn't even remember falling asleep or when the storm had finished. Just across the room I could see Michael was still fast asleep and at the bottom of his bed was the football we had been playing with just before the storm had started.

Arguably Bordeaux is the most famous wine region in France, so it was no mistake that my dad had picked this area as our holiday destination; okay, it was still a good drive from Cadouin to Bordeaux, but we were right in the heart of some of the most famous French vineyards and my dad was going to do his level best to visit as many of them as possible. I didn't mind going out in the car as I always enjoyed listening to my music as we passed through all the beautiful countryside and along the wonderful Dordogne River. But I found it was becoming more of a habit that I would take off my earphones while I was in the car so I could properly focus on the surrounding beauty of the place. There were just so many places where you wanted to stop and spend time just to take in these breath-taking views. And it wasn't just the river itself, there were so many beautiful villages and market towns up and down the Dordogne to visit. It comes as no surprise that so many people from the UK would eventually come to live here and make it their home – it was the second most popular place to live behind Paris and you only had to look around to understand why.

Now as the van was driving past Bordeaux my mind was thinking about that last holiday. I couldn't forget how the Dordogne had left such an impression on me, I can still remember wondering if I'd ever see the place again – little did I know that over forty years later I'd be driving past it in a van with someone I'd only known a few days and three of my dogs.

The excitement of crossing the French border had dissipated and my mind was now thinking about the rest of my family in Kinghorn. It was incredible the years that had passed since that holiday, and that Michael, Kenneth and my mum and dad were still living in Kinghorn. Then there was me, forever bouncing from pillar to post, never knowing where I was going or what I was going to do. I was starting to feel sad, slightly lost and a little sorry for myself.

My mind drifted back to the second last night of our holiday in Cadouin when we had all gone for a meal in a local restaurant. It seemed quite small and was quite noisy – there was a long table which was full of local French people who were all happy and enjoying each other's company, they didn't seem to notice us. My dad picked a table farther back into the restaurant, next to the window which gave us a nice view onto the square outside.

Already in the middle of the table was a huge bottle of red wine. At first my dad thought it might just be there for decoration but a waitress walked up to the table, handed us our menus and without asking turned over our glasses and started to fill them with the wine; the bottle was so big and heavy that she had to hold it with both hands. At first this startled my dad – yeah, he was going to order wine but he was confused as to why she would start pouring wine from a bottle that we hadn't asked for. The girl smiled and said in her broken English, "Ahhh, don't worry, this wine comes with the table. If you want other wine you need to buy it from the menu." This really amused my dad. "Christ, that's not bad free wine," he said laughingly as my mum turned the bottle around to show it was actually a two-litre bottle.

Just to make sure nothing was lost in translation my mum asked the waitress again, in French this time, to make sure that this incredibly large bottle wasn't going to be on the bill. The waitress reassured us again in her broken English that the wine came with the table, it was actually wine that was made by the restaurant owner and he was happy for his customers to drink it. Well that was certainly a good start to the evening! Now it was just down to my mum to translate everything on the menu.

It was fairly obvious that most of the stuff seemed fairly inexpensive and with it being the second last night of the holiday my dad was certainly not hanging about. We ordered little bits of this, and little bits of that, extra portions of this and extra portions of that – there was certainly plenty to go around, and of course my dad was pretty impressed with the wine list so he picked a few bottles of Bergerac Cabernet Sauvignon. This was actually one of the vineyards we had visited a few days earlier. All in all it turned out to be an absolute feast. There's nothing better than going into a good restaurant when you are really hungry and being able to eat as much as you want – and it didn't stop any of us picking from the dessert menu. It was just a wonderful night and everyone had a great time. It wasn't lost on me how happy everyone was, in fact I'd probably not heard all the family laugh as much as I did that night.

Yeah, for that night alone I was glad I went on that last holiday. Looking back I remember that things around my family weren't always great, especially with my mum and her problems, and our lack of knowledge in how to deal with it. Everyone would just bury their heads in the sand and hope it would all go away, or that some sort of miracle would happen and everything would be alright again. Even with all the things that had happened over the years between then and now, it was still really hard to compute.

Sitting there staring out of the van I found myself thinking about things I hadn't thought about in years. I was finding it disorientating, a strange feeling. Of course, I was really tired, it had been a long day travelling, but it was the same little feelings that had crept up on me every now and again over the years. It's difficult to put into words, but I felt disenfranchised from everything – my family all living in Kinghorn, Nicky happy with her family in Bridlington, and me in the middle of nowhere feeling completely insecure about the future.

It's really hard to explain what was going through my head, but it felt like I was sitting on a hill watching all the people going in and out of their nice houses. It's dark outside but I can see all the light coming from their little warm-looking windows. I can only sit and watch, but every now and again I can chat with the passers-by, it's all very amicable but they look at me in such a way that I should know I can't go in. I'm given a very cold shoulder as if I should understand that I'm not part of their thing, they know I think about things that they completely disagree with. It feels like I'm always asking questions they don't want to hear, that I'm vilified by the voices that always seem to chatter in the shadows. I'm not out to cause trouble, my inquisitiveness just wants answers to the things that worry me, things I just don't fully understand.

Knowing now that I have ADHD comes as a relief for myself, but it doesn't change anyone else's opinion. In fact while I may excitedly tell people that I've discovered that the ADHD is the reason why I am how I am, but it only confirms for other people that their suspicions were correct, that there is something wrong with me. The most frustrating part is they just treat me the same, they still don't have any understanding of what I'm going through or what I suffer from – the over-thinking and sensitivities, always over-explaining things, and the negative feelings I suffer from after each disappointment.

Once again, I realised my head was slipping away into a world of self-pitying nonsense and I was only saved by Jim saying, "We're going to be stopping soon." This was great news, I needed one of those strong coffees again. As I turned to look at the dogs, I could see they were all still sleeping so I thought it best not to disturb them – the last thing Jim needed was for them all to start barking, the last leg of the journey had been really peaceful and there was no point in spoiling it now.

The petrol station was just off the motorway, so it was just a short slip road and then straight to the petrol pump. Once Jim had refilled the van, we parked at a quieter bit of the service station. It was dark now and noticeably much cooler than what we had experienced at our earlier stops, with no bright hot sunshine beating down on us when we climbed out of the van. This was much better for the dogs and it seemed to relax them more. Thankfully they were less excitable now while I was getting them in and out of the van for their little run around. Evie in particular was behaving better, not going mad every time I took Harry away from the van; even Charlie was on his best behaviour. When I took each of them for their walk they were not in that panic mode, which was thankfully allowing Jim to enjoy his powernap in peace.

Again, I was just blown away with Harry and how well he was handling the journey. As I was walking with him, I spotted a bench that looked fairly comfortable in a nice spot just at the entrance of what looked like a picnic area at the end of the car park. Although it was dark the area was nicely lit up. I could still hear some of the traffic passing on the motorway not too far ahead of us, but it just looked so nice, surrounded by bushes and trees and wooden picnic tables, so as I knew Jim was relaxing, I thought I'd grab a seat on the bench.

Harry obviously didn't mind as he jumped up beside me. It was such a nice moment, just Harry and me looking off into the distance. I stroked his head and said to him, "Wow, who would've thought, me and you sitting on a park bench in France?" It was one of those moments I was never going to forget. Even though I was extremely tired I could feel myself moving into another hyperfocus euphoric state, the magnitude of the whole journey and what it meant was just rushing through my head again. I looked back over to where the van was parked, a hundred yards away from us. Again, it was crazy to think Evie and Charlie were both in there, I could feel myself smiling as I looked back down at my best friend Harry and said, "C'mon pal, I'll need to go and grab a coffee."

We got up from our seat and slowly made our way back to the van. Without making any fuss I lifted Harry back into his cage. All three dogs had now been out for a little walk so I closed the van door gently behind me so as to not disturb Jim. Making my way into the service station I could see it was a little bit busier than the previous ones; it was mostly French kids hanging around. It looked like most of them hadn't long learned to drive and this was a place they all came to show off. The service station was certainly big enough, and it sold just about everything you could ever think of – souvenirs, car accessories, towels, books, music, food and even wine, who would have thought that you would be able to buy alcohol at any time during the night or day from a service station?

I'd calmed down now and was again feeling really tired. I was quite surprised as I browsed around the aisles to find I wasn't feeling that hungry. Of course, I wasn't exactly burning off lots of energy sitting in the van, so I just decided to buy a small bar of chocolate. The thing I really wanted was one of those super-duper large coffees. Standing in the queue I could see it was now nearly nine thirty. I couldn't believe it was over twelve hours since we had left the ferry in Cadiz.

Before I could dwell on the situation any further it was my turn to get served. I asked for my large coffee, "un grand café, s'il vous plait,", which caught me unawares – I hadn't even thought about asking for my coffee in French; maybe I was inspired as all I could hear was French accents around me. Leaving the service station, I was feeling pretty impressed with my efforts at talking French even though it was only asking for a coffee.

Approaching the van, I could see Jim was awake now. "How are you, Jim?" I asked enthusiastically. "Yup, feeling pretty good," he said smiling. "Now there's a hotel not far from here I use that's not too expensive, or do you want me just to keep going? I'm feeling fine, but I notice you've not slept yet." He fired it out there, just like that. I was taken aback and didn't know what to say. "Ermmm, I'm not sure," I replied trying to look thoughtful, but really, I was gobsmacked. "If we keep going at this rate, we could probably catch an early-morning ferry tomorrow," he said, again, just like that. How was I to reply? "Ehhhh..." I was struggling to come up with a coherent answer. Mind you, he did say ferry tomorrow morning, that would be us getting there a complete day ahead of schedule. "Uh, if you're okay with that Jim, I'm quite happy to keep going," I said tentatively. "Yup okay, we'll keep going pal. I'm just going to grab a coffee."

At that he jumped out of the van and made his way into the service station. I could hardly believe it. This was something I'd been putting off asking about throughout the whole journey – where we were going to stop and when. Every time I had thought about it, I'd gone into a panic. The biggest issue of course was the dogs. There was just no way I could go to sleep in a hotel knowing I'd left the dogs out on the street in the van and I knew Nicky wouldn't be too happy with me if I did that either. I mean, there would be no point in me even finishing the journey if someone pinched the dogs. It just didn't bear thinking about. I could imagine Nicky shouting at me, "How did they manage to steal the dogs?" and my reply being, "I don't know how it happened, that double bed was so comfy I just fell asleep and I couldn't hear a thing." That would probably be the point where Nicky's temper would explode and she would cut my head off in some cruel but deserved execution.

On the other side of the coin, Jim would think I was a total weirdo if we parked outside the hotel and I said to him, "No, you go in and get a room Jim, I'm going to stay out here with the dogs." Or what if the police came along and there I was with the dogs in the back of the van looking like a bunch of stowaways? These dreadful thoughts had been getting pushed to the back of my mind for the whole journey, and now, just like that, it wasn't a problem anymore.

As I sat there enjoying my large coffee, I was starting to see the positives of keeping going. First and foremost shaving a day off the journey was just fantastic, and the idea of getting a ferry in the morning was just so exciting, I mean it was like we were really beginning to see the finishing line. I didn't want to get too carried away as we still had more customs to go through, and there was no way that this would just be a case of slipping over the border like we had managed entering France, but still there was no dampening my spirits, this was another unexpected piece of good news that seemed to be a game changer.

Jim was now feeling more refreshed after his little sleep, and I was feeling more refreshed because of my very large coffee; add to that the weight that had been lifted off my mind of worrying about where and when we were going to stop and I was feeling much happier. We still had a long journey to go but for the moment I was feeling positive about the whole situation. The only thing bothering me was whether Nicky would understand that we seemed to be taking on this journey in one fell swoop. I hoped it would be a nice surprise, us turning up early. It wasn't late and I knew Nicky would still be awake, but still I thought I'd leave texting her till the morning, there was no point in having her worrying about us and the journey.

The roads were still very quiet with little traffic in front of us, the only difference now was it was dark, so the journey had certainly become less scenic. Over to our left we could see a sign for La Rochelle. I remembered my dad taking a detour through the city on the way back from Cadouin all those years ago. It was a beautiful city, right on the Atlantic coastline which lay within the Bay of Biscay. I remember it being hot and everyone being agitated and grumpy; all we wanted to do was get home as fast as possible, the holiday was over in everyone's mind apart from my dad's. Little did we realise how far we had come off the beaten track for this visit to La Rochelle.

Even back then, it was very busy. The old town had really narrow streets with plenty of cafes and restaurants, and I remember the smells making us feel hungry, which only added to our disappointment as my dad insisted we didn't have time to stop and eat and we would "get something further up the road" as he put it. This was adding to the potential of a mutiny as the rumblings of discontent were now being murmured among the rest of us. Thankfully my mum was fully on our side as she was now pushed into playing the part of Fletcher Christian. Fortunately, the mutiny was a success, and we were all happily bought off with chips, which really helped and made the day much better as we walked around the picturesque harbour with its two towers. This was obviously the most popular part of La Rochelle as people just seemed to be flocking to the old port.

The last place we visited was the old U-boat bunkers at La Pallice, which was very striking and very recognisable. I remember my dad and I watching the original series of *Das Boot*, it was all in German, so we had to really focus on the subtitles. Each programme finished on a cliffhanger so you couldn't wait for the next episode, which was always a week later. The series ended with most of the crew being gunned down by allied planes just as they had returned to their base in La Rochelle; it wasn't what they expected after everything they had been through. It wasn't just the harsh living conditions, but the number of times they had managed to survive by the skin of their teeth the constant attacks and death-defying moments at the hands of allied depth chargers.

I don't think there's ever anything good about war but watching these programmes really gave me an insight into just how horrible it must be to be stuck in one of those submergible tin cans. It wasn't just the cramped, smellie, unhygienic living conditions, but as it got close to the end of the war these things were just sitting ducks once sonar really came into operation. There was something like 1162 submarines built, yet by the end of the war there 785 had been destroyed by allied ships with the loss of 28,000 crew members. It's hard to feel too sorry for them though as they created havoc for all the supply ships crossing the Atlantic, and a lot of the people who were killed by these U-boats were only merchant seamen and not actually military personnel. It was amazing to see those old bunkers still standing though, you could see how much smaller the submarines were during the Second World War compared to the ones they build now. A lot of the submarines now are nuclear powered and can stay out at sea for months at a time, just in case you are wondering why you hardly ever see these modern-day vessels.

I don't suppose I feel too bad about the La Rochelle visit now as it is part of the memories of that last holiday, but as I've mentioned before, I don't think I would've been happy at the time if I'd known how off course we travelled that day. It most likely added another three hours on to our trip home, but like I pointed out earlier, my dad had it all planned out from the beginning.

The van was now heading away from the Atlantic in more of an inland direction so the next place of significance that we would be passing was the city of Poitiers. Although another fantastic place with a long and rich history, it is also very up to date with its feet firmly placed in an integral part of the future. With nearly 30,000 students who are mostly studying in the biotechnology and health fields, it made sense that the main industries around the city were electronics manufacturing, printing and food processing, everything was working hand in hand in a very progressive fashion.

Now knowing my own education most probably faltered because of my ADHD hasn't stopped me feeling very positive when I think about solutions for a better future. I strongly believe that education should be free across the board and that universities should have a (metaphorically speaking) revolving door so people of all ages can be educated and re-educated. And of course these are not just places of learning, but places of developing as well. It's not just about creating jobs and helping grow business investment, it has a far wider role in supporting the backbone of society.

And while I'm on my utopian rant, they should do the same for the health service. I know any captains of the health industry would be coughing into their coffees reading this, but it has not escaped my attention that private health insurance is just waiting to devour what's left of our already dying and crumbling health service. Well, it doesn't have to be like that. Let's just cut to the chase – imagine there was no profit to be made from people's ill health, imagine all drugs were developed and controlled through government bodies across the globe, imagine saving lives was actually helping save money – then our approach to healthcare would be completely different.

Learning about my ADHD hasn't exacerbated my problem, if anything it's been a very enlightening experience and has opened my eyes to things I'd never understood before. I may have already covered some of this thinking previously but bear with me. ADHD can be helped with regular exercise, whether it be physical or mental exercise, and it's also important to try and have a better diet, but a lot of mental health issues are exacerbated by the environment the patients are subject to. It may be down to pressures from work, bad relationships or even difficulties with living conditions. Sadly, no doctors are in a position to deal with these outside factors, which means those little pills made by the large drugs companies and prescribed by doctors are having little or no effect. Yup, it's literally all just a waste of money from start to finish. I know what you're thinking – could I be any more pessimistic?

Let me give you another little insight into what I'm talking about. I remember one time standing at the reception of the hotel I worked in. I was speaking to a long-time member of staff when a customer walked up and asked for our help regarding some tablets he had got from the local Spanish chemist. Our receptionist Eduardo, helpful and professional as always, offered his friendly service. The gentleman's problem was that he couldn't read the instructions that came with his tablets as they were in Spanish, so he wasn't quite sure how many he was supposed to take. In one hand he had his small box of tablets and in the other hand was his nearly finished pint of lager. Our receptionist carefully read out when he was supposed to take them and the correct dosage, so you'd think that was good job done and the gentleman could carry on with his holiday safe in the knowledge his health management was all good.

After the gentleman left us, happy and satisfied with the help of our receptionist, I turned to Eduardo and asked, "What were the tablets for?" He smiled at me and nearly started laughing as he told me they were for gout. What was the point of the guy going to all the bother of going all the way to the chemist to spend money on tablets that were just going to be washed down with loads of lager?

It's like watching people in mobility scooters smoking cigarettes – could you imagine the abuse you would get if you approached these people and said, "Not only is it bad that you're smoking cigarettes, but smoking while sitting in the mobility scooter is really bad for your circulation." You would no doubt be told to mind your own business, all because you were giving them some relevant information that might be advantageous to their health while at the same time saving them and the taxpayer a lot of money. Look, I don't want to come over all judgemental here, and I certainly don't always practise what I preach – I probably drink too much and my diet is horrendous at times, especially now that I know that I have ADHD and I should definitely look after myself a bit better.

Okay, I think I've made my point, so now here is my fantastic solution to all those people's ills. Now obviously there's never a perfect solution, people will always find fault in anything you do, but at least if you try to make things better that's an improvement in itself. Now to start this, because I'm Scottish let's just take Scotland as an example. I believe every town in Scotland should have a swimming pool with a sports centre, the bigger towns and cities would require more pools and sports centres. Each of these sports centres would have sports scientists, psychologists and dieticians who would work alongside lifestyle coaches. All these sports centres would be available to all ages, young or old. There would be the usual stuff – football, tennis, badminton, squash, table tennis, volleyball and of course fully equipped gyms. The swimming pools would be used for swimming lessons and aqua-therapy, which is massively important for sports injuries, and of course aqua-fit classes, mostly for the elderly or for anyone who wants to join in. There would yoga classes, tai chi and aerobics classes. It could even be a starting point for people who wanted to go out on hikes or just gentle walks.

Now most of you reading this probably see all it as a bit over the top, but I certainly don't. Let me explain this in further detail. A lot of people in this day and age suffer from real stresses and pressures from just general living; work can be a place where it builds up, which can add to any strain in your homelife or vice versa. Certain illnesses, whether physical or mental, can manifest over a period of time which can just make things worse, leading to other ailments developing, and it all slowly becomes a slippery slope. So wouldn't it be great if instead of a doctor (when you get the chance to see one) prescribing drugs or referring you to another long waiting list at a faraway hospital they could send you to a lifestyle coach who could make an assessment of your physical capabilities, even just find the little things you could do just to get started. It could be someone you could talk to about your bad habits, even discuss how to make changes in your lifestyle, somebody there to listen and to point you in the right direction. A lot of the time people just don't know where to start.

For me personally I've discovered that I need to find ways to exercise my cerebellum which is a part of the brain which is right at the back of the head. The cerebellum is primarily responsible for muscle control, including balance and movement, but they've now found out that the cerebellum is emerging as a key anatomical structure underlying normal attentional and cognitive control mechanisms. Sorry if this is beginning to sound a little technical, but dysregulation within cerebellar circuits may contribute to the core symptoms of my ADHD. Previously, they thought that ADHD all stemmed from the frontal cortex, but now they are convinced it's the way that the cerebellum sends messages to the frontal cortex. The good news is that I can personally exercise that part of my brain which helps to improve my functionality. On top of all that, the exercise also helps produce dopamine which is important for keeping me happy and a bit more balanced.

But it's important to realise that people's environments are all different, so each person's problems need managing in different ways, and although most mental health disorders cross a very wide spectrum, there are always little things that relate. So what I'm getting at here is that once people find a strong line of support and begin to make changes, their health improves in a way that their body begins to look after them as they look after their body, it's just important to find the path that works for you. Once people start to see and feel the benefits of this, it begins to have a knock-on effect, meaning that when someone begins to recognise the changes and improvements other people are showing, it makes it easier for them to get on board.

So again, let's get back to the basic premise here – the healthier people are, the healthier they stay, hospitals stop becoming overcrowded, people take fewer drugs (legal and illegal) and the country slowly becomes a happy, healthier place. Look, I recognise this can't be a cure for all ills, as people have accidents, and certain illnesses need a completely different approach, I just feel moving in this direction would help a lot more people than we realise. And a real game changer would be having health education classes for all ages in every school at least four hours a week, where children would learn about healthy foods and the importance of a healthy environment. I could write a book on this subject alone so I'll just leave it with this last important point. The Amazon jungle, which plays a very important role in supporting the world's ecosystem, is being destroyed all for the purpose of hamburgers...

Things were so different as we drove through the night and of course the tiredness which was growing over me was playing havoc with my thought processes. I found my mind was floating strangely over so many different subjects. I wondered how the apartment was getting on, this was the first time it had been completely empty in over twenty years. Even if Nicky and I were not there, the cats and the dogs would usually be looked after by Nicky's mum. The cats had all gone now, and thinking about them left me feeling really sad. Even thinking about the poor apartment, left empty of life, made me feel sad – one thing was for sure, things would never be the same again.

At that moment, my eyes were drawn to the left of me. We were just leaving Poitiers and the place suddenly seemed to light up, all I could see were brightly lit-up space-age buildings with coloured waterfalls and very modern-looking statues. It looked like some futuristic city had just landed from outer space, with so many different colours filling the night sky. I turned to Jim. "Geez, what's that?" I asked. My whole train of thought had changed and my mind was now awash with the bright lights and wonderment. "That's Futuroscope," Jim said knowingly. "Yeah, I've been there with the wife," he said.

Futuroscope is a technological theme park full of multimedia, cinematographic and audio-visual techniques; there's a mix of 3D and 4D cinemas as well as other attractions and shows all based around new and upcoming advancements in technology. Some of the shows people were getting to see were the only examples in the world. There were fun rides and games that all ages can enjoy. "In fact," Jim said laughingly, "we didn't want to leave!" He looked at me and said jokingly, "No, we are not stopping, and anyway it must be nearly closing up for the night." But what a brilliant idea, it looked like great fun. My mood had changed again. I was wondering if we had been a little farther on in the journey, had it been a little earlier, whether Jim might have agreed to visit Futuroscope. I'm sure he wouldn't, and I think to really enjoy it you'd have to spend at least half a day there.

The van was heading back into the darkness as we left Futuroscope shining behind us. The dogs were quietly settled in the back and I think they must have been feeling a little more comfortable as the van was noticeably cooler now, a sure sign we were heading northwards into colder climes. There were certainly no worries with Jim's new van which was coasting effortlessly up the motorway, you couldn't even hear the purr of the engine, only the music of Radio 2 coming out of the speakers. I wasn't sure exactly where we were headed but Jim assured me we were still making good time and that we were headed in the direction of Tours. Looking at my watch I could see it was nearly eleven o'clock, it was obvious we had a long night ahead of us. I was desperate to stay awake, something in me just wouldn't let me relax enough to sleep – for some reason, I just had to stay awake.

We were now approaching Tours and although it was dark you could make out the surrounding hills of the Loire Valley region. Tours itself was another university town with a collection of landmarks that all dated back to the twelfth century but unfortunately it was dark and we would only be circling the city, so it was far from a sightseeing trip.

My eyes were now fully focused on the road ahead; the long beams of light coming from the front of the van were stretching far out into the oncoming darkness. My mind was drifting across a number of different subjects, trying to figure out what lay ahead. I mean, I knew where I was headed – I was with the dogs, and we were off to meet up with Nicky in Bridlington – but paradoxically, I didn't know what I was doing or where I was going. Everything that had happened over the last few months had been a bit of a blur.

The more I thought about it, the more the whole last five years seemed a bit strange. Ever since they closed the old Dunas Caleta my life had changed, and if I was to admit it, probably not for the better. Whatever I had made of my life – my job, my pets, my relationship – it all seemed to be fragmenting in front of me. It was like I was actively helping to dismantle my life. Being tired wasn't helping and most of my thoughts were confused, but I knew that by the end of this journey things were most certainly going to change and there was no going back.

I think the change started way back in April of 2016 when my place of work, the Dunas Caleta, was closed down for a refurbishment. It seemed like a breath of fresh air that the Dunas was going to be given a new lease of life. It was a fantastic place, loved by staff and holidaymakers alike; we had so many repeat guests that it had a really fantastic atmosphere, not only that, but the relationships between the staff members and the guests were second to none. The only problem was that our poor old hotel was badly in need of refurbishment. Looking back now, if they had just done up all the rooms, our guests would have been more than happy. But unbeknown to me at the time there were bigger plans afoot.

During my time there as an entertainer I had worked hard at building a strong relationship with the guests and would always promote the idea that they should use the Dunas Caleta as their home from home in their own little paradise. In fact, the hotel became affectionally known as the Pleasure Dome, another of my daft little ideas but fortunately it seemed to strike a chord with our many repeat guests.

As the years went by, we all began to stay in contact, and with the advent of social media and with a little help from a friend it wasn't long before we started a Facebook group called Friends of Dunas Caleta. This was massively successful; I would upload silly videos which I would make around the hotel, along with pictures of well-known staff members. As you can imagine, this was great for promoting the hotel and keeping everyone in touch with the goings on at their beloved Pleasure Dome.

Unfortunately for the hotel, the world around it never seemed to stay still, things were always changing – holiday companies would come and go, flight operators' rules and regulations were always changing. But no matter what happened, we were always lucky enough to stay busy through the loyalty of our hotel-loving repeat guests. Dunas Caleta was part of a small chain of hotels, some of which were further south on the island of Fuerteventura. These other hotels were a little less fortunate and it was our success that was helping keep the wolves from their doors so to speak so there was never really any extra money around for the much-needed refurbishments.

But then help arrived in the form of a rather large company that had decided to invest heavily in the island of Fuerteventura and when they came knocking at our door, our bosses were falling over themselves. I think when the new bosses first set eyes on Dunas Caleta, they were surprised to see how popular and busy we were, especially when they could see the dilapidated state of the place. The apartments were always clean and the rooms were really bright because of their large glass doors, and the swimming pool area was well laid out and certainly looked good from first impressions, but once you started to scratch under the surface you could see there was a lot of work needed.

When the hotel first opened it was really only fit for self-catering: the apartments had small built-in kitchens and there was a conservatively built restaurant close to the bar area for half-board, which was all fine and dandy for the time. But all-inclusive was now the order of the day and the hotel's restaurant wasn't really big enough for dealing with such large numbers of people and was beginning to creak with the strain.

I was over the moon when I first heard that we were going to close for three months for a much-needed refurbishment; not only were we getting a three-month break but once it was over, we would be returning to a brand-new shiny hotel that would be the belle of the ball. At the time, all this was great news, and I couldn't wait to get on Facebook and keep everyone up to date with all this exciting news. I managed to create a lot of excitement, everyone was looking forward to this new bright and shiny Pleasure Dome. They had all loved the place so much that they were willing to overlook the little problems the hotel had; it was a very special place that brought lots of people happiness so it didn't matter if it was a little shabby in places, it just added to the hotel's character.

I'll never forget the day the old Dunas Caleta shut its doors. Somehow, I knew it was the end of an era, one that had served myself and the guests well for so many years. I had sensed even then that things would never be the same. I remember being in the hotel on my own on that last day; it was sunny and warm with no wind, the pool was like a millpond shimmering in the sun. There was no music playing, no people smiling and laughing, only the doves cooing high up on top of the apartment roofs. As I looked around that old, quiet complex, I began to realise how many happy years I'd had working there. Everywhere I looked had some sort of memory attached to it, the things I had done, all the faces I could remember, the families I had watched growing up over all these years, it was all coming flooding back. I began to feel very emotional as it was beginning to dawn on me that I was possibly saying cheerio to the best years of my life.

Of course, I didn't know that I had ADHD then, but looking back on that day I now know that my mind was going through a hyperfocus euphoria moment, it was racing through all sorts of crazy scenarios and was desperately wondering how I could possibly reverse this refurbishment. The most frustrating thing for me was that had we not had the refurbishment then we would've still gone on to have another successful summer to be followed by a great Christmas. At no point was the hotel losing business – in fact, the demand was going up, year on year we were suffering from more and more over bookings. As far as I was concerned, I had the best job in Corralejo. Okay, I was nothing special and yes, I was only an entertainer, but I was helping people to enjoy their holidays. I effortlessly thrived on my work, again probably not realising that I had found a match for my over-excited ADHD brain. Earlier in my life I had bounced in and out of so many jobs, not understanding why, not knowing what I really wanted to do, always crashing through life in a manic fashion, and then, just by luck, I eventually fell into something that suited me down to the ground.

Through the grapevine I was slowly beginning to hear little bits and pieces about some of the proposed changes. The first major one was that they would be changing the name of the hotel to the Corralejo Village. As the days went on, I watched them begin ripping down the old Dunas Caleta. This only added to my doubt about the changes that were afoot. The old tennis courts where we had played so many fantastic games of football tennis were now being built on. Slowly but surely, I was watching my old hotel change beyond recognition. In fairness, the apartments were all in the same place and the hotel hadn't lost its shape, the swimming pool would never change, but whatever was happening it was well and truly out of my control.

Now it's obviously important to point out that as this new company was taking over the hotel there was no point at which they had to inform me of any structural changes to the hotel. I was just an employee like all the other employees – in fact, realistically, I was probably one of the least important people still employed there.

Then the grumbles began to start on my Facebook group. Some of the group members started to post that from what they could see of the building work, in their opinion it would never be finished in time for its re-opening on the first of July. People started to panic. Some started to post pictures of the work being done around the hotel so other people could make judgements on whether it was going to be ready or not. People started messaging me with concerns about whether their holidays would be going ahead as planned. I did my best to keep reassuring people, telling them everything was going to plan, but not everyone was convinced. I even started taking photos of the building work down from the group page as it was starting to worry people. Personally I felt the pictures were a little undignified anyway, I didn't want people seeing the old girl in such distress. Unfortunately other people didn't see it this way, they thought I was trying to hide something from them. People started accusing me of not being honest about when the hotel was going to be ready. It got to the stage where I was cycling up to the hotel, going in and checking with any of the bosses who were there supervising the building work and asking them if everything was going to plan.

Then, just to make things worse, I found out that eighty percent of the hotel's occupancy was going to be taken up by an Italian company that would be bringing its own entertainers. What I thought of as my guests, all the people in my Friends of Dunas Caleta Facebook group, were going to be in for a massive shock, and it was beginning to feel like it was all my fault. I had everyone believing Dunas Caleta, their little bit of paradise in the sun, was going to be bigger and better, all shiny and new. Everyone believed it was going to be there, just waiting on them coming back.

Nobody had told me about these new changes before we had closed; I was just an unofficial mouthpiece from the old Dunas Caleta. I was not an official spokesperson for the new company, and again, at no point was the company duty bound to inform me of anything that was happening with the new hotel – this was their business not mine. Sadly, but painfully, I understood this, but how was I going to explain this to all the many repeat guests we'd had over all these happy years?

Then, only a few weeks from the re-opening, I had a meeting with a representative from the company. It was all very amicable, but I was asked if I'd like to maybe try my hand at working at one of the other hotels. I politely declined and, as you can imagine, left that meeting with a huge emptiness in my heart.

Eventually, the brand-new hotel, the Corralejo Village, opened its doors on the first of July as promised. The hotel was fantastic – all the apartments had air-conditioning, fabulous new bathrooms, the living rooms were all much bigger and all the old kitchen facilities had been ripped out. It was now a four-star all-inclusive hotel; the restaurant was very spacious, bright and so clean looking and the food that was prepared was gorgeous, with an Italian theme. The old bar had gone – it was hard to even remember where my old DJ unit and stage was; the reception area had also been moved. A lot of it was just unrecognisable from before. Because it was now a four-star hotel, there was obviously a lot of new staff – double the amount of kitchen staff, cleaners, reception staff and maintenance people; the entertainment team was now six-strong, with one guy who would deal with all the music and lights.

16

As we got through July and then into September, things were already not going well for me. Lots of the repeat guests who had booked previously to stay at the complex were being moved to alternative hotels. This enraged quite a few who were expecting to be returning to a bright new Dunas Caleta, and the ones who were lucky enough to get through the door were not entirely happy with the changes – and that's me putting it politely.

I found myself caught right in the middle – I was having to defend the changes to my guests and on the other hand to defend my guests to the hotel. I was in an unenviable position. It was a real double-edged sword; my bosses couldn't understand why people who had previously booked a two-to-three-star hotel that was in poor shape were not happy that they were being upgraded to a far superior four-star hotel with much better amenities. And it was hard to explain to the guests who did get to stay at the Corralejo Village that the customers who had booked through the Italian company had paid about four times more for all the Italian styled entertainment.

As I tried to keep the previous guests sweet while dealing with my new bosses I just ended up exacerbating the problems. I had no control over the music in the daytime, I was having to work around the Italian team's activities, I was literally crawling around in the shadows. I hadn't just become surplus to requirements, it was worse than that. Where once I thought I was a happy-go-lucky swash-buckling buccaneer who was always there to steady the good ship Dunas Caleta, I had now turned into this less fortunate character who was about as popular as a confused out-of-control referee at a Celtic Rangers match.

Now back in the real world, most of the new guests who came from the UK and who had never stayed at the Dunas Caleta, loved the Corralejo Village. Okay, the entertainment wasn't brilliant for them, but there were free buses to take them to some of the island's most beautiful beaches, the rooms were spacious, air conditioned and very comfortable, and the food was fantastic. As the weeks and months went on, things were just dragging on for me. The twenty percent of the guests who I was supposed to be dealing with were a mixture of English, German and French and they were spread amongst a busy hotel that was mostly Italian. With all the noise and excitement coming from the six Italian entertainers, I didn't stand a chance trying to communicate.

The other members of staff who had previously worked at the Dunas Caleta were getting on fine – there was lots for them to do and they were learning so much more about the changes and new working conditions. But I was hanging about like a bad smell, I was like the ghost of Christmas past, walking around with very little to do, and time was just dragging on. I found myself going into the gym and training on my own. It was a terrible position to be in, knowing that your bosses are hoping you'll maybe just disappear.

I'd even had to arrange the return of the cats who had lived in the old Dunas Caleta, although it wasn't a great place for them to return to. Especially the black and white one who was aptly named Stagecat as he would sit on the end of my old stage at the Dunas Caleta basking under the warm stage lights. Or little Tabs, who was the grand old age of thirteen, she was such a cute little thing and well loved by all the guests. I had no option but to bring them back to the hotel as the homes I had found for them during the refurbishment couldn't look after them anymore. It was really sad as you could see they weren't enjoying their new environment either. Little Tabs eventually became very ill; I tried my best to look after her but trying to keep the poor wee thing alive seemed to be going hand in hand with the futility of my job.

In all the time I'd been on the island, I had never experienced anything like this. At the time I didn't realise how unhappy I was, but even to this day when I think back to that period my heart just sinks. Don't get me wrong, some of the young Italian entertainers were lovely, but what must they have thought of me? This old wacky entertainer with the strange accent. They must have wondered why I was there. I mean, they didn't know any of my history, they didn't even know that Dunas Caleta had existed, or that I had done all of the daytime and evening entertainment mostly by myself.

Maybe I wasn't having a great time, but things on the island itself had really begun to pick up, especially in Corralejo. There must have been another four hotels which had gone through a successful refurbishment and were receiving lots of bookings. And it wasn't just all-inclusive establishments, a few swanky boutique hotels had also suddenly appeared in town. Even the local government was spending a fortune pedestrianising most of the high street, which in turn saw a lot more street cafes and bars popping up along the way. And because we were getting so many more tourists, this was also encouraging a lot of investment in the property market. Yup, there was no doubt about it – Corralejo was booming.

In 2017, there was a little glimmer of light at the end of what had become my long dark tunnel – our company had decided to take control of the Alisios Playa. This was a hotel my original bosses had managed for a number of years and now my new bosses had picked up the mantle and the good news was that all the rooms would be occupied by a dynamic new English company called Jet2. This hotel was right bang next door to the Corralejo Village and was somewhere I was more than familiar with as I'd worked over there in the pool bar not long after I first moved to the island.

At first, my bosses were very reluctant as their new venture wasn't geared towards entertainment, and as far as I knew, nothing had been negotiated with Jet2 apart from having a quiet relaxed hotel with no entertainment. But luckily for me, there were a few teething problems in the beginning. The hotel again was rather old and it lacked any atmosphere to distract people from picking faults. Complaints were starting to come in thick and fast from guests and reps alike and it was all becoming a bit of a headache for my bosses as there wasn't a lot that they could do.

I hassled and I hassled and repeatedly e-mailed my bosses and implored them to let me go over there. My point was basically what was the point of me moping around the Corralejo Village being paid for doing very little when I could go to the Alisios and try and put a few smiles on faces while working as a conduit between the hotel and the guests. It worked!

I took the month of September off so I could spend some time with Nicky and the dogs and get my head into a better frame of mind so I could move over to the Alisios refreshed and ready for another challenge. I hadn't been at the Alisios for long when I found out that they had decided to move Sally over to work as public relations person and to oversee the upgrade of the apartments. This was great news for me, not only was Sally brilliant at her job but she knew me and would act as a buffer between me and my bosses. Although to be honest we also had a new hotel manager and he was a great guy so things couldn't have started any better.

17

The next three years were fantastic. The Alisios became a mini version of the old Dunas and all our repeat guests returned. The pool area was a little smaller than at the Corralejo Village so everything was just a little bit more intimate. The Facebook group was working once again as a great advert for the Alisios and Jet2 couldn't be happier with the service they were receiving. A lot of the staff from the Corralejo Village were doing their level best to come over and work at this hotel as it was a much friendlier environment. Personally, it was a triumph for me, as the hotel was going from strength-to-strength and even the Italian entertainers were beginning see what I was really about. Sally also played a massive part in making sure everything ran smoothly and everyone's needs were catered for.

Then bang, it happened again. Everything had been going so well, the demand to stay at the Alisios was going through the roof, but something happened between our company and some of the major owners of the Alisios Playa. They couldn't reach an agreement for some reason or another and it was all just about to end when the pandemic struck. All of a sudden, the holiday companies were in a mad rush to clear the island of their guests as we prepared to go into an unprecedented lock down.

And now here I was, sitting in the van, heading to England with our three dogs, not a clue what the future held for me. Everything was so confusing. The Corralejo Village had re-opened but a number of us still hadn't been called back; it felt like I was being held in a perpetual furlough situation. I didn't have a clue when I'd be called back or what they would do with me if they did. All I knew was once

I got the dogs back to Nicky I would be in England for a week and then I had a flight booked to take me directly back to Fuerteventura from Manchester. But what about after that? Sell the apartment and move back to England permanently so I could be with Nicky and the dogs? Rent the apartment out? Or stay in Fuerteventura and see what happened with Nicky and hopefully they would all come back to the island.

To be honest, I knew the last option wasn't really on the cards. Nicky and I had always spoken about moving back to the UK with the dogs, in fact right from the beginning, when I first met Nicky, I had said that one day I would definitely be moving back to Scotland. She seemed to be okay with that suggestion, especially after visiting my hometown of Kinghorn on the Fife coast. But as the years had gone by, my thinking had softened a little, especially with Harry having epilepsy and there being no way we could get him back on a domestic flight. My idea had been that eventually, once I'd got enough money, we would all fly back on a private flight. Nicky's thinking was always more practical; she had worked out how much and how long it would take by road and sea, it was something she was really wanting to do.

Nicky thought it would be a fantastic adventure for us all but every time she spoke about it, I would nod my head and quickly change the subject. In my mind there was no way I could cope with being cooped up for days on end driving back to the UK, it just wasn't me. Anyway, my ADHD-fuelled procrastinatory tactics would never allow it to happen; we would all be better off if we just waited till I could hire that private jet, or so I hoped. So, of course it was quite ironic the way it all worked out, with Nicky having to fly home on her own and me doing what I had felt would be the dreaded journey by road and sea with my three furry friends. And now here I was, doing it during a pandemic just as Brexit was kicking in and a volcano was threatening to bring our part of the world to a standstill. You just couldn't make it up.

The idea of selling the apartment was another major headache for me. There was no way anyone could walk into the apartment the way it was at the moment. With Charlie not long having had knee surgery, we'd almost had to turn the house upside down. To protect his knee from any further injury, we had to cage rest him so he couldn't run about too much in the house; we kept the cage in the living room because that's where we spent most of our time. So he wouldn't damage his knee jumping off the couches, we had brought in a mattress and put it on the living room floor. In our main bedroom, we had taken away the bed base so he wouldn't hurt himself jumping on and off the bed, so we were just sleeping on a mattress on the floor. There were clothes everywhere, as well as bikes, surfboards and wetsuits. The place just looked a complete shambles. And it wasn't just the general untidiness of the place – it needed quite a bit of work done as well. I really didn't know how long it would take me to get it ready to put on the market if I did choose to sell it.

Even the thought of having to sell it saddened me – that apartment meant so much to me. I still tend to call Kinghorn in Fife home as that is where everything began for me, my very life blood came from that wonderful little town and there were hundreds of years of family history wrapped up in the place. But the truth of the matter was I'd actually spent more of my life living in my apartment in Fuerteventura than anywhere else; not only that, but every member of my family had spent time with me there. My mother and father had come over and spent lots of Christmas holidays with us, and they had been fantastically happy times for everyone. So my apartment wasn't just my home, it was a representation of my life.

Now I know that probably sounds a little dramatic as it was only a three-bedroom apartment in a little town called Corralejo, but it had a very special place in my heart. And of course, there were all our previous pets who were intertwined with the apartment's history. I could never forget all our cats, Big Kinghorn, Courtney, Scraggy,

Alex, Harvey and Sophie, all now passed away but all with burial sites around my volcano Bayuyo. It was like my apartment was a living thing and I didn't want to leave it all lonely and empty, it was a big part of me.

So here I was, once again suffering the downside of ADHD as I began to ruminate over my past and the uncertainty of my future. It's very difficult trying to switch these thoughts off as it all seems to be so very real, again my life slowly fragmenting in front of me, powerless to do anything about it.

Sitting in the van looking out into the darkness I could feel that mental change coming over me that indicated another burst of hyperfocus euphoria. There seemed to be a real clarity as I pieced together all the different scenarios. I couldn't envisage any future with the job that had played such a large part in my life, I didn't feel part of that hotel anymore, it just wasn't the same place. I wasn't inspired to go through all the same nonsense as when it first re-opened in 2016. Then there was the apartment. What if I did get it knocked into shape, how long would it take before it was sold? There were apartments within the complex where I was living that had been on the market for over a year. Then I started to think about my relationship with Nicky. What if she started really getting on with her life? A new job, all her old friends – did she really need me coming over a year or more later and spoiling it all?

I turned round to check on the dogs. I think I was hoping Harry would be awake and I was going to ask him, "Hey Harry, what do you think?" But the three of them seemed to be comfortably curled up and sleeping. As I turned to look at Jim, I could see he was focused on the road, both his hands firmly fixed onto the steering wheel as we sped along the road into the night. Strangely it felt like the dogs, the van and Jim were all as one, all following the same purpose, they all had somewhere to go, they were all on the road home. Then there was me, I was feeling very detached from their journey. Even though we were all on the same road, they were all going somewhere else. Jim would soon be back home with his wife after another job successfully completed, and the dogs would be ecstatic once they were re-united with Nicky, but my journey wasn't even close to being finished. There were a few other twists and turns ahead of me. As long as that volcano behaved, I'd be back in Fuerteventura in a week's time with a lot of unanswered questions milling around my head and some serious decisions to make. No amount of procrastination could stop the inevitable now.

It's funny how quickly my mood swings can change from one thing to another, the slightest distraction and "ping" my mind is off somewhere else. We were now in the lower reaches of the Loire Valley and this time it was the bright lights shining up from Tours that were grabbing my attention. We had just driven out of the long darkness and the skyline was now littered with brightly lit castle towers, structures of Gothic design and of course remnants of the Roman Empire all neatly packed together like they had all been built hand in hand so people could saunter by and marvel at their splendour.

But these incredible feats of architecture were actually part of a darker and more serious side of history. These were monuments to the real power struggles that had gone on over the centuries, and although beautiful in stature, they were all steeped in blood from the many historic battles that had happened through the ages, and Tours was certainly no different. In fact, Tours probably more so than most had seen its fair share of warfare, and it's worth remembering when the Roman Emperor Augustus came a calling you didn't have to send him an invite, his armies would march and stop wherever they liked. Any rabble-rousing resistance would be quickly put to the sword as his generals made sure they organised their own brand of law and order and enslaved the local inhabitants at the crack of a whip. And even as the Roman Empire retreated during its collapse, the Germanic tribes didn't come calling any quieter as they picked away at the retreating Roman forces. And let's not forget the Islamic conquests that were driven back in the seventh century; even the Vikings parked themselves at the mouth of the Seine after ransacking Angers, Tours and Marmoutier Abbey.

Yet today, walking around these magnificent old buildings, things always seem so peaceful. Away from the hustle and bustle of everyday life, you've more chance of listening to birds singing, or the raised voices of tour guides as they show off their knowledge of their surroundings. Photographers with expensive cameras trying to eye up the perfect shot as young students admire the work created by these Renaissance elites and take notes every now and again so they can finish their thesis.

There's no getting away from it, the architecture is always stunning, the stone masonry is always carved to perfection and to think this craftmanship has all but disappeared. It's as if those days gone by were times of great people with superhuman skills creating such beauty with great artistry but no apparent technology, and all in these very peaceful surroundings. Yet nothing could be further from the truth. Many of these incredible buildings were built by the victors of war, literally trophies to be worshiped in. Most of the time, the people lived in perpetual fear, enslaved to their masters till they became of no use. Don't get me wrong, I find these building fascinating, but I do feel people should be more aware that these monuments of success were built on the backs of people who lived in absolute squalor with no form of democracy or right to protest to alleviate their circumstances. You never know, it might even help make us realise how lucky we are that certain elements of the future have been a bit more beneficial for the less fortunate amongst us.

Driving away from Tours, we were now heading back into the darkness; the roads were very quiet as we were now moving into the hours of early morning. Not only that, but we were now being hit with rain. Being tired I found watching the rain cross the path of the headlights quite mesmerising. "We'll be pulling over for another stop soon," Jim said suddenly. That was music to my ears, I was most certainly needing another of those fantastically large coffees to keep me awake; the more tired I got, the more determined I was to stay awake, and it was a battle I wasn't going to lose. Jim was in fine fettle – he had been grabbing power naps every time we stopped and had slept most of the way on the boat so he was well prepared for this long journey. Even though I was feeling extremely tired, I still felt better knowing we had four eyes watching the road as opposed to two.

We were on the French A28 motorway and it was easy to pull off into the service station as there was hardly any traffic on the road. Much the same could be said of the service station – being so late at night, the place looked lifeless. It was well lit and nicely placed in amongst very leafy trees; I could see them swaying lightly in the breeze and hear that very recognisable sound of the rain hitting their leaves.

To my surprise the dogs were all fully awake and attentively sitting upright; thankfully, they had given up on barking every time we stopped. As usual, Harry was first out of the van, he didn't seem to flinch an inch with this change in the weather, he was more interested in pulling towards the trees. He had obviously picked up on some new smells and was keen to investigate – he must have picked up the smell of a rabbit as he was literally dragging me into the wet trees. I still only had my t-shirt and shorts on so this was definitely a lot colder than I was used to. Slowly but surely, we eventually circled the whole service station then I tried my best to get Harry quietly back into the van. Before taking Charlie out, I opened the side door and quickly put a pair of jeans on and grabbed an old jersey – I certainly wasn't used to this colder October weather in northern France.

Getting Charlie out of the van was somewhat different to Harry, he just seemed to freeze to the spot. I could tell he wasn't a big fan of this cold wet surface and had to be coaxed to move. Once we got going, he was fine, but it wasn't lost on me that the fastest he moved was when we started heading back to the van. Evie wasn't any different, she too wasn't happy about this cold wet surface on her paws, but what I also noticed was that she was reacting to the noise of the wind blowing the rain through the trees, that's when I realised that would've been bothering Charlie as well. None of this had had any effect on Harry, he would've happily stayed out there much longer had I not dragged him back to the van. Once again Harry was proving that he had been taking this journey in his stride. All the worries about his epilepsy and him being a sensitive little thing had gone right out of the window, there was no doubt about it – he was still very much the leader of the pack. I certainly wasn't taking anything for granted though, we still had a long way to go, and I knew there was plenty of time for him to give me some very unnecessary surprises.

Once I had got the dogs all back and settled into the van it was time for me to go and grab some grub and one of my very large coffees. I wasn't really hungry but when you're travelling long distances from home, eating some sort of comfort food always helps get you through the journey. With not moving around in the van I certainly wasn't working up an appetite, but one thing was for sure, being so tired from the lack of sleep my head and body were screaming out for a large dose of caffeine.

The service station looked almost empty with only two lorries and our van in the car park so I wasn't really expecting to see too many people milling around. First things first though, a much-needed bathroom visit. The toilets were pristine and looked like they had just been cleaned five minutes before I'd entered. It was warm and smelled very fresh which helped make me feel that bit more comfortable.

I spotted a long mirror that ran along the top of the hand basins and decided I'd give myself a once over as they say. Being a bit older and balding, mirrors were certainly not a thing I used to help me feel better about myself. Thankfully I didn't look too bad. I was still quite slim and suntanned, but I could see there was a little bit of sun damage beginning to appear under my left eye. "I need to get some coconut oil on that," I thought to myself.

Having said that, when I considered the amount of time I had spent running around in the sun with no suntan lotion on I had probably been really lucky. Every day I'd leave my apartment around ten o'clock in the morning wearing training shoes, socks and surf shorts with my bag on my back. I'd jump onto my bike and off to work I'd go, shouting hello to the usual people on the way as I cycled along Corralejo high street. That was my attire, my uniform, every day for years. I even remember having to go down to the bank to sign for my mortgage, rushing out of work dressed in my shorts and training shoes to get to my bank which was luckily not too far away from the hotel. Fortunately, most of the staff in the La Caixa bank had worked there for years so they knew I was a little off the wall. I always made the effort to be courteous and polite, so this hopefully made up for my very unorthodox way of being.

As the years went on, my hair began to thin out and it wasn't long till I began to shave it down, so to protect my increasingly shiny dome from the sun I began to start wearing caps. I was never one for lying in the sun but I was out in direct sunlight almost every day all day and for years I didn't use even a drop of suntan lotion. Not that I wasn't aware of the dangers of the sun, I just never got round to using the many bottles of suntan lotion that were always at hand. Ironically, nearly every day I would be on the microphone making a point of warning everyone of the dangers of the sun, especially the people who were going to visit our fabulous beaches. I even had a library where I would ask people to leave any leftover suntan lotion for others to use which was a handy cost-free little service that was well appreciated by our guests – but not me, not once did I pick up a bottle and use it.

In my defence, I never stood still long enough, and if you are running around while covered in suntan lotion you just feel and look a sticky mess. One minute I'd be charging around the poolside like a madman trying to keep everyone informed of our daytime activities, the next I'd be running around the tennis court winding everyone up during a lively game of football tennis. Once that was all over and done with, I would then be directing a raucous game of water polo as a loudmouth competitor who refused to lose, all done very much tongue in cheek. In fact, I was just playing the pantomime villain, which was all about bringing people together. There just didn't seem to be any time for me to apply any suntan lotion.

I recognise now that of course it was probably my ADHD that was driving me on, and that most sensible entertainers would actually take the time to make sure they stayed protected and applied some suntan lotion. It wasn't just my skin that was unprotected from the elements – being in the sun all day your eyes are constantly squinting. Now don't get me wrong, I think over the years I've owned every popular brand of sunglasses known to mankind. But with me moving around all the time, the minute I put them down I'd never find them again; never being in the same place for more than a minute it was almost impossible to retrace my steps. Another problem was that I'd break them while I was frantically running around, although I did eventually start buying really good-quality sports-styled sunglasses that wouldn't fall off. The other issue I had was that I felt it was important to look people in the eye when I was working around the hotel and speaking to the guests. In between all my absolute nonsense I always tried to be as genuine as possible with these people and didn't want anyone thinking I was hiding behind my sunglasses.

And of course, spending most days around the poolside I was always playing water polo and like many other people I would keep my eyes open while under the water so they would become reddened from the chlorine and other things such as suntan lotion, kids' pee and an assortment of spilled drinks. And once that was all finished, I'd probably go swimming in the sea not too far from my apartment which was close to an area known as Harbour Wall. This was the place I probably swam most in all the years I lived on the island. It's just on the northside of Corralejo's main harbour. The strong currents would wash over the reef which was great exercise when you were trying to swim against it, but this was made even more difficult by the large waves that would come crashing down on your head. If I'd been playing water polo beforehand and then swam in this very salty water it didn't half make my eyes sting, they would literally be red raw for hours afterwards. I'm not complaining because I'll certainly look back on these days as probably the best in my life, but at times it just felt like my body was being dragged around from pillar to post by every daft idea my head would have.

As I peered into that service station mirror it dawned on me that after everything I'd been through, I was lucky to still be in one piece. Oh, it wasn't just the sun damage under my eye, there were a few other little battle scars I could pick out – chipped teeth, a mark where my nose had been broken a few times, a small scar on my top lip, an indentation on the top of my head, another scar where I had split my chin. Now I know I used the term battle scars but to be completely honest, most of these visible little flaws came from extremely stupid accidents. For instance, one of my broken nose incidents was me running up some stairs away from a girl and catching a fire extinguisher that was fixed to the wall. To be honest I could still look at my refection in that mirror and smile; in fact, once I was scrubbed up and in the right attire, I could still look quite distinguished – well in my mind anyway.

All cleaned up and ready to go, I left that service station toilet feeling a bit fresher although still tired and desperate to get my hands on one of those large strong coffees that my body was now beginning to rely on. Thankfully I still wasn't feeling too hungry, so I managed to avoid my usual choice of fat stodgy sandwiches or pastries and grabbed a container of selected segments of fruit. I knew we were nearly on the last leg of this part of the journey but it was going to be even more difficult trying to stay awake so I made sure there was nothing heavy in my stomach, which would make it easier to fight off that feeling of sleep.

Standing at the counter I was approached by a young lady who started to charge me for my little carton of fruit. "Would you like anything to drink with that?" she said in English, which caught me by surprise. I hadn't spoken to her so how did she know I was from the UK and I'd just been admiring my tan in the toilets? "How did you know I spoke English?" I inquisitively asked. She smiled back at me and replied, "I saw you outside running about with your dogs, and I heard you talking to, I think it was Harry?" I started laughing and remembered I had been a bit loud when I'd asked Harry if he could smell the rabbits when I was out running him around the car park.

Of course, that got me blabbing away about why I was talking to Harry about rabbits, and that led on to where we had just travelled from and where we were going. She seemed quite happy to talk and appeared to be glad of the company and it wasn't long before she started telling me a little about herself. She was a good-looking girl and was obviously very bright, she had not long finished her course in the summer and was just waiting to join some department in the police. That bit I didn't really pick up properly as I'm never too good at listening, my mind begins to wander after a few minutes. So there I was, nodding my head like I was taking everything in but I did actually pick up that her name was Romilly and she had studied sociology at Paris-Saclay University. It was a nice situation as we were both happy to chat away; she even poured herself a coffee and was excited when I mentioned Edinburgh. She went on to tell me it was one of her favourite places and she had promised herself she was going to go back one day.

I had obviously mentioned that my hometown wasn't too far from Edinburgh, and it was obvious we shared a love for that historic city. It wasn't long till she had her phone out and was showing me photos of the time she had spent there with her friends. I knew I wasn't in too much of a hurry as the longer I took, the more time Jim had to sleep. Eventually Romilly and I said our goodbyes as I had to awaken Jim. I told her he would probably be in for a coffee before we left.

It was good timing – as I got back to the van, Jim was just waking from his slumber. I mentioned I had been talking to a girl in the service station and that she seemed friendly with almost perfect English. Jim just kind of looked at me with that sort of "what are you on about, I've just woken up?" look, that unfocused stare with no thought behind it. "Right, I'll go and get freshened up and grab a coffee. Are the dogs all okay?" he asked. "Yeah, they're fine cheers Jim."

Sitting in the van, just me and the dogs, I was feeling fairly upbeat again – not only had my big coffee kicked in, but I had just been looking at my watch and realised we were maybe only four hours away from Calais. As tired as I was, I couldn't help feeling a little excited. As I turned to look at the dogs, I could see they were all sitting staring back at me. I'm sure they could sense my excitement.

I saw Jim heading back to the van still eating something and with a coffee in his hand. I turned around to the dogs again and said, "Not long now gang." At that, Harry started barking which in turn started Charlie and Evie. As Jim opened his van door I quickly said, "Ahhh, they're pleased to see you, Jim." He turned and looked at the dogs and smiled, then he looked at me and said, "Here, this is for you." I looked down and he was handing me a little piece of paper. "It's from your friend in there," he said. I looked at the piece of paper and could see it was a note from Romilly: This is my Facebook page if you want. Say hello to Edinburgh for me, Romilly x. "Wow, that's really nice of her," I said to Jim.

To be honest, I was over the moon. Even as I was coming out of the service station, I was thinking to myself, "I bet she's glad to see the back of me, I bet she thought I was never going to shut up." Now understanding ADHD, I'm very aware and concerned if I start talking too much, and I find myself constantly apologising for everything. I've never been one for blowing my own trumpet, I've certainly no need to, I'm not actually any good at anything to boast about, but that doesn't stop me rabbiting on and on. In fact, I can't think of anything I'm good at, I'm just me and that's it.

Oh don't get me wrong, I can certainly get quite opinionated and quite enjoy trying to put the world to rights and if I'm not doing that, I just love talking rubbish. It's not because I love the sound of my own voice, I just can't help it. I don't even need to think – my mouth just keeps on going and going. I'm always pleased to see people, and will always greet them with a smile, but I know it's a one-way street, not everyone's glad to see me. In their defence, most of the time they're probably busy with the things that are going on in their own lives, and with me being an entertainer everything's just a big laugh and a joke. I enjoy nothing more than winding people up with my nonsense, so yeah, I put my hands up, I'm probably really tiresome for some people. But genuinely I just want to get along with people.

I now understand that because of the defects of ADHD, I just want to be liked, but I lack certain filters. The more excited I become the faster I talk, I foolishly agree to do things that I just really don't want to do and I'm forever putting myself down. So when people are genuinely nice to me, it's hard for me to accept it, as I don't feel I deserve it. So I was really happy that Romilly had given me her Facebook details, I obviously hadn't pissed her off. With the constant paradoxes of ADHD, we can be very aware of things that normal people just don't see, but on the other hand sometimes we just don't listen and sometimes we just don't read situations very well.

As we drove out of that service station, I must admit I was feeling pretty good about things. The only concern I had now was that I'd noticed the rain was coming down a lot heavier than it had been previously. Thankfully the roads were still quiet and the van seemed to be handling the conditions effortlessly. It wasn't till we passed a heavy goods vehicle and could see the amount of water kicking up from its wheels that I noticed how much water was lying on the road.

This began to make me feel just a little anxious as the visibility wasn't brilliant either. I wasn't sure if it was extremely low cloud, or a heavy mist. The weather conditions had certainly worsened as we were beginning to pass the city of Rouen. It wasn't so bad if we saw a lorry up ahead and the lights on the back of the lorry gave that distinctive rectangular shape and we could judge how close or how far away we were from the vehicle. But in some cases, the lorries had lights that flashed from all different parts of the vehicle like some intermittent flashing Christmas tree. I don't know about Jim, but I found it very disorientating, in fact almost mesmerising. The last thing I needed in these horrible conditions was to start feeling discombobulated.

Many years ago, way back in the late 1980s, I was in a fairly serious car accident and was very fortunate not to be seriously hurt, although the same couldn't be said for the other two people in the car. It had started off as a normal evening. I had been working for a direct sales company, one of those jobs where you go for the interview and they are actually selling the job to you, and the renumeration package is sort of "Sky's the Limit" commission only.

Don't get me wrong, the people were all very personable, but the salesperson they had become had begun to take over the rest of their lives. They started to believe their own stories, there was no difference between fact or fiction. A lot of the people I met had been married on numerous occasions, some were alcoholics who lived a very debt-ridden shambolic lifestyle. To be honest it could've been an incredibly dangerous environment for me, but thankfully I didn't stick it out too long. These people could make incredible amounts of money very easily and quickly ended up throwing it about like it was confetti. As far as they were concerned, they would just make even more tomorrow – until their wayward lifestyle started to trip them up.

Anyway, our main objective was to sell burglar alarms. Looking back, they were fun times but not the sort of work I'd wish to get involved with again. We were literally going into people's houses and scaring them witless about burglaries. The alarms were great, they did what they were supposed to do, and for those times they were state of the art. But it was the, let's just say, the unorthodox tactics we would use when we went into these houses to speak to people. For instance, we would tell them that statistics showed that one in three houses would be broken into over the next five years, and we would add that it could be one of their neighbours either side of them, but of course not mentioning that it could be them, knowing full well that's what they would be thinking.

We were even selling finance deals which would make it even easier for them, especially if you had the husband-and-wife sitting together. If you knew they had children, you would then turn to the husband and say, "Yes, this burglar alarm system is less than the price of a pint of beer a day, and you can't put a price on your family's security." After a very good demonstration of how easy it was to operate, and with his wife won over at how good it was, how could he say no?

On the evening of the accident, Peter the driver, a girl called Susan and I had been working near a place called Cramond which is not far from Edinburgh. It was a Sunday evening and Susan had managed to get us an early lead. If it was successful, we would call it a night as there was no point in having Susan out working in the rain. Susan did warn us that she didn't feel we would have much chance as the guy she spoke to seemed rather weird and she felt he didn't communicate very well, in fact she was really surprised that the guy had agreed to speak to us.

So, Peter and I went to the house thinking we'd give it a go, there was nothing to lose. It was one of those wet, dreary nights and we weren't really expecting much and were looking forward to calling it a day so we could all just pack up and head for home. We agreed that I would do the talking and Peter would display the burglar alarm, while poor Susan waited in the car. On arriving at the house, we rang the bell and right enough without saying too much the guy hurriedly got us into the house. He seemed strange and was very reluctant to look us in the eye.

Although the guy seemed a little rude at first, Peter and I stayed very professional and remained polite and courteous. The man was very tall and was dressed in a kilt so the first thing I did was compliment his attire and told him I was a big fan of kilts which was true, in fact I'm always happy to discuss all things Scottish. He began to relax a little and told me that he was in a pipe band and that he hadn't been long back from practice when Susan called.

I realised there wasn't too much point hitting him with any sort of heavy sales pitch, in fact I thought any would-be burglar would get a real fright if they broke into this house and stumbled across this guy as he was massive. The only disconcerting thing for Peter and me was that every time he asked us something he would get up and disappear into the other room which we found strange. We didn't hang about but quickly gave him a demonstration of how the alarm worked. Our alarm system was all neatly packed into a silver aluminium case which was all padded out with foam, it was the sort of case you would keep expensive camera equipment in, so it all looked very impressive.

After he watched Peter go through the demonstration, he quickly did his disappearing act out of the living room again. I could tell by the way Peter was looking at me that he didn't think this was going very well. I didn't know what to say either, I could only shrug my shoulders and shake my head back at him. At that moment, he came back into the living room. "Can I just pay for it after the installation?" he asked. "I'm not interested in the finance package." As cool as you like, I replied, "Of course, that wouldn't be a problem."

At that he seemed to totally relax. It then transpired that he had been going through and talking to his elderly parents who were in the other room. He said they had been thinking about an alarm system for ages and couldn't believe their luck when our company had called at the door. It was now just a case of filling out the relevant paperwork. We told him that someone from our company would call him the next day with an instillation date. He enquired how long it might be and I assured him not to worry, our engineers would be with him within the week.

Once everything was done and dusted, I decided to ask him how long he had been playing the bagpipes and how often he practised. He told me they only practised once a week unless they had events coming up and then it was a bit more often. "Would you like to hear them?" he asked. "Of course, that would be brilliant," I replied, so he went off to grab his pipes. Peter was smiling now. "Is he going to be playing them in here?" he asked. At that, we heard the loud shriek of the bagpipes starting up and into the living room he marched with the bagpipes now howling at full volume. It was incredible, I've been to plenty of parties where the music is loud but never had I been in a house where someone has been playing the bagpipes full pelt. With it being such a strange scenario, Peter and I couldn't help but laugh out loud although of course you couldn't hear us for the skirl of the pipes.

Once we got back to the car Susan couldn't wait to ask what had been going on – she said that even sitting in the car in the rain she could hear the pipes really loudly. Peter and I were still laughing as we did our best to explain to Susan everything that had happened, it all seemed rather surreal. As far as we were concerned, that was enough excitement for one night and, with the rain beginning to get worse, we were definitely going to call it a night.

Susan didn't live too far away from Peter so it was decided they would drop me off at South Queensferry first which wasn't too far from Cramond so it would probably only take ten minutes to get me home first. Peter's car was a red XR2, which was actually a sporty Ford Fiesta, and to make it look even better, Peter had put spacers on the wheels which made them stick out a little more. I suppose looking back now it was a very boy racer sort of thing to do.

The rain was now falling heavily and Peter's windscreen wipers were going ten to the dozen. We pulled out onto the A90 and drove past the then Cramond Brig Hotel; the roads were quiet with it being a Sunday and Peter wasn't shy about putting his foot down on the pedal. I'd been in the car with Peter lots of times and we would usually be flying along with music playing loudly, so I was confident with his driving. It was a dual carriageway so the road was fairly wide but once you get to the top of the hill the road begins to decline downhill slightly.

We were doing roughly eighty miles an hour when we felt the car lift and pull a little to the left. It was then we realised that there must be quite a lot of water on the road as the car had just ever so slightly aquaplaned. We didn't think too much of it and kept going at the same pace, but then all of a sudden it happened again, only this time the car started to spin. Before we knew it, the car was completely out of control and we were spinning full circle. Round and round we span. I had my seat belt on as I always did but I decided to brace myself and hold on to whatever I could. But then everything happened so fast. I remember heading onto the grass verge still spinning and then, with a loud crash, the car was rolling and rolling. Even though I had my seat belt on, I was flailing around like a rag doll. No one was screaming or shouting but it was dark as the lights had gone off and the car just seemed to keep rolling. I didn't know what was going to happen. I remember just waiting for something to either knock me out or stick into me.

Finally, everything came to a stop. I could see the car was upright, and I could feel the rain coming in where the windscreen used to be. I looked across to Peter who was slumped across the steering wheel and not moving, and I looked behind to Susan who was slumped across the back seat and making a groaning noise. I decided to check myself over. I could feel the wet stickiness coming from my left arm; I'd felt it go through the door window, but I was moving it okay. I checked my legs and both seemed fine. I ran both my hands across my head and face; everything seemed to be in place – my teeth felt okay, my nose was fine and I couldn't find any other wounds.

With the car badly smashed up there was no way I could have opened the door, so I had to climb out of the window that I'd just smashed with my elbow. Luckily the car had landed just in front of a gate which was the entrance to the field we were now in. I quickly checked to see how Peter and Susan were. Peter was coming around but was covered in blood from his wounds, Susan was still slumped in the back of the car and I could see she had a bad head injury. I ran out to the side of the dual carriageway and tried to grab the attention of any passing vehicles, but as the cars were passing it was like they were either ignoring me or they hadn't seen me. I remember shouting as loud as I could through the rain, trying to grab anyone's attention, just hoping someone might stop.

Someone had obviously seen me as eventually I saw blue flashing lights heading towards me. First was a police car, so I pointed out that the car was upright at the entrance to the field. Then the ambulance turned up and I did my best to help them get Peter and Susan out of the car. Peter wasn't too bad, he had a few nasty cuts but seemed to be awake and talking, but Susan was more of a concern. In the dark, the horrible gash across the side of her head just looked horrible, instead of being bright red it was a black colour and of course before they could move her, they had to make sure there was no other serious damage.

After giving Susan a good check over it wasn't long before we were all hurriedly making our way to the general hospital's emergency department. My memories of being in the hospital are pretty thin on the ground now. I remember talking to the police and then being asked by a nurse if I could sit with Susan. Not wishing to sound horrible, but I wasn't looking forward to seeing Susan's head injury as I knew how bad it had looked in the dark when she was lying in the back of the car.

As I walked into the room there were a couple of doctors and two nurses attending to Susan. Being me, I wasn't sure what to say as she looked up at me, I could see she was really scared. "Wow, I see it's only a flesh wound," I said, smiling at her. "Well this has been a different Sunday, it's just like being in *Casualty*, er the TV programme I mean." At that, Susan smiled back. "You're such an idiot. How's Peter?" she asked. "I've just spoken to the doctor, and he says he's still ugly." Thankfully even the nurses and doctors saw the funny side.

Susan and I chatted away for the next twenty minutes as the doctors finished pulling fragments of glass out of the wound with tweezers before finally stitching up the horrible gash in her head. Although she was putting on a brave face, I could tell she wasn't enjoying having the stitches done. Once they finished, I said farewell to Susan and said I'd come and see her in the morning. Incredibly she needed fifty-four stitches in the end, I was amazed how cool she had been all the way through the ordeal. Mind you, I suppose she had me to annoy her all the way through the process.

Before I left the hospital I decided on a quick visit to the bathroom. As I opened the door, I couldn't believe it when I saw my reflection in the mirror – my face was covered in dry blood, bloody hand marks to be precise. Obviously my hands must have been covered in blood when I had checked my face immediately after the crash. I looked a mess, with bloody finger marks all over my shirt as well. As I began to wash all the blood from my face, I felt a pain in my elbow; I rolled my shirt sleeve up to take a look and saw a nasty gash in my arm. Oh well, I wasn't going to show that to the doctors now. I had just watched them stitching Susan up, and I didn't really fancy going through all that. It had stopped bleeding anyhow so there was no point in wasting the doctor's time.

I never did get to visit Susan the next day as I couldn't lift my head off the pillow to get out of bed – my back, my arms and legs were all in pain after the accident and I had marks and bruises all over my body. The car had rolled down the embankment for over seventy-five yards we eventually found out. Thankfully we all made a full recovery but sadly that poor wee car was a total write off. The police also told Peter that it was probably the spacers he had put on the wheels that had helped the car to aquaplane so easily.

I hadn't told Jim about the accident, and he probably didn't realise how nervous I was as we drove through the rain. One thing that did come to mind that I remembered from the accident was feeling concerned that the ambulance was going to crash because of the rain. I was feeling very agitated and I remember the relief I felt when we eventually got to the hospital. I think it was that relief that helped me deal with the hustle and bustle that was happening around our situation – checking on Peter and being able to chat and reassure Susan that everything was going to be okay. And let's be honest, looking back on that terrible night, things could've been a lot worse. We were all still alive, and I had certainly got off quite lightly; the scar just above my elbow has now gone a dark brown colour from the sun. I just wish I'd gone straight to the bathroom when we first arrived at the hospital so I wouldn't have been walking around looking like a babbling Zombie.

Staring out of the van I was just hoping the weather would let up. The memories of the accident were still reverberating around my head – and it wasn't just the memories, it was the emotions as well. I had felt more panic in the ambulance than during the accident. It was these exact same feelings I was managing to dig up as I sat in the van. And of course, the journey had been going so smoothly, so something had to go wrong. Was it about to end literally with a bang?

Even though I was watching the signs with an eagle eye as we were travelling along this now wet and misty road, I still had to ask Jim how much farther it was to Calais. I tried to sound as calm as possible when I asked, "Do you think the rain's getting heavier Jim?" As I said that, I was stretching my head towards the front of the windscreen and looking upwards, although obviously I couldn't see anything but darkness. "It'll probably be like this all the way into Calais I would imagine, anyway we should be there in about an hour." I looked at my watch – it was just after five in the morning. Again, my mood changed drastically, like someone had just snapped their fingers and I'd woken up from some nasty bad dream. I was back in the world of happiness as it dawned on me that we were only an hour away from Calais.

The coffee had worn off long ago and it was only the excitement of finally getting to Calais that was keeping me awake. All I had to do was hold it together for getting the dogs through customs. We could see the bright lights of Calais now shining around us as we made our way eastwards around the outside of the city. The roads were still quiet, but I wasn't too surprised as it was still so early in the morning. It was still raining but that foggy mist had gone and with so much more bright light around, my worries about the bad weather had dissipated.

"Will the harbour be busy Jim?" I asked. "I shouldn't think so, not on a Tuesday morning, but you never know." Jim was now turning the van northwards towards the coastline and I could sense we were not far away from the port. After watching lots of news reports over the years, I was half expecting to see lots of refugees heading in the same direction as us but there was nothing – just long fences and well-positioned bright lights, and still not much in the way of traffic.

I turned to check on the dogs who all seemed to be curled up and sleeping. I thought it better to leave it that way. Just at that moment, Jim turned left and that was us heading into the port. Even though it was dark you could still see that the place was massive. We were on a long, well-lit, smooth, double-laned road; everything looked very clean and organised, with tall fences either side of us.

Eventually we came across a row of about five kiosks with the lights on in only one of them. As Jim pulled up, he asked me for all the paperwork for the dogs and my passport. Thankfully I had it all prepared in front of me. "There you go Jim, I think that's everything." He took it all off me, winked and said, "Right, sit there and don't move."

I could see Jim was at the kiosk window where he was speaking to a well-wrapped-up English lady. Yup, the cool breeze was blowing off the sea which was cold. I heard Jim saying, "You stay there, I'll do it; I've got my own little scanner." He was helping the lady out, and I'm sure she was glad she didn't have to get off her seat and go and check the dogs' chips with it being so cold and miserable outside. It all seemed mad to me, I was expecting burly French customs officers all armed to the teeth, I had expected them to be in radio contact with watchtowers placed in different positions around the entry gates to the port. But there was nothing – this was more akin to being at your local picture house picking up tickets from a disinterested lady in the kiosk.

I looked around outside the van to see if I was missing something – maybe this was just some pre-security thing, but nothing, everything seemed low key, almost like everything was shut. At that moment, Jim went round to the back of the van, opened the doors and scanned the dogs. He did Evie first, then Harry; he had a little trouble finding Harry's chip as over the years it had moved down to the front of his collarbone. Once he found it, he then did Charlie's. I heard Jim saying, "That's it" and then he closed the van doors again.

He must have been only another two minutes chatting with the lady in the kiosk, then before I knew it, he opened his door and was passing all the paperwork back to me. I pulled the folder from under my seat and started to put it all away. I heard Jim having a last few words with the woman and then he quickly jumped back into the van with a piece of paper which he attached to his rear-view mirror. "That's just a lane hanger, although there's not much need for one today." I wasn't sure what a lane hanger was and, to be honest, at that moment, I wasn't really interested. "Have we just gone through customs?" I asked, trying not to sound too excited. "Yup, that's us officially crossed the French border – we are now in the UK." Obviously, we were still in Calais, but I knew what he meant.

My biggest concern about the whole trip had been getting through customs, it was either me not having the correct paperwork, or something we might have overlooked or even law changes while we were on the road. And let's not forget, it was only four days ago my blood was dripping all over the floor in the vets as I was failing miserably to put Charlie's muzzle on. But the shootout scene from *High Noon* didn't play out either – the dogs kicking off and being shot down in a hail of bullets was just another symptom of my vivid imagination. There thankfully would be no need for me to weep down the phone to Nicky, saying, "They fought and died together so bravely." I reminded myself I could never tell anyone about these mad thoughts as people would just laugh at me.

Jim started up the van and drove into what looked like a massive empty car park which was where we would wait to board the ship. Apart from a couple of lorries, we were right at the front. "We should be boarding in about twenty minutes," Jim told me. This was incredible – we'd made it to this moment which only a day or so ago had felt a million miles away. Jim could tell I was in a good mood as I babbled on about being so relieved at getting through customs so easily, and of course about the dogs behaving so brilliantly as well.

It wasn't long till someone was waving at us to start the van as we were about to board. Behind us there had been a last flurry of activity as a few more vans and lorries had arrived for the journey. The boat was much bigger than the ferry we had been on from Fuerteventura to Cadiz but of course the traffic between Calais and Dover was so much busier, I think Jim said there were about seven or eight ferries that did this journey every day. The ship that we were driving onto was called the *Spirit of France* and was over two hundred metres long and could carry over two thousand passengers. Getting onto the boat it seemed massive inside, there was no wonder they could fit 180 lorries on here.

As we parked up among all these huge vehicles, I checked to see the dogs were okay. Thankfully they didn't seem to be as fazed as I was at being surrounded by all these noisy lorries. It was fairly dark and the van was still warm and comfortable, so the dogs were still snuggled up nicely paying no attention to what was happening around them. Luckily, we were parked right next to a stairwell which would take us to the upper decks of the ship. Still feeling really good about everything, I was looking forward to grabbing some breakfast which Jim had promised me was fantastic.

As we left the van and moved up into the ship you could tell it was probably usually really busy with the many tourists who do this journey, but at the moment it had an industrial feel to it with most of the passengers being lorry drivers. At first, I thought most of the drivers were English, but I soon discovered the accents were from all over Europe. As we moved into the boat, we passed a very comfortable seating area where a few passengers were already snuggled up and trying to grab a little sleep, even though the journey was only supposed to last an hour and a half.

Eventually we came to the restaurant where we could see they were already serving breakfasts. I was looking forward to this – as tired as I was, there was no way I was missing out on a hearty breakfast I told myself. As a member of the ship's staff asked me what I would like on my plate, I struggled to contain the smile on my face. I had been doing my best through the latter stages of the journey not to eat too much so I could stay awake, and this had left me feeling very hungry – there was no way I was holding back. So, it was two fried eggs, two large sausages and two hash browns; to accompany that were fried tomatoes and two well-buttered slices of toast – hot, thick, buttery toast was something I loved and was something I first fell in love with early in my childhood. Morrisey of the Smiths once put it beautifully when he said that one of his favourite things was to have hot buttery toast on a late winter's Monday afternoon when it's raining and a film is just starting. Well, this was my moment – it wasn't even half-seven and the boat hadn't yet left the harbour but everything in my world was just fine and dandy.

I pulled out my phone and took a couple of pics and excitedly sent them to Nicky. I knew she'd still be sleeping but as far as she was concerned, we should still have been somewhere in the middle of France. I was obviously feeling quite triumphant at what we had achieved, although the real hero of this was Jim for getting us this far so quickly and so smoothly. To think Nicky wasn't expecting to see the dogs till Wednesday afternoon but hopefully we should roll into Bridlington sometime today, more than twenty-four hours ahead of schedule. Yup, this was a nineteenth of October I was never going to forget. As I sent the pictures, I wasn't expecting a reply straightaway but no doubt I would chat with her once we were on the road.

Finishing off my large mug of coffee I could see by looking down that I hadn't left a morsel on my plate, the breakfast had been excellent just like Jim had promised. Again, paradoxically, it probably wasn't the best breakfast I'd ever had but it was maybe the greatest! With another big smile I got up and walked away from my table.

It was time to have a wander around the ship and get out onto the deck to watch it pulling out of the harbour. I knew Jim would be wanting to get his head down before the final stage of the journey, but I was too full of the joys of spring to be trying to settle down and sleep, and anyway I really wanted to get out and watch the ship pull out of France, just so I could savour this fantastic moment. It was almost daylight now, but the weather was still very dreich. On the west side of the boat heading towards Dover it was still slightly misty with a light rain blowing in. There was a lot of white water on the sea with the wind blowing across it. I say white water but with the dull light it actually looked quite dirty, a muddy yellowish colour – it certainly wasn't the bright clear seawater of Fuerteventura that I'd become so accustomed to.

After we left Calais, I had a little nosey around the ship. Most of the rooms and services were shut or closed down, but you could tell it was obviously busy during the summer season as the rooms were massive. Everywhere you looked were comfortable seating areas. I could see some of the drivers I had passed on the stairwell were hunkered down and trying to grab some sleep. Most of them were pleasant enough but nobody really spoke, everyone just seemed to keep themselves to themselves. The furniture was all browns and reds, very well worn in places, probably unnoticeable when it's really busy.

Eventually, Dover came into sight, and I could see those very prominent white cliffs, made famous by that wonderful song by Vera Lynn. The entrance to Dover harbour looked surprisingly small considering the number of boats that travel in and out every day. Looking into the harbour area, I could see there were a few ferries docked up. Once we moved into the port, I could see it was much larger than it first appeared before we passed the harbour walls.

It wasn't long till I realised it was probably best to get back down to the van as soon as possible as the port authorities don't hang about once the ship gets docked. Thankfully, more through luck than anything, I found the stairwell which we had used when we first got on the boat. Just ahead of me I could see Jim on the stairs which was good timing, now there was no chance of me getting lost at the last minute. I ran down the stairs a little just to catch up with him. "How's things?" I shouted. "Yeah, good, we should be off the boat pretty sharpish once we dock." I was glad I'd caught up with him, the last thing we needed was me causing any delays.

Once we opened the heavy door to the parking deck, we could see most of the drivers were climbing into their cabins and starting their engines. I was still blown away by the size of the parking bay, especially with it not being full – it made these large lorries look small by comparison. Once Jim and I were settled in the van, I turned to the dogs. "Is that us off to see Nicky?" It probably wasn't the best idea as it started Harry barking and of course the other two had to join in as well. I apologised to Jim for starting them off, but he didn't seem to mind. "To be honest, they've been no trouble at all." That was good to hear as I wasn't sure how Jim felt about the dogs – the way I had been going on, I thought he possibly felt I fussed over them like they were babies. I mean that's okay if you're a girl, but very emasculating for a guy, well that's my take on it anyway.

It wasn't long before Jim was being directed from the ferry by a team of very efficient port officials. Everyone knew what they were doing and they all seemed to work in unison, pointing and shouting to make sure everything ran smoothly. We followed the exit signs which took us through the UK border force controls where someone directed us towards a large hangar which resembled a big empty warehouse. "Looks like we've been chosen for a random inspection," Jim said. I looked at him and said, "Is that bad?" Looking quite serious, he said, "I hope you've got clean underwear on because these searches can be very thorough." Jim turned to look at me and could see I had a rather puzzled and uncertain look on my face. "I'm only joking! They'll just want to check over the van."

Being really tired, I didn't know what to think – one thing was for sure, it would've been a massive inconvenience. "Let me do the talking," Jim said, as we were directed where to park. He switched the engine off and we both climbed out of the van. Jim walked round and opened all the doors to make it easier for the guys to have a good look around. Both men were very pleasant and reassured us that it was only a routine procedure as they quickly looked through the paperwork.

As the older of the two officers walked round to the back of the van I said, "You're lucky, they're usually barking their heads off by now." I then started babbling on about how I'd been really impressed with their behaviour during the journey. I could see Jim staring at me as if to say, "Just shut up and let the guys get on with their job, they're not bloody interested if the dogs have enjoyed themselves." The older officer just looked at me and smiled. I think he could tell by my over-simplistic take on the whole situation that I was hardly criminal number one. In fact, another car had now pulled up behind us and they were keen to move us on.

It wasn't long till we were climbing back into the van. Of course, I had to say cheerio and wish the guys all the best. Jim looked at me and smiled as he said, "It's nice to be nice, but the more you talk, the longer things take. These guys just want to focus on what they're doing and keep things moving." I got it – obviously I didn't at the time, but I could see everything was just due process. I explained to Jim that I fully understood what he was saying. "I just wish I could learn to shut up more!" Jim just laughed and said, "I don't think there's much chance of that!"

As we left the port at Dover, I was able to look back at the *Spirit of France*. The road leaving the harbour is on a hill, so I was literally looking down onto the ships that were docked in the harbour. It was getting much busier with cars and freight lorries all jockeying for positions in the ferry parking areas.

Jim pulled away from the harbour and we were now heading for the A20 which would eventually lead us onto the M20. The major thing that was very noticeable after our journey through Europe was that the roads were incredibly busy. I had hoped that if we were lucky and timed it right, we might miss the early morning rush-hour traffic. But as Jim reminded me, Calais had been an hour ahead, so instead of it being just after ten o'clock, we were back on UK time and it was only just after nine o'clock. This didn't sound too bad to me as I believed we would now be arriving in Bridlington an hour earlier, even though I didn't have the foggiest idea when we would actually be arriving there.

Although I had already noticed that the traffic was much heavier, it wasn't till we eventually got ourselves onto the M20 that it really hit me – the traffic was incredible! I couldn't remember being on a road this busy, the last time we had seen any real traffic was as we were pulling out of Cadiz, but even then, it didn't take long to fizzle out. We were obviously right in the middle of rush hour with hordes of vehicles charging their way into London.

And it wasn't just the number of cars, lorries and vans that were on the roads, it was all the different types of vehicles that were catching my eyes. I mean, years ago, the different makes of cars had been very distinctive, whether it be Ford, Volvo, Vauxhall or even the Mini, but things had changed drastically. I don't mean in a bad way, just that Range Rovers, Jeeps and even Minis now had models that were all about the same size, they all looked very sleek with their new modern and dynamic designs. It wasn't just the shapes of these vehicles, it was the new modern technology and incredible colours that was fairly standard with them all. Even with the small businesses, or what used to be known as white van man, you could see the changes there as well, with their fancy new vans all covered in great advertising slogans all splashed with incredible graphics.

Jim had the radio on so we could keep up with the travel news and all we heard was reports of hold-ups here, there and everywhere, most notably there seemed to be a lot of delays due to lorries breaking down. So far, we had been lucky and our traffic was moving along quite smoothly although it was very much nose-to-tail as we were getting closer to the M25. Again, listening to the radio, we could hear that there were a few problems on certain sections of the M25 although as far as we could make out, they were all happening in the west, which wasn't too bad as we would only be using the north-eastern section.

While it's true that the M25 is a ring road that goes all the way around greater London, the words "ring road" don't really do it justice, in fact they prefer to call it an "orbital motorway", which is probably fairer when you consider it's actually over 115 miles long which makes it one of the longest ring roads in all of Europe. Like Rome, it wasn't built in a day, in fact they started building parts of it in 1975 and didn't complete the final section until 1986. Being one of the most important roads in the UK, it will not surprise you to hear it's one of the busiest, which means, to put it politely, it has its challenges, and a couple of hold-ups in the wrong place can certainly cause tail backs that can go on for miles. I don't know from experience but I can only imagine it must be soul destroying at times for people who have to drive to work on a regular basis using this ring road.

It was now time for us to make our way onto the famous M25 and we were jumping on at the Dartford junction. As we were doing this, we were keeping our ears open and our fingers crossed that the updated traffic news coming our way would be favourable. There had been a few stories coming through the airwaves that the traffic was very slow on the M11 which wasn't good news for us as this was the road we would be heading onto eventually. We could only hope that it would have sorted itself out by the time we got there. We knew we were still very much in the rush hour traffic and could only hope that it would eventually begin to thin out by the time we started heading further north. But for the time being, it wasn't looking too good as all around us the traffic was beginning to slow down.

Eventually we reached junction 27 and this guided us straight onto the M11 and into heavier traffic. There were more reports coming through of hold-ups all over the southeast and southwest of England. Again, the most common reason for these delays seemed to be the numerous breakdowns of lorries. Thankfully it sounded like our road ahead was clear, although from where we were sitting it certainly didn't look like it.

Another thing that kept happening, much to our annoyance and I would suspect for many of the other drivers, was when one lorry decides to overtake another, especially considering how busy the roads were. From what we could see, one lorry would be very close behind another for what seemed like a considerable distance but as soon as they hit an incline the lorry behind, if it was marginally faster, would decide to overtake the slower and possibly heavier lorry in front. When a car overtakes, it usually drops a gear and very quickly gets past the vehicle in front of them. But for the lorries it was a far longer process and would take what seemed like forever. Sometimes being stuck behind them as it was happening it almost looked like the lorry doing the overtaking wasn't going to make it, which was a complete nightmare if the road was going uphill for any length of time. This only slowed the very busy roads even further.

I must say, I take my hat off to Jim as his patience was fantastic. I know if it was me who was driving, I'd be shouting and swearing very much like I know my dad would. I think what was surprising us most was that while it was understandable that the roads going towards the M25 and possibly going to London would be very busy at that time, we had thought the roads heading north would've been much quieter. I had travelled many times from London to Edinburgh by coach and as the bus was heading onto the M1 our road ahead was always relatively quiet compared to the traffic going in the opposite direction. We would quickly be making our way up the motorway but as I looked across to the other side, I would always see the queues into London steadily building up.

We received more bad news in the next travel report which said something about an accident on the northbound carriageway of the A1 – it was the last thing we needed to hear. All the excitement of finally arriving in Blighty was a thing of the past as I struggled to count up the hours I hadn't slept. Slowly but surely, we were crawling in the direction of the A1 and we could only hope that the accident wasn't serious and that the traffic would be moving freely again.

Jim felt confident that by the time we got onto the A1 the traffic would have eased a bit. After listening to all the depressing travel news, Jim decided it was time to change the channel and put something a bit more upbeat on. As he was going through the channels, we heard someone discussing the problems that the roads were having at the moment. "This'll be a laugh," Jim said.

We were half expecting to hear some politician making half-baked excuses to cover up for the usual mismanagement of the roads system. But it wasn't, it was a university professor explaining why the roads were so busy and why we were facing so many problems; he seemed to be speaking a lot of sense. First of all, he pointed out that since the pandemic there was a massive backlog of freight that hadn't been delivered. Everyone was in a mad rush to get these things to where they were supposed to be, but you still had the present-day deliveries on the roads as well. He pointed out that there was another unfortunate problem too – lots of people were concerned for when Brexit eventually kicked in. So it was a sort of pre-Brexit rush that was compounding the transportation problems and the haulage companies were just overloaded with work and demands. With such a heavy demand, these companies were not wanting to lose out on the business as they were in a position where they could charge an arm and a leg with the demand being so high.

So, the professor suspected that when the phone calls were coming into the haulage companies, their replies would be, "Yes, no problem, leave it to us, we can have that delivered for you" and as soon as the phone went down, they would be shouting to their mechanics, "Just get that bloody thing up and running pronto!" So a lot of these lorries might not be in good running condition before they're fast tracked back onto the busy roads to fulfil the heavy demands.

This actually made a great deal of sense and would certainly explain the very high volume of lorries breaking down left, right and centre on the UK's roads. Jim had to agree as he said he couldn't remember the last time he had seen the roads so busy. It all a made a lot of sense, it was a case of pandemic back log + the usual high demand on normal services + pre-Brexit panic = pandemonium.

Later than expected, we finally got onto the A1, the Great North Road as it's known. It was designated in 1921 and has been an important road for over a hundred years, although history believes it's on the same route that the Romans first used in 43 AD. This was an incredibly important road for them and was of great use up until they left in 410 AD.

Strange as it may sound, this is a road that is close to my heart. Way back in 1974, I remember travelling with my dad all the way from Kinghorn to London. I was on my way to spend a week with my Uncle John in London and my dad was off to spend some time in Luton as the company he was working for had offices there. It was just me and my dad; with it being such a long journey, I think he enjoyed the company. My dad's car at the time was a blue Vauxhall Victor with a 2.3-litre engine; being quite a small kid, that car seemed massive to me. It was great getting to sit in the front seat all the way, this seat was usually reserved for my mum who was always second in command in our house. Of course as I was just sitting in the car, there was no way I could really misbehave which meant I couldn't upset my dad at any point. It was a memorable journey where I got on well with my dad for over four hundred miles, which was a feat in itself.

My Uncle John was the brother of my grandmother on my mum's side. He was living in Bethnal Green at the time, although he had lived in many different parts of London during his life. His wife, who I don't remember ever meeting, was called Peggy but had died when I was really young. An incredible but sad fact about my uncle is that during the war he was bombed out of his house seven times – how's that for unlucky? Sadly, his father was killed when one of the bombs blew the front door in with such a force that it hit my great, great grandfather, killing him instantly.

So every time I ever travelled on that road back and forward to London, I would always have fond memories of that journey, and it'll come as no surprise that certain sections of that road are very familiar to me. That's one of the special things about the A1 – because it's so old, apart from the repairs that have been done over the years, nothing much else has changed; there are still all the same houses and farms that had always been there by the side of these well-used carriageways. But there was one thing for sure – this was the busiest I had ever seen this road. Not only was I very tired, but it was difficult trying to harp on about the good old days with this motor madness going on all around us. Yes, I could pick out the little places I remembered but the traffic in both directions was a sight to behold, it looked like the whole country had upped sticks and decided to move on the same day.

With the traffic being heavier than we had anticipated, Jim knew we were not going to be able to do this last leg in one go and was resigned to the idea that we would have to make another stop.

Looking across to the southbound traffic, we could see that nothing had changed for the last hundred miles – it was still nose-to-nose traffic on both sides. "There's a pretty good service station up here we can stop at," Jim said.

I looked round to the dogs as I knew that was good news for them as I thought they must be bursting for the loo. I could see they were all sitting to attention with their ears alert. It was great to see them all looking so well. Harry looked funny as he still had that pink mark on the end of his nose where he'd scraped it trying to get to the spilt biscuits.

Pulling into Blyth service station it was now quite sunny, not what I really expected for mid-October. As Jim parked up, the place seemed to be quite busy but fortunately I could see a large picnic area that nobody was using; this would be perfect for the dogs once I got them out of the van. Leaving my side of the van, I walked round and opened the back doors to let Harry out first. This was actually quite a big moment as this was the first time Harry would be setting his paws down on English soil. I could see he was quite excited and couldn't wait to get out. I didn't get a chance to make a celebratory speech as he dragged me off into the picnic area. I could see he'd latched on to all these new smells, there were lots of damp freshly fallen leaves on the ground. No doubt he would've picked up on some of the local wildlife and could probably smell squirrels as there were a lot of chestnuts lying within the leaves.

I was feeling surprisingly fresh considering my lack of sleep, but I think that just stemmed from my excitement at realising how far we had travelled, and I was over the moon to see Harry looking so well. Getting him back to Nicky in one piece was now looking like it was going to be a reality which only days ago I didn't want to tempt fate thinking about. He wasn't so much the crown jewels, he was more the Jewel in the Crown. No disrespect to the other two, but Evie and Charlie were the new kids on the block compared to Harry, and with them being so young, I hadn't foreseen any problems with them regarding the journey. Little had I thought that it would be the other way around with Charlie and especially Evie being out of sorts.

I got Harry back to the van and then it was Charlie and Evie's turn to make their first steps on English soil. They did much the same as Harry and couldn't wait to get over to the picnic ground, as per usual picking up on Harry's scent and taking the exact same route as he did. Getting Evie and Charlie out together was working just fine, and it wasn't long till I had them both back in the van. Once they were all fed and watered, Jim and I decided it was time to go and see what we could grab to eat in the service station.

The first thing we noticed was how busy it was with lots of people coming in and out, a far cry from the service stations we had visited in Spain and France. Even though it was busy, the atmosphere seemed quite relaxed, in fact we noticed a lot of people seemed to be using it as part of their day out. A lot of the couples we saw looked as if they were retired and were just milling around in a very relaxed fashion.

Once we got into the service station, we saw that there was no way we were going to struggle for something to eat and drink as it was beginning to resemble a food hall in a large shopping centre with so much on offer. They had Burger King, Costa Coffee, Greggs, Costa Express, Krispy Kreme and, if you wanted to do a bit more shopping, there was always M&S Simply Food and WH Smith. It didn't take me long to make my mind up – I knew exactly what I was after. "Let's go and grab some steak bakes Jim," I said excitedly. "I've never had a steak bake," he replied. At first, I thought he was joking but then I could see he was deadly serious. "Right, my treat, trust me you'll love them!"

I walked enthusiastically up to the counter and jokingly shouted to the lady behind the counter, "Can you believe it, Jim here has never had a steak bake?" My charm offensive seemed to be working as she said, "It's nice to see a happy face." As my eyes searched along the counter for the steak bakes, I said, "Smile and the world smiles with you." I'd always remembered one of my grannies used to say that to me. "Oh, I'm sorry, we only have three left," she said in an apologetic voice. It wasn't a problem, I could see that there was a chicken bake so I would have one of each and, as it was Jim's first time, I'd let him have the two steak bakes. It goes without saying that we also ordered two of their largest coffees, probably the last ones of the journey.

Even before I'd got back to the van, I'd managed to scoff both my chicken and steak bakes, much to the amazement of Jim who hadn't even noticed me eating them. Steak bakes were something else that evoked memories of my childhood. When I was younger, one of my favourite things was getting steak and kidney pie at my grandmother's; if I was doubly lucky it would be followed by either rhubarb crumble or rhubarb tart. It wasn't just the steak and kidney I loved, it was the soft soggy pastry on the underside of the crust that I loved the most.

As a young lad, I eventually got a job with Millars the bakers which was right in the heart of my hometown of Kinghorn. It was an easy enough job, all I did was sit on the back of an old Austin van which I'm sure was from the sixties and deliver rolls to the houses that had ordered them. After a year of doing that, I moved into working in the actual bakehouse, doing a Saturday job from six in the morning till twelve midday. The hardest part was getting up at that time of the morning, but as soon as I walked into that warm bakehouse, the fantastic smells had an electrifying effect as the aromas pierced my senses. I've always felt that for those unfortunate people who are left in a coma, instead of playing their favourite tunes to try and get a response, they should just start cooking bacon at the side of their bed. Obviously I'm no doctor but I'm sure that would work for me.

The best part of the job in the bakehouse was when all the stuff eventually had to be moved down into the shop. This would involve loading up long boards with all the different cakes and pies – these boards would be filled with chocolate eclairs, apple charlottes, jam doughnuts, cream doughnuts, custard doughnuts, sponges, cream sponges, fondant cream cakes, fondant-covered sponges, and an assortment of pastries and cream pastries. Then of course there were all the different breads, like French halves, the ever-popular Scottish morning rolls, the soft white ones and my dad's favourite, the well-fired ones. And then there were the Scotch pies, the bridies and my favourite, the kangaroo pies or to use their official name, the steak rounds.

Once the board was loaded, it would then need to be picked up carefully and balanced centrally on top of your head. As I would take the boards down to the shop, I would pass a little area that was out of sight of the bakehouse and the shop and I would stretch my free arm up onto the board on my head and grab one of those delights and eat it as quickly as I could. There was obviously no way I could sneakily finish off one of those incredible kangaroo pies – it wasn't for the want of trying though! Those famous steak rounds are written into Kinghorn folklore history as they became the town's infamous kangaroo pies. And yes, being steak and pastry, they were obviously a favourite of mine.

The bakehouse would open late on a Friday night and the first things they would get started on were the kangaroo pies, so every Friday night as the pubs would shut, people would make their way to the back door of the bakehouse to purchase a steak pie with its softly glazed buttery pastry and its hot meaty filling. Folklore has it that one evening as people were queueing outside the bakehouse somebody looked into the storeroom and spotted the large tins all marked "Australian beef" and from that day on that famous pie was christened "the kangaroo pie" and Friday night in Kinghorn became known as kangaroo pie night.

I'm sure as I recited that story to Jim in the van, he must have thought I was either mad or making it up, possibly even both, but I'm sure I must have recited it with the passion and love I had for these wonderful pies.

18

This was now the final part of the journey, and we were making our way onto the M18. Although excited and happy that it was nearly over, I was also tinged with sadness. It was hard for me to get my head around the fact that in another five days I'd be flying back to Fuerteventura (well, hopefully, assuming that volcano didn't massively erupt and end up grounding all flights to the Canaries). I still felt sad about it all, from now on, nothing would ever be the same. No Nicky, no Harry, Evie or Charlie, just me and the apartment and no idea what the future holds, an uncertain future in a very uncertain world.

There were still a few of us on furlough which felt strange with the hotel being open, but did I really want to go back there? It wasn't the same place, at least for me. But the worst part was my mind kept going back to the apartment as it dawned on me that living in that apartment was probably the happiest time of my life. I'd lived there for more years than I'd lived anywhere else, and there was still this deep yearning for it. I didn't want to lose the apartment, it was such a big part of me. Everything felt like it was out of my control. I was losing Nicky and the dogs, at least for a while anyway, and the more I thought about that, the more I realised there was always the chance I could lose them for good. It felt like everything was possibly slipping away.

First there was my job. Okay, it wasn't the most fabulous job in the world, far from it, but within me, I felt it was the best job on the island and I was lucky to have it; and of course it suited me down to the ground. I was playing football tennis and water polo, and fulfilling my main vocation of laughing and helping other people laugh. Because of my ADHD, I would never feel I was doing a good job, the way my head was wired I could only make an assessment that I was just being me. Would things have been better if I'd found out earlier that I suffered from ADHD? I just don't know, there's an argument it was the ADHD that gave me the longevity in the job.

A lot of uncertainty and feelings of not fitting in had certainly faded over the years without me even realising it. I had a life and my apartment; I had lots of people around me, and things in my life had found a sort of balance. There were always things going on, and I never had too much time to dwell on all my insecurities. This was something I'd become acutely aware of way back in 2016 as the pillars of the old Dunas were beginning to crumble, the realisation that a huge chunk of me was going down with the ship. There was one thing for sure – if or when I went back to the Corralejo Village, nothing could really be the same, it was a totally different environment. Inside, I just didn't feel I had the fight needed to make it work. The obvious problem was that I was getting too old for it – the demands had changed, the people had changed, and what's the saying? You can't teach an old dog new tricks. Although the sword of Damocles hadn't finally fallen on my time at the hotel, it was certainly in the post, and I could feel the postman wasn't too far away.

Again, that paradox was biting on me hard. I knew exactly where I was taking Harry, Evie and Charlie, but I didn't have a clue where I was going. I was reminded of the words to one of the Beatles' songs: "You never give me your money …. Oh, that magic feeling. Nowhere to go, Nowhere to go."

Time was passing slowly but surely, and we were getting closer and closer. We had just left the M62 and were now on the A614, the road that would take us into Bridlington. Even with all the confusion and feelings of an uncertain future, I was feeling quite upbeat. Some of the views we were passing were great. For the time of year there seemed to still be lots of leaves on the trees, the areas we were driving through were lovely. We were crossing beautiful rivers and some of the houses were fantastic, built with those old-fashioned red bricks and with huge gardens. All these amazing colours and the sun shining brightly was giving the whole place a really summery feel.

Jim and I were chatting more regularly; he was telling me about his dogs in Fuerteventura, but I was finding it hard to think straight or focus on some of the stuff he was telling me. The effects of the coffee had long worn off and the hours of no sleep were hanging over me like a very heavy weight. Just at that moment, I saw a sign for Bridlington, and with that there was another burst of excitement and my feelings were lifted again. "The satnav says we're only six miles away," Jim said as we passed a sign for Burton Agnes. We turned a corner and drove past a lovely pond full of geese, swans and ducks. The water was sparkling, yet full of feathers, but it was such a beautiful setting, the pond was surrounded by trees with just a few old houses close by. The last time I saw anything like that would've been when I was watching TV.

I was getting that hyperfocus euphoric feeling again. I could feel myself sitting upright in my seat, I could even feel myself smiling. It's funny, my memory is terrible, I can rake through my brain for ages sometimes trying to remember something, but as soon as I get that hyperfocus euphoric feeling, everything just seems to fall into place. It weirdly ties up all the special moments I've had all through my life and I knew that passing that pond would be one of them.

We were now on quite a long straight road, and I could see Bridlington ahead of us. The traffic was still really busy, but it was all moving along quickly. In the distance I could see what was possibly an old church; whatever it was, it was massive and looked like it could be very old, weirdly it looked old enough that it would've probably been around about the same time as the wonderful buildings we passed as we were going through Spain. Jim was smiling as he gently tapped the satnav. "This is going to take us right to the front door," he said as we pulled into Bridlington. I wasn't sure exactly where we were as I'd never been here before, but I could tell we were moving around the outskirts of the town.

As we turned to enter Bridlington properly, I was quite impressed with what I could see – lots of very old large house with well-kept gardens. At that moment, Harry started barking as though he somehow knew we were close; as per usual, Evie and Charlie joined in. "Oi, shut up," I shouted, but that just seemed to add to the din.

Jim started to indicate, and we took a left onto a quaint narrow street called Bempton Drive. The dogs were still barking away. "Harry!!" I shouted again. "Don't worry, we're nearly there now," Jim said laughingly as he took a right-hand turn into Bempton Crescent. And there, just at the corner, I could see Nicky. "There she is!" I said, trying to act calm in front of Jim, but inside I was bursting with excitement.

As we drew up, I literally jumped out of the van and nearly bowled Nicky over as I gave her a massive bear hug of a cuddle. We were both fighting back our emotions. "I've got someone here to see you," I said. Well, as soon as we opened the back doors the dogs went ballistic, and as soon as they were out of their cages, Nicky was once again almost knocked to the ground, this time by her best friends. Luckily Nicky's mum was there to help out. The neighbours must have thought there was a riot going on.

Nicky agreed to get the dogs into the house quickly while I helped Jim clear out the back of the van. It was hard for Nicky and me to talk as the dogs were like a torrent of madness, but as our eyes met, Nicky and I knew it was job done. We both knew what was going through the other's mind, we had done it! Something which only a few months earlier had seemed like a dream was now a reality.

Nicky and her mum took the dogs and the bags with their stuff in and quickly ushered them into the house. Jim's van wasn't too bad, the only messy cage was Harry's as he'd knocked over his food and water dish, but the other two cages were fine, especially Evie's. I packed all the rubbish into a black plastic bag and was able to squeeze it into a bin which was close by. Jim then passed me the only big bag I had with me. And with that I shook his hand and thanked him for getting us all there safely and ahead of schedule. "Brilliant Jim, cheers," I said gratefully. "No problem, you take care fella," he said. And with that, he jumped back into the van and drove off.

I waited till he was out of sight and gave one final wave and then looked around. I was standing on the street on my own. Just me and my big blue hold-all. Suddenly it dawned on me – looking down at that old blue bag, I realised it was the very same one I had used when I first arrived in Fuerteventura twenty-six years earlier. I was frozen to the spot, staring down at that old bag, millions of thoughts rushing through my head all at once; in fact, I couldn't have moved, even if I'd wanted to. But eventually there was just one thought springing to the top, just one burning question on my mind: what now?

ABOUT THE AUTHOR

The author has had a varied life and ended up settling down on the island of Fuerteventura working as an entertainer in a small but popular hotel in Corralejo. Now in his later years he has decided to put his creative energies into his writing.

Printed in Great Britain
by Amazon

18670225R00169